My GUARDIAN ANGEL Drew the SHORT STRAW

A girl's journey to adulthood and
the Best Friend she met along the way

CHANTAL LAVASSEUR

SILVERSMITH
PRESS

Published by Silversmith Press—Houston, Texas
www.silversmithpress.com

Copyright © 2024 Chantal Lavasseur

All rights reserved.

This book, or parts thereof, may not be reproduced in any form or by any means without written permission from the author, except for brief passages for purposes of reviews. For more information, contact the publisher at office@publishandgo.com.

The views and opinions expressed herein belong to the author and do not necessarily represent those of the publisher.

ISBN 978-1-961093-55-3 (Softcover Book)
ISBN 978-1-961093-56-0 (eBook)

INTRODUCTION

When you read the title of this book, I imagine it elicited different responses. Some people might immediately snicker and think to themselves "I know how that feels." Others may laugh and say "I can't wait to hear this one." Still others may say (the younger generation I would assume) "I don't know what that means." Well, I'm here to tell you that you might experience these responses and a myriad more if you read my story. This is the journey of my life, with all its highs and lows and moments of joy and sadness. It is kind of an emotional soup if you will, and I've chosen to share it with you, the reader, to help you feel hope and love in the most hopeless of times.

Did you know that from the moment of our conception each one of us is assigned a Guardian Angel? That Guardian Angel stays with us our whole lives. He doesn't go on vacation, he doesn't leave us for a different gig, and he doesn't ask to be moved to another human being, one that's easier and more obedient. I must thank God for that. Angels are pure spirits with intelligence and free will. There are nine legions of angels, and they exist to serve God in all capacities, including, but not limited to, being his messengers. So then what is the job of a Guardian Angel you ask? Quite simply it is to get us to Heaven—not so

INTRODUCTION

simple, the how-to part. When an angel is assigned to a human being like me . . . well . . . let's just say he probably wishes he could get hazardous duty pay or a yearly bonus.

As I sit here writing with my coffee in one hand, chocolate in another, and sunshine blasting through my window (which let me assure you is a rarity when you live on the coast in Washington State), I am preparing to take you by the hand and walk you through the memories and experiences of my life. I would love to tell you it is going to be enjoyable, but honestly, whose life is enjoyable all the time? I want to tell the truth about my life so that maybe it can help comfort you or give you a different perspective. Most of all, I want to share my life with you because we are all connected and need each other, and if I share my personal experiences, it might help others not feel alone and not feel like they're the only ones going through hardships. Above all, I want you to know there is someone who loves you and is always there for you, no matter how bad you may act or how bad life feels.

It is a difficult story for me to write, as it is very emotional and close to the heart, so it has taken me ten to fifteen years to get it done. I love to write, so the idea it has taken that long to put down (on "paper," so to speak) the story of my life just gives you a little window into how much these last fifty-seven years have hurt and how much I tried to avoid reliving them. While I realize I am under no obligation to share it, I can't help but feel as though the Holy Spirit has guided me in this direction and wants the story told. As I proceed forward, I just want you all to know I'm very blessed to have been born into my family and to have the friends and experiences I have had. Alas, however, it is not without some pain and suffering, so the story will be a mixture of joy and pain. Without further ado, let us begin our tale.

CHAPTER ONE

TURTLE SICKNESS

In my bedroom one night at about the age of five, I was awoken by an incredible pain in my stomach like nothing I had ever experienced. It felt like someone twisted my insides repeatedly and would not let go. I was so scared and confused, and I didn't know where I was when I woke up. When I finally became alert, I realized I was lying sideways in my bed, kicking the wall with my legs and moaning uncontrollably. I shared a room with my two sisters, and next to our room was our brother's bedroom, which also housed three boys. If anyone reading this has ever lived in a big family, and a small house, you know how impatient siblings can be. They started yelling at me to shut up, and they started throwing pillows at me, and overall were just annoyed. What can I say? I was causing them sleep deprivation. But none of that mattered because in short order I was up and running to the bathroom. I proceeded to "toss my cookies," "lose my lunch," "Ralph," whichever of these expressions you most prefer. Naturally, as a kid, you throw up and move on with your life, right? . . . Wrong!

My mom came into the bathroom and prepared a fizzy

1

CHAPTER ONE

concoction to settle my stomach, and within minutes of ingesting that out came a fizzier version of the original stuff I was depositing into the toilet. I can't remember exactly what happened the rest of that night because I'm ashamed to say that was fifty-two years ago, but it must not have gone well considering the back-end of the story.

At some point along the way, my mom and dad must have figured this was not just some kind of stomach bug and would require more medical intervention. She took me to the doctor, and I remember him saying I had some kind of fish disease and sent us home with a big ole bottle of pink liquid. I was required to drink this a couple times a day, but all I can remember is I kept depositing that back into the toilet as well. I'm not sure how long, but I think I vomited every day for a couple of weeks. I just remember feeling so tired and worn out that I didn't want to try and eat or drink anything ever again. It was way too much work for my little body to handle.

I have this moment etched permanently in my mind, where my mom sat down next to me on the couch to administer yet another round of pink liquid, and when I looked into her loving, motherly, and caring eyes, I saw fear. It was an overwhelming feeling for me because, to a young child, parents never seem afraid of anything, and if a parent is afraid, a child knows there's something very serious going on. I spoke to my mom about that years later, and she said she tried to hide the fear from me. I told her it wasn't her fault because I've just always been that person who sees and feels things in the invisible world—you know, sixth-sense type of skills.

What I learned later from my parents was I had contracted a bacterial infection known as salmonella poisoning. I won't include the encyclopedia definition of that here, but the general

TURTLE SICKNESS

definition of it goes like this: it is an intestinal infection that causes lots of vomiting, diarrhea, stomach cramps, fever/chills, and more severe symptoms in specific cases. The source of salmonella also affects how sick an individual gets.

So what was the source of my salmonella infection, you ask? Well, turtles of course, as reptiles carry a lot of salmonella on their shells. Did my mom and dad know this when they bought the turtles for us back in the '70s? Yes, they did, which is why my mom told us over and over again to wash our hands after handling the turtles. So how did that translate in my little five-year-old peewee brain? Play with turtle, suck my thumb; play with turtle, suck my thumb. The bummer for my mom is she couldn't pull the old "I told you so" card because I was too sick. My mom got jipped twice. She couldn't throw it back in my face as evidence of "You should have listened to your mother," and she almost lost her daughter in the process and had to live in fear of that for a couple of weeks. Wow, kids are fun, aren't they? I bring this story up for a couple of reasons: because it was always such a strong memory for me and a source of emotional trauma, and because it would cause me health issues for the rest of my life.

My older sister Anne just told me a couple of years ago she noticed a significant change in my personality after that. She said for the five years preceding I was a happy-go-lucky child and super friendly and fun, but after that, I became angry and edgy and seemed temperamental. She said I became a difficult child to raise. It's amazing how circumstances in our lives, out of our control, can have such a lasting impact.

So I finally started getting well and slowly returned to school. When all was said and done, I think I missed two months of kindergarten (well, I wouldn't say I missed it, if you know what I mean). It took quite a while for my strength and appetite

CHAPTER ONE

to come back, but man was I excited to get back to school and see all my friends. Kindergarten is the best because you get to play with friends, color, paint, create things, go out for recess, take a nap, and repeat the process all over again.

I think that's how we should design our adult lives. Wake up in the morning and eat breakfast, drink coffee, go to work with your friends (hopefully friends, not just colleagues), color, paint, make stuff, go to a playground and have recess, come back to work for a brief nap, and then repeat until it's time to go home. Then when we get home, we should go outside and play with our friends all night. I vote we should skip adult things like grocery shopping and buying toilet paper, paying our bills, and fixing our cars. Instead, we should spend every day playing outside when possible, talking with our families and friends about the meaning of life and stuff, and eating and drinking what we want. If we could all find a way to make money doing that, I think we'd be much happier.

HEALING SLOWLY BUT SURELY

Slowly but surely, I started building my way back up and went on with life as a normal five- and six-year-old would do. Naturally, it took me a while to start making friends when I came back to school as I had missed the early opportunity to do it, but as luck would have it, I made some decent friends.

Once I finished kindergarten, I was moved to another school my siblings attended. This was a Catholic school roughly three miles from our house. From my memory, the best part of the school was the amazing gravel playground. It had monkey bars, a swing set, a jungle gym, and a bunch of wild boys and girls willing to play kickball and dodgeball or race each other on the asphalt parking lot. It started out being a pretty good school, but unfortunately even that changed fairly rapidly.

It was only my first-grade year, and I had an incident that occurred during class time. I believe it was only a few months into the school year when it happened. To this day, I don't remember much about what was going on around me as my focus became very internal. I remember going to my teacher (who was an intimidating individual and didn't seem to like kids very much) and asking if I could go to the restroom. Apparently I had gone to the restroom several times, and she was very distrustful of why I was asking to go yet again. I remember sitting in my seat after a very harsh "no" from the teacher regarding my request, and I started to feel an uncontrollable urge to urinate right there.

I was shifting and wiggling in my seat, trying as hard as I could to control the urge to go to the bathroom when all of a sudden I could feel warm fluid running down my legs and onto the floor below my desk. It made a small puddle around my feet and my desk, and right then the bell rang. Oh, that evil, hateful, cruel bell which refused to ring five minutes sooner to save me from the most embarrassing moment of my life. That bell robbed me of my dignity, pride, and respect in a horrific moment that will stay lodged in my brain forever.

As soon as the bell rang, all of the students got up and started heading for the door, but not before they made a very wide berth around me, my desk, and most importantly, my pride. It's almost as if time stands still and you are locked in that moment for what feels like an eternity. That was the experience I had as a little six-year-old girl seeing all of the faces of the other students looking at me, horrified and disgusted at what had just happened. While those moments in our youth don't seem like much of anything, when we become adults, they somehow shape and form us, for

CHAPTER ONE

good or for bad, in all that we do moving forward. That is what it did for me, and I can assure you my formation wasn't great.

I certainly don't remember what happened in the next couple of hours or days, but that memory sure hangs out there like a giant cobweb I cannot wipe away. I don't know if my mom came into the school to get me that day, or if I somehow managed to clean myself up and get out to the car, but either way, I returned to the loving arms of my mother. What I do know is once I returned to my mother she seemed very concerned and protective of me, which is always a nice feeling. She must have taken me to the doctor after that to try and find out what was going on. Remember the salmonella poisoning mentioned earlier? This infection was another aspect of it.

After the doctor did some tests, it turned out I was suffering from a urinary tract infection, which of course can cause a person uncontrollable urination resulting in frequent visits to the potty. In other words, the good news was I had a real medical issue, and I wasn't just trying to take advantage of the teacher to get out of the classroom. The bad news was none of this would make any difference in restoring my reputation.

After my mom got the results of the lab work from the doctor and an explanation for why I had to go to the bathroom so frequently and what caused the accident, she decided to go visit the school. Now I assure you, unless my mom is coming to talk about PTA events, no teacher or school administrator would want to face down my mother when one of her children has been mistreated. To the best of my memory, we went to the principal's office, she called the teacher in, and proceeded to read her the riot act regarding her treatment of me. Surprisingly my very scary teacher did not look so scary anymore—she looked scared. My mom told the teacher that she better treat me with respect and never let something like that happen again to me or anyone else. Needless to say, my first-grade teacher was very kind to me after that and for the rest of the school year.

Those are the moments you most appreciate having a mom and dad as a safe place to return to, and someone who will be there for you in good times and bad. I hurt for those children who have never had that experience. Having said that, however, I did not always have the best relationship with my parents, and we didn't communicate very well. We fought a lot during my formative years, and it made for some serious hardships. I experienced bouts of extreme loneliness and depression throughout my life, which will be fleshed out throughout this book.

I returned to class shortly after the event had occurred, and eventually, after a couple of months had passed, it appeared the kids had forgotten about my embarrassing incident. They started treating me just like every other kid, and I think I even made some friends. I must have made some friends because I was at that same school for the next five years, and I do remember having friends when I left.

Slowly but surely life started to get a little more normal. As the years continued, however, I missed a lot of school and was sick a lot. Looking back on it now, I can see how those formative years affected my education down the road. Because I was sick a great deal, which looking back on it now probably had to do with my initial illness, I ended up missing a lot of the building blocks needed to learn upper-level math and to understand the natural sciences. The only thing that didn't seem to need the early building blocks was writing, and that's where I seem to be strongest. Which I guess is the reason I am using this mode of communication to share the story of my life with you.

It is very difficult to struggle in mathematics when both of

CHAPTER ONE

your parents are mathematicians and all of your siblings seem to understand math as well. To my dad's credit, he did try to work with me, but he lacked the patience and ability to communicate basic-level math skills. He was a high-level computer programmer and worked at a defense contracting firm with some of the brightest minds in the field. How's that for an unleveled matching of intellects? My dad's poor communication skills coupled with my inability to comprehend and execute rudimentary math functions made for a very difficult setting. And if you haven't deduced this yet, I was, and still am, a very emotive individual, which caused me to internalize my pain and made me feel incredibly insecure, inferior, and ultimately stupid, very stupid.

CHAPTER TWO

DAD

Moving along in the story, I think it's time for some background information. Now while no one wants to air their dirty laundry, or that of their family, if I am going to tell my story truthfully, then I will do just that. So I think it's important to give a little bit of my parents' childhoods and experiences. When it came to trying to understand my parents, that was a difficult task. They were not always very quick to share stories of their past and childhood. I don't know if this came from a desire to avoid reliving some of their hardships or if it was just a matter of living in the present and not in the past, but either way, the details of their childhood were spotty at best. So I will piece together what I remember from my dad's and mom's lives.

My parents were both raised during the Great Depression, albeit in two different types of settings and home environments. It is a well-known fact those who grew up during the Great Depression were tough, of strong character, and not very subject to emotional expressions or outbursts. They handled difficulties, struggles, and suffering like kings and queens with stoicism and elegance. There was a reason they called them the "Greatest

CHAPTER TWO

Generation," and having been raised by two of them myself, I do believe it was. Who knows if we'll ever have that type of generation again?

Having said that, the shortcomings of this generation, and their perspective on life, also need to be addressed as it had a major impact on the kids raised in that environment. Let's dig into the history of my father a little bit. He was raised by immigrants—one French (my grandfather) and one Irish (my grandmother)—and let's just say home life was lived at a very high decibel as I understand it. As expressed by my dad, and quite a few of my aunts and uncles, there was a lot of fighting in the home, and that fighting sometimes turned into abusive behavior, both emotional and physical. As one can imagine, this caused a lot of anger and hostility amongst the family members, which would stay with them for their entire lives.

My dad grew up in Upstate New York, a great distance from my mom's small town in Colorado and an entirely different environment. We went back to visit a couple of times when I was young, and although I don't remember much, I do remember it always seemed to be cloudy there and was very dark without much sunshine. The winters were frigid cold, with lots of snow. As for the summertime, I think it was always miserably hot and muggy with lots of bugs and not much relief from the staggering temperatures. My dad and his family grew up in very extreme weather conditions, which made them used to those hardships. When he was little they endured some difficult times, that is for sure.

There were seven kids in the family, and because it was during the depression, his father had a very difficult time getting work daily, so food was scarce and money was in short supply. From what my dad shared with me, it sounded as though all of the families in the neighborhood would work together to take care of one another. If somebody had enough food to make dinner for more than just their family, they would invite others in and take care of them. The stress levels were no doubt very high, and I'm sure it made it very difficult to raise a family that size, but the stories that were told to me, few as they may have been, were not pleasant ones.

I was told there were times when my grandfather would lose his temper and get very angry at the kids. No good things would come out of those moments. In addition, my dad said both Grandma and Grandpa fought a lot in the home. I'm sure it was a very intense and stressful environment to be in, so that's very understandable, but these things can have a long-lasting effect on a child.

When my dad was growing up, he started to have some health problems. He ended up with a bone infection called osteomyelitis, and it took a long time to treat and heal. The net result of this disease is he spent a lot of time in and out of the hospital when he was a teenager. It was during these episodes in the hospital my dad became an avid reader and studied mathematics and science. He learned a lot during that time and became quite an advanced mathematician, which would serve him well later in life. It's lucky for him he had such a thirst for learning, as he probably missed a good deal of school and may not have gone very far in his academics had he not been self-taught.

I don't know if he had many friends when he was growing up as he never spoke much about them. He did, however, mention he went to a couple of Buffalo Bills football games with his brother-in-law. Even during the time I knew my dad, which was obviously my whole life, I never saw him with a lot of friends. In all actuality, the people he spent all of his time with were his

CHAPTER TWO

immediate family and all of his in-laws. He had a couple of work friends we got to know fairly well, but they were much more business partners than what I would call "buddies."

I do remember my dad mentioning to me he had a difficult time with his mom. It wasn't that there wasn't affection and a lot of it, but because he was so sick, he said his mom spoiled him too much. He wanted to stand on his own two feet and make his way in life, and it sounds like he didn't feel like he could do that if he were in close proximity to his mom. So when he turned eighteen he entered the military and left home.

My dad told me his dad and mom were still paying off his medical bills up until the very day they died. I can only imagine the strain that must have put on them and their marriage. They died when I was just a little kid, so I have only one memory of my grandpa rocking me on his knee and no memories of my grandma. They were only in their seventies when they died.

My dad was a very tough individual, and I would even go as far as to say scary at times. He had a pretty gruff appearance and looked a bit angry most of the time. I would find out later that a lot of that was just his thinking face. He always seemed to be solving problems in his head and had a hard time being present and in the moment. I don't know for sure what he was thinking most of the time, but it left us all wondering.

He grew up with five sisters and one brother, and his sisters never stopped talking. To be honest, they remind me a lot of the way my sisters and I can be, which got passed on to the next generation as well. I think that is why my dad was so quiet and so mentally distant; he probably couldn't get a word in edgewise, so he retreated to his safe space inside his mind.

My dad and I never got along when I was growing up. He had a lot of bottled-up anger (I unfortunately shared this trait), and he took it out on his kids—especially my defiant brother and I. In the last five years of his life, however, we started to get to know each other and formed a very close relationship. We were finally able to let down our guard and accept each other for who we were. This gave us a great opportunity to talk about kids, religion, and politics, and much to our surprise, we were aligned on most of those things. He was so informed and well-read that he knew what was going on in the world. I was just learning about it all, so I could bounce things off of him. My dad was a strong man, a good provider, and a good protector. He loved his family and wanted us to be successful in life. I think he was one of the most misunderstood human beings I knew.

After my dad left the military, he worked for General Electric and was assigned to Turkey for two years. The stories told during that time were pretty entertaining. There was a lot of drinking, a great deal of smoking, and something about a drunk donkey, a high-ranking officer, and my dad at the apex of both of those events. My dad used to laugh pretty hard when he would tell us that story, and I think he prided himself in talking his way out of that crisis. That was always surprising too, maybe because he wasn't exactly what I would call a gifted communicator or charismatic.

Sometime after that, he moved to Colorado and eventually met and married my mom. Let's just put it this way; even with his wads of cash and his flashy sports car, my mom was not too impressed. She was the type of woman that expected a lot out of people and gave a lot to everyone. So some flashy bachelor showing off his bravado was not going to sweep her off her feet. The story of their first "date" goes something like this.

My mom and her best friend Avery were busy getting ready for their double date, when lo and behold, who shows up at my

CHAPTER TWO

mom's door but my dad. Just for clarity sake, he was not my mom's date for the evening, but he had taken it upon himself to become her date. So he made himself a nuisance and stayed until her date arrived, at which time the date, having stepped into this awkward situation, decided he should leave. And that's when my dad thought, "Now is a good time to move in and steal her away." However, things didn't go according to plan because my mom was so mad at him she said she never wanted to see him again. I think the fact I am writing this book as their biological daughter proves who won in the end.

MOM

My mother's background was a little bit of a different situation. To begin with, she was an orphan, and her brother, sister, and she were raised by their aunt. Their mother died of spinal cancer, and their father died after a prison riot. The prison riot was a very historical event. It happened in 1929 in a maximum security prison outside of Canyon City Colorado.

My mother's father (my grandfather) was a security guard at the prison. One day the prisoners rebelled and took over the prison. They killed most of the security guards and held up the prison for four days. The prison riot broke out when a number of convicts decided to take over the prison. They managed to kill eight prison guards, and five prisoners were also killed in the process. My grandfather managed to stay alive with two other prison guards in one of the cell houses. The prisoners burned down the dining room, chapel, and two of the other cell houses. As you can only imagine, the trauma from this event stayed with my grandfather until he died, which unfortunately did not happen to be very long.

The above story was what I found in one of the online

MOM

newspapers from that time period. The additional information came from my mom's dad when he returned from the jailhouse riot. As my mom explained it to us, the prisoners had killed a lot of the guards and my grandfather, in an effort to save himself, lay next to the bodies of the men who had been killed and pretended to be dead for four days. In other words, it was a very smart game of "playing possum," and it kept him alive. The sad thing was the trauma he suffered from the event would never go away. We were also told they finally pumped tear gas into the prison to take back control. It worked, and they were able to get back into the facility. My grandfather didn't live much longer after that, and no one knows for sure if it was from the trauma of the event or the inhalation of tear gas. I guess we'll never know.

I don't know very much about my grandmother either other than she suffered a great deal as well. My great aunt told me my grandmother had a form of spinal cancer, and my aunt had to nurse and care for her for two years until she died. I think she was bedridden most of this time. My grandfather died three years after the prison riot, and my grandmother died another four years after that.

This situation left my mom, her sister, and her brother orphaned and their aunt, uncle, and grandfather to raise them. These were very difficult times for the family. My mom also had another aunt that she was very close to, and whom she had attached to after her parents died. When my mom was a teenager, tragedy struck once again, and this aunt of hers was hit head-on by another vehicle and ended up dying in the hospital four days later. This event took place roughly ten years after my grandmother died. So in fourteen short years, my mother lost both parents and one of her favorite aunts. That is so much pain for a young girl and teenager to go through.

The way some of this trauma seemed to play out in my

CHAPTER TWO

mother's life is she had a hard time opening up, and she had a hard time allowing herself to cry and express her emotions. As I may have mentioned before, I am a very emotive person, and being designed that way makes it hard for people to hide their feelings from me. It was because of this that I could feel the pain and sadness coming from my mom most of the time I was growing up. She did a quite righteous job of holding it together for the sake of our wellbeing, but her hurt and pain never escaped my attention, and I think I internalized it and blamed myself for it. I guess that's what happens when people aren't able to communicate their feelings.

As for my mom's personality, well, that's just a whole beautiful story in and of itself. She was a fearless woman and very strong-willed and self-sufficient. She grew up during a time when it wasn't so easy for women to do the things they desired, but that did not seem to stop her. She used to tell stories about how she liked to compete in "foot" races against the boys in her neighborhood. She would laugh and tell us how she would make bets with the boys that she could outlast them running. Inevitably, because what boy doesn't like a good challenge, and I imagine a little bit of their pride in question, they couldn't resist the temptation to say "yes" to her challenge. So as the story goes, they would race her, and she would keep running and running until one by one they all dropped off.

She would then proceed to pick up her winnings (possibly some candy or soda) and head home—trophy in hand. To this day I do believe I carry that willfulness with me. Once I've committed myself to something I will dig my heels in and stay focused until it's completed or a very large brick wall stands in my way. When my mom was growing up she had interests in lots of different areas. She was interested in sports, exercise, and activities, but apparently, she was also very interested in mathematics. (I do sometimes wonder if that may have been a contributing factor in my dad's interest in my mom.) She also grew up on a farm with lots of animals as well as apple and cherry orchards and a large garden. Let's just put it this way, they never stopped doing physical work, which my mom swore kept her from getting in trouble.

My mom was a big proponent of hard labor to fix any depression issues a person might have or any desire to be careless and reckless in their lives. She always said she never had enough time in the day to do any of that, and although I fought her every step of the way when she asked me to do chores, I am now the biggest proponent of hard labor. "Mama, I know you're listening, so be happy, and accept the fact that I just said you were right, and you can enjoy it for all of eternity."

When my mom became an adult she decided to move up to Denver. She moved in with a close friend of hers and got herself a good job working for the telephone company. My mom was well into her twenties and still not married when my dad came into the picture. The fact she wasn't married never seemed to concern my mom, even though on numerous occasions she was told she was going to be a spinster. I don't think she was concerned with any of that and might have been content to be single if it wasn't for the fact that she secretly—and maybe not so secretly—always wanted to have children. My dad and mom managed to have six kids, which I think suited them quite nicely. Although I was not what they expected, an absolute handful to raise and way more emotional and less logical than either one of them had bargained for, I think they both considered all of us to be their biggest blessings.

CHAPTER THREE

MORE SCHOOL FUN

As I continued my very simple journey through my grade-school years, I had some very goofy, and fun experiences and continued down the road of embarrassments as well. Let's just say the Lord kept me humble. I remember a very funny incident that happened in my grade-school cafeteria.

One day as I was heading to lunch in the cafeteria a couple of the kids and I decided it would be an extremely brilliant idea to race each other to the front of the line. If you're old enough to remember what schools were like in the '70s and '80s, they had a lot of hard tile floors and unforgiving concrete. This cafeteria was your classic old-style tile floor with about as much bounce and absorption as a retaining wall. In addition, for some ridiculous reason the janitorial staff thought it would be smart for them to do their job and mop and wax the floors.

So a couple of friends and I came booking it around one of the corners, hit the straightaway, and decided to run as fast as we could to the front of the line. I prided myself on being the fastest, evidenced by all the blue ribbons I won during track and field day, and I thought I could out-race anyone at that school. Oh, but that's when the cockiness does you in. I slipped on the very slick floor and was immediately taken down to the ground. I still had a ton of momentum behind me, so that had to go somewhere, and it kept pushing me forward until I slid into the wall—knee first. Wham-O, I hit the wall and finally stopped moving. I rolled over on my back and stayed frozen for a moment. You know that feeling you have when you know something very bad has happened to your body and you're afraid to look at the injured area?

Finally, after what seemed like an eternity, but was probably only thirty seconds or so, I looked down at my knee. I expected to see it all bloodied, but the opposite had happened. It was completely white, unnaturally so, and was dented in. I stared at it for a while, waiting for the blood to come seeping back in, but it didn't. Someone helped me up and took me to the office to see the nurse. By the time I hobbled up there, the color came back, but there was very little blood. It looked more bruised than anything and remained dented.

To be honest the dent in my knee stayed there for years to come, although I can't be sure how many exactly. It scarred as well, but I find it hard to see evidence of this injury as I look at it now. So my stupid, crazy, actions took my body years to recuperate from. Luckily for me, it wasn't a major injury. What can I say? I used to love living life in the fast lane and taking things to the edge.

PLAYGROUND FIGHT

Now I don't know how many of you out there grew up with a lot of siblings, and I certainly don't know if you all ended up going to the same grade school when you were growing up, but let me assure you it can be bad sometimes as well as it can be good. I'm

CHAPTER THREE

sure it's no big surprise to hear my siblings and I went to the same grade school. And while it seemed pretty cool at the time when you're a first- or second-grader, etc. . . . it can get kind of ugly as well.

What do I mean by ugly? It means your siblings do and say things to you and about you that can ruin your very precious reputation. So when did that happen to me, you might ask? Well, it happened a few times at the hands of my not-so-cool and not-so-popular bros (they may have been popular after all, but they never knew how to play things cool). This will require a few more details to help you understand.

Naturally, as we were all going to the same school, we had gotten fairly close with other families that attended the same school as we did. My brothers had a couple of friends who used to hang out at our house regularly, and we considered them just like additional brothers. On a couple of occasions, however, some new boys came into the picture that my sisters and I found cute and interesting, but because we were younger than them, they didn't take much notice of us. If that was the worst crime that had been committed, I could have lived with that, but the truth of the matter is my doofy brothers decided it would be a great idea to embarrass me even further. Now when you're the second-to-youngest sibling out of six, you can't wait to prove yourself to your older siblings and to be included. Little did I know how that would backfire on me.

We used to arm wrestle in our house for entertainment, and I, for some reason, seemed to have a knack for "bringing people down," if you will. It was pretty entertaining when I was young because it made my dad and brothers so proud (well maybe not all of them), and it put me in the spotlight. So one day when we were at school my brothers talked to some of their more macho friends and asked them if they wanted to arm wrestle me. I had won a few times over the years, but on one particular occasion, an incredibly strong and prideful friend of my brothers lost to me in an arm wrestling match in front of a lot of kids. He was so mad, and I'm quite sure so embarrassed, that he didn't talk to me for the rest of the year. It was very sad, and even though I enjoyed being the hero, I felt guilty for embarrassing him like that. The nice little bonus I didn't know would come along with that reputation was none of the boys were interested in me because what guy wants to get beat up by a girl? So even though it's not really my brothers' fault, they ultimately ruined my popularity and chance of having any young boy interested in me. This wasn't the only time they did it either.

A few years later, after the arm-wrestling incident, was another opportunity for me to crush another male ego and make another boy mad. Sadly, this time it was one of my very good friends. He was a really funny and sweet boy, and we used to talk to each other all the time. On one occasion, he thought it would be hilarious to make me laugh. I said very stoically to him that he couldn't make me laugh, even if he tried, which of course was an open challenge. So I closed my mouth, held my breath, and waited to see what he had. He cracked a few jokes; I didn't laugh. He cracked a few more—yada yada—until finally he said something so funny I couldn't hold it in anymore. I exploded with laughter, which did not bode well for me as I blew snot out of my nose on the exhale. I was humiliated and hid under my desk until I could get some Kleenex, and all my friend could say was "See, I told you I could make you laugh." That's the kind of kid he was, funny and sweet.

So this friend of mine just happened to have an older sister who was not so sweet. She was a couple of grades ahead of me,

CHAPTER THREE

and she was kind of a bully and loved to pick on people. On several occasions, she and I would get in verbal fights out on that very same playground where I had some of my other fights. She was so mean to people, and it just made me burn with anger. So on one occasion, while we were out at the playground and she was doing her bully stuff, I started yelling at her. Her brother came over and heard me and decided at that moment to defend his sister. This was kind of strange because he didn't really like her, and she was kind of mean to him, but you know the old saying blood is thicker than water.

So we started yelling and arguing with each other, and my brothers came over and started yelling, "Fight, fight," which managed to get the whole group of kids yelling the same thing. I don't remember much after that other than to say he and I started to fight. I have no earthly idea why we did it because we liked each other, and were good friends, but pressure got to us I guess. All I remember is I started to win, and he finally got mad and walked away. We never really recovered from that and never ended up restoring our friendship. So that was yet another big loss for me and a moment of being labeled as one of the most undateable girls alive. Where were you on that one, Guardian Angel?

CHAPTER FOUR

FIELD AND NEIGHBOR BOY

As if the school wasn't hard enough, you would think that one would get some relief by being at home. That was not the case of course. I mean overall my parents certainly did the best they could, but the problem was my parents had their own problems from their childhood they had never dealt with, so it ended up front and center in our lives. My dad had a huge temper, and my mom was very closed off regarding her own emotions and feelings. That didn't make home a very safe place for a child to express her emotions.

We (the siblings and I) seemed to fight a lot when we were young . . . well, even when were older. I think we all were very prideful and very stubborn, and we had a hard time accepting the fact we made mistakes or were wrong. I experienced emotional things at a very high level. I was very good at reading people and knowing how to talk to others. I was without a doubt a very social creature. The interesting thing, though, is instead of seeing that as a gift or a blessing, I considered it a negative because all of my family seemed to be more scholarly and cerebral. Now that I'm an adult, I can appreciate the gifts God has given me, but that's just not how things are when you are young.

CHAPTER FOUR

PLAYING IN THE BACK FIELD

When I was a child, I so much enjoyed playing in the open field behind our house. We lived in the inner city of Denver and had a very unique situation in our four-block neighborhood. Right in the center of these four streets was a huge open field covering the length and width of the city block. It was enclosed all the way around by all of the houses in the neighborhood except for one spot, which ended up being on our property. This spot, or access point (which is what the city called an easement), ran along the length of our property and led into this open field. So if anyone wanted to take a vehicle back there or walk back into the field, they had to come and ask permission from my parents. Luckily for everyone, my parents were very open with this easement and allowed people in and out as the need arose. This entire area, the field as well as the easement, were owned by the city.

My parents tried for years to get the city to sell it to them so they could allow access from other pieces of property, but the city wouldn't sell. It was such a strange situation because the field was relatively useless to the city, and they never maintained it anyway, but alas, there it was, a big open field to play in for hours on end, and play we did. As a family, we liked to play a lot of different games. We loved to play Football, baseball, cops and robbers, and cowboys and Indians. My mom had planted a very large garden in this field as well, and during the summer, as we played our many games, we would run over to the garden to snack on sweet cherry tomatoes, peas straight out of the pods, and delicious beefsteak tomatoes, as well as onions. And yes, believe it or not, an onion fresh out of the garden can be eaten just like an apple and tastes sweet and satisfying.

PLAYING IN THE BACK FIELD

Sometimes we would run out into the field and hide in the tall grass and weeds so that our family couldn't see us or find us. We even snuck out the window of our house, sometimes at night, to play hide-and-seek or to pretend we were breaking out of our house without our parents knowing. Of course this never lasted very long as our parents had built the fear of God into us that we might get picked up by the police and arrested. So most of the time we would just run out there into the field, hide for a couple minutes giggling and laughing, and then head back to the house, sneak back in through the window, and crawl into our beds, feeling confident in the knowledge we had bested our parents. I think they always knew what was going on but didn't worry too much because they knew we wouldn't go too far. It seemed that every time we crept back in the house there were my parents sleeping comfortably in their bed, unfazed by the goings-on of their children and our wild escape into the night.

That, however, was not true of one of my brothers who decided to sneak out of the house one night and venture out much further than the rest of us had (he was my male counterpart and always liked to test the limits). I still do not know exactly what he was doing when he left, but that goofus managed to get himself picked up by the police and transported back to our house. Our parents got a knock on the door in the middle of the night and were met by a police officer and their son on the front stoop. They were so mad, and my brother was so scared, that we all had to pay the price for his action. All I could think to myself was why my brother couldn't manage to get better at sneaking around and being more discreet, which is I'm sure not the "take-away lesson" my parents were hoping for.

As I continue to reminisce about the memories of that giant field and all the fun and activities we had experienced, I

CHAPTER FOUR

remember something that actually made me unsettled. I don't remember what age I was, but I remember being young and a young boy approaching me in the field and asking me to come over by some trees. It sounded like fun, so I headed over there with him, and when we got underneath the trees and out of sight of everyone, he approached me and kissed me on the lips. I was too young to really understand what that was, but I remember not feeling good about it. The boy seemed proud of himself and ran away smiling. Any of the times I saw him after that, he always looked at me weird, and it made me uncomfortable.

While these may be common events that happen to little kids, it made me very nervous to go and play in the field by myself anymore. Little did I know how later in life these types of behaviors would grow in size and seriousness and leave an indelible mark on me, like a permanent marker does on paper. Unfortunately, this mark and others like it were left on my soul, which had a much deeper impact and lasted for a lifetime.

FRIEND OR FOE

While I prefer to reach into the folds of my memory and return to the happy times I had with my family, the beautiful house and big backyard we had, and the very fun neighborhood filled with lots of kids, unfortunately, that only tells part of the story. It's just like everything else in life; the sweet and the sour always mix, and there's just no getting around it. I was told I was a very gregarious child with a spunky personality and super extroverted. I know I loved talking to people and found every opportunity I could to do that. In addition, my parents and siblings always told me I was so pretty and cute. They were just complimenting me, but later in my life, it would become a negative trait, and for quite a while one that I wished I didn't portray because I thought it brought me unwanted attention.

I have this memory that has flashed in my mind on many occasions throughout my life. It's about a very dark place I ended up in on more than one occasion. I would like to say I have all the details figured out, and know exactly what happened, how it happened, and who it had happened with, but for many of you reading through these lines, you know that is not how sexual injuries play out in one's life. I can share the memories of these experiences, but it's fragmented at best. So I would liken it to being in a dream state where everything comes to you in pieces, not sequentially, and it comes in one flash after another and nothing seems to make much sense. I'm not sure of my age as events like these seem to be devoid of a timeline, but I think I was probably around eleven or twelve, and I remember somebody of the opposite sex exposing himself to me (not that I knew what exposing meant) and wanting me to do the same. It was scary and unsettling. I don't know why I took part in this activity, and why I didn't fight him off with everything I had, but I must have trusted this person. Isn't that usually how it is?

The worst part of all is it never really left my memory—even when I got older. The flashes would continue to come to me and bury me in sadness, shame, and guilt. I wish I could have gone to my mother and talked to her about it, but I was afraid to. If she had ever known I was going through this, I'm sure it would have broken her heart to think I didn't trust her enough to share it with her. I know I would feel that way if it was my child. The reason I didn't tell her was threefold: I felt guilty and responsible for having participated; I was afraid my dad would have gotten so mad he may have killed this person; and finally, I didn't think she and the rest of the family liked me very much. I was a stubborn

CHAPTER FOUR

child and was always getting in trouble, and the family talked about me a lot—and not in the best light. I assumed they didn't like my personality, or in general the person I was. Add to that the fact I was closest to my brothers at that time, and no girl wants to go tell her brother something like that.

It's the strangest experience when you are a young child to be so curious about such things, but to feel with every fiber of your being it is wrong. I always felt a closeness to God in my heart, and I knew he would find this physical behavior bad. Sadly it happened more than once, and on these occasions, I felt fear and trembling and absolute shame down to my core. That is how I felt, and I never told anyone about it. I was trapped in my subconscious memories, and it just added to my self-doubt, insecurities, and self-hatred. That is the problem with these kinds of abuses. The shame is so great it drives the victim even deeper into themselves where they have to carry the burden alone. I think that's probably the first time I started to think God was disgusted with me and couldn't possibly love me anymore. It drove a wedge between me and my savior that would only widen and deepen as time went on. Now that I have gotten older, I realize my Guardian Angel tried to protect me from this, and in some ways I think he wanted to weep. Thank you for always being there and being my friend, even when I didn't realize it.

CHAPTER FIVE

FIGHTING MY WAY TO FIT IN

Along with everything else, I had some other pretty difficult changes in my life. When I was in grade school, a new priest came to the school when I was in sixth grade and decided he was going to close it down, and he did just that. He seemed to have it in for the school and the parents, so I'm not sure exactly what was going on with him. Needless to say this left me and my younger sister to find a new grade school to go to. She was placed in a school about two miles from our house, and I ended up having to go across town to a school where we didn't know anyone. I entered the school in seventh grade and stayed through eighth grade.

If anyone has ever gone to a private school, you know exactly how cliquish it can be. This school was no exception. Right from the get-go these girls pretty much hated me, and I felt as though I had a target on my back every day. People were not very friendly, nor were they welcoming. I was an outsider to them, and they preferred to keep me on the outside. I hated being there, was miserable, and I wanted to come back and go to school with my sister, but that was not an option. Add to that the fact I had to

CHAPTER FIVE

ride two buses just to get to school, and you have a pretty clear picture of how miserable seventh and eighth grade were for me.

I had a couple of fights with some of the girls at the school; luckily though it was nothing physical. Then finally a couple of girls befriended me. They were on the outside fringe of popularity, so they were the perfect candidates to take in a misfit toy like myself. They were both so sweet to me and such kind and loving girls. They made the rest of the time I spent there very pleasant and even happy. I will forever be indebted to them. As time went on and I graduated from eighth grade, it was time for me to move to high school. The only problem was the private high school my parents wanted me to go to was even further away from my house. I do remember being upset and not wanting to go, but for whatever reason, my parents sent me there anyway. I was an outsider again because all of these kids had grown up together. Most of them went to the grade school attached to the high school, so they were all one big, happy family without any extra room for me.

Surprisingly I got invited to several parties in my ninth-grade year of high school, but I chose not to go. I don't remember the reasons exactly, but I do think it had to do with the fact I didn't like a lot of the girls, it was such a long distance from my house, and my parents probably wouldn't have taken me over there. Either way, I found out later how good it was I didn't go. A couple of the girls I had made friends with said they were doing cocaine at the parties and other lewd and inappropriate behaviors. One of these girls witnessed some of these boys and girls having sex in the bushes outside of the house. Aside from the fact that seems ridiculously painful, I thought it was disgusting and didn't want to have anything to do with it. While this may seem like a normal high school event, the reality was these young kids came from very wealthy families and had very little monitoring or parental involvement. They had money and could get and do whatever they wanted, and it was at a very heavy cost to their souls in my opinion. My parents never really believed how bad it was, and I think they just wanted to stay removed from it.

By this time I started getting used to change and adapting to new environments, so I tried to make the best of it. I was able to make some good friends at the school and find a way to navigate through that ninth-grade school year. I even decided to go out for track, which was a surprise to me as well. The track coach was very tough, and our practices were extremely hard. If that had been the worst of it, I could have accepted that, but there was more to the story. I showed up to every practice and did whatever the coach told us to do. I don't remember if she was new to coaching or what, but she prided herself on trying to make practices as difficult as possible. I think it would have done her some good to have run some of the practices with us. It was not unusual for any of us to throw up during practice as that's how hard she pushed us. When I came home at night, I was trashed and had a hard time getting my homework done. My mom seemed surprised by my exhaustion levels, but both of my parents had raised us to finish what we started, so the idea of quitting track seemed impossible, so I just kept working at it.

As the meets were getting closer, I kept asking to run in the 100- and 200-meter dash and the coach said no. I would ask her why, and she said I had to be faster than everyone if I wanted to run it. So I told her to time us all in these events at the next practice, and guess what? I ran the fastest times of any of the girls—even the seniors. Foolishly, I thought this would make a difference because what coach doesn't want to win, but it didn't. The first meet came, and she put me in the 400-meter dash,

CHAPTER FIVE

the 800-meter dash, and the mile relay. If anyone knows me, they know I am not a middle distance person, but because I was competitive, I still performed well. I was so angry at this point because it seemed like this coach disliked me and was reacting out of emotion. It reminds me of the teacher in the movie *Freaky Friday* who treats the student unfairly, and the mom doesn't believe her until she becomes the kid and has to deal with him.

Luckily my mom was finally starting to see what was happening, so she said for me to stick it out through the next week's meet, and if the coach didn't let me do either of my two races, then she'd let me quit. So I went to practice every day that week, and when the next meet came, the coach refused to put me in those races. Even the girls on the team were starting to wonder what was going on because I was the fastest runner they had. Nonetheless, I ran in that meet, and then for the first time ever, I quit a sport mid-season. It was very disappointing for me because I had a chance to do really well that season. The coach, however, was just playing favorites, and there was no other way around it. It really made my mom angry as well, which was nice to have her support.

After I finished that school year, my mom and dad gave me the option to go to public school by our house as they had my other siblings. I jumped on that opportunity immediately and couldn't wait to be back in my "hood" again. The funny thing is my neighborhood was a very nice place to live when I was growing up, but later, it really did turn into an inner-city hood. Nonetheless, after three fairly miserable years in private school, I was ready for the change. So starting tenth grade I ended up at the local high school, which was roughly two miles from my house. Wow, what a change that was for me. Even if I couldn't get a ride to school on any given day, I was still close enough to walk.

Later on, that was actually something my friends and I did quite a bit. I had to, however, get some new friends first.

MY BESTIE

So one of the greatest parts of my childhood had to do with this super-cool girlfriend of mine. We met when I was thirteen years old and she was twelve, and we hit it off right away. We actually met at softball practice, of all places, where we were playing a pickup softball game. This was one of the girlfriends that attended high school with me. I definitely went through a very tomboy phase in my life, and in some ways I think the tomboy is still in me. Needless to say I had my hair cut very short at this point. Remember the Dorothy Hamill haircut? Well that's what I had when my girlfriend and I met. I loved that haircut and wanted to be Dorothy Hamill (who didn't), and I thought it looked really cute on me. Let me tell you the way it translated for my friend (I will call her Jenny). She thought I was a boy, I assume a very cute boy, however a boy nonetheless. She said it took her a while to realize I was a girl with short hair. That explains why she was so weird with me when we first met because I was up on the pitcher's mound, and she just stared at me like something was wrong with me.

As time went on, we became best friends and hung out regularly at each other's houses. My memory was she was at our house quite a bit, which was completely accepted by all members of my family. They liked having Jenny around. Even to this day, I think you would be hard-pressed to find a person that didn't like her. She was bubbly and effervescent, like Alka-Seltzer, very charismatic, and loved people. She had a lot of friends, but for whatever reason, I was her best friend at that time.

CHAPTER FIVE

We loved riding our bikes everywhere, which gave us a sense of freedom, and we could be found on our bikes most of the time. I do want to take this moment, however, to mention the fact that when we rode our bikes up and down hills and all the back streets, I rode a heavy-duty Schwinn muscle bike if you will, and she rode a ten-speed. This meant I ended up getting double the workout and moved at half the speed. This is still something I laugh about even to this day. Jenny would nag me to ride faster whenever we were trying to get somewhere. I should have made her ride my bike so she could find out what it felt like. Who knows, maybe I did.

There were a couple of instances we had along the way forever embedded in my memory as some of the funniest things I've ever seen or heard. On one occasion, on a fabulous day, my sister Lisa, Jenny, and I decided it was time to play dress up in my mom's clothes. What young lady didn't at some point go and put on their mother's dresses and dress shoes and prance around like an adult? So we paraded around like we were in a Miss America pageant and presented ourselves to the judges as we walked around the house. We had in our house a deep, dark, creepy basement, and the only access to that basement was one of the steepest, most treacherous staircases you've ever seen (emphasis all mine).

Let's just say that as we were parading around, Jenny was not the most natural in heels. Let's put it this way. She was so clumsy in heels that just watching her walk was a great deal of entertainment; although, I don't think she appreciated us teasing her about it. Needless to say as we were making our rounds in front of the judge's table, it was suggested we take a trip down the stairs. I assume to see how elegantly we handled a staircase. We were about two steps in when all of a sudden down went

Pageant Queen Number 3 (Jenny) tumbling down the stairs and onto the hard concrete below.

A natural reaction after such an event should have been panic and hysteria, but my obnoxious sister and I (being equally obnoxious) weren't exactly the most compassionate. So we started laughing and could not seem to get ourselves to stop laughing. There was Jenny at the bottom of the stairs, with the strap from her hat stretched across the face of her lifeless body. The longer this went on, the more we started to realize she might actually have gotten hurt. So just as we started to make a move toward her, we heard our dad yell in a very disturbingly gruff voice (which was always his normal voice), "Who is that making all that noise; stop screwing around." Jenny proceeded to jump off the floor as if sprung out of a Jack in The Box and yelled, "It's okay, Mr. P; it's okay." Well that was the final straw for us, and we all dropped down on the floor and started rolling around in laughter—all three of us this time.

The next fun adventure is what we called the "Spider Hunt." As I mentioned before, the basement of our house was dark and creepy, which was a perfect place for spiders to live. And since I haven't mentioned it now, it's as good a time as any to tell you I had severe arachnophobia. I regularly dreamed spiders were crawling all over me and were going to attack and kill me. So to sleep in a basement where the spiders outnumber the humans by a disgusting amount was a very difficult thing.

So as was always the case, Jenny came up with a brilliant idea. She decided we should get dressed up in Safari clothes, borrow our brother's BB guns, and go into the basement and shoot spiders. I'm pretty confident most of the people reading this have done some ridiculous form of a spider hunt in their own lives, so you can relate. I don't know how many spiders we killed

CHAPTER FIVE

that day, and I don't know if we ever did it again, but I do have to admit that dressed in the appropriate clothing, and armed with those sophisticated weapons, I finally started to feel empowered against the arachnids. It didn't change my fear of them until much, much later, but they didn't have the same power over me they used to.

We had many of these adventures and played as much together as any two kids could play. We were both very close with each other's families, and she went on trips with us, and I went on trips with them. On one particular trip, we took an RV to the mountains with her family. I don't remember much about the trip, just that we were having fun as always, but I do remember an extraordinarily funny event that happened with her brother.

Jenny's brother was . . . well . . . what shall we say . . . an older brother! He lived to harass us and get in our business all the time. We considered him a dweeb and wanted him to stay away from us, but years later I realized he was just a big brother enjoying the tormenting of his younger sister and her best friend. Needless to say, on this particular camping trip, he was on his fifteenth or so episode of fighting and irritating us, and low and behold came Jenny's grandmother to the rescue. Now this grandma of Jenny's was an amazing woman with an amazing heart and love for all kids, but she was also what I would like to call a tough broad. I like to use the term we're all familiar with, but I think soaking wet she may have weighed a hundred pounds. She was a scrawny old thing. When Jenny's brother started in on us again, and I think made me cry, she got so mad she grabbed him, started shaking him, and then started punching him with her little bony fists. She started yelling at him, "You need to be a better person and stop picking on the girls," and on and on. He couldn't do anything except stand there and take it, but in that moment the three of us, Jenny, her brother, and I, all looked at each other and burst out laughing. There is nothing quite like the vengeance of a grandmother. I will always remember that woman and love her dearly. I never had a grandma to grow up with, and she filled that spot for me.

As time went on, and we got older, we started drifting apart, especially around the time of high school. We seemed to hang out in different friend groups. I don't know what caused us to separate at that time. I do think high school drama had a hand in it, but nonetheless we always cared for each other and were always very grateful for the friendship we had and the depth to that friendship. I can't remember clearly how often we spent time together, but it waxed and waned. At one point she started dating the ex-boyfriend of another close friend of mine, and unfortunately, it put me in the middle of things. I tried to tell both of them I didn't want to be in the middle, but you know in high school it's very adversarial; you're either with me or you're against me.

Nonetheless Jenny was always and will always be my closest childhood friend. She was my confidant and trusted source of support, compassion, and overall joy. She made me happy when I was at my lowest points, and I feel like she gave me a reason to keep going on. I know my Guardian Angel was working with her to help keep me sane and functioning. I wish we could have stayed close when I went through the even more difficult times that arose in the future because who knows how different that would have been for me, but either way, she was my life preserver, and I think I was hers. There's no doubt in my mind God put us in each other's lives.

CHAPTER SIX

THE SUFFERINGS OF A TEENAGER

As mentioned in an earlier chapter, with all the drama of my schooling years I arrived now in a public school setting for the first time in my life and on to a new adventure. When I arrived at the school after having left a grade school consisting of a total of five hundred students from first grade all the way to twelfth, this school of two thousand students was a bit overwhelming. As is always the case when it comes to me meeting new people it became a challenge I readily accepted. I was, however, very nervous trying to figure out how to fit in. But then again, what young teenager isn't?

It took a little while for me to meet some people, but luckily I had my sports. My favorite sport was gymnastics. I begged to be put into gymnastics classes when I was young, but my mom and dad said they didn't have the money to do it, so I didn't actually start taking gymnastic classes until I could work and pay for it myself, which unfortunately wasn't until I turned thirteen. Now I have known some thirteen-year-olds that entered gymnastics at that time and went on to do a great deal in the sport, but I do believe they had a tad bit more natural talent for it than I did.

Because I started late and was behind the mark on the training, I could not go as far as I had intended. I would have loved to have gotten a scholarship and gone to college in the sport, but that was not in the cards. Needless to say, I loved the sport so much, and I worked harder than anyone else in my inner circle to do the best I could. I was at least good enough to compete in high school, so that is what I did.

It was during that sport that I met what would later become my new best friend (Sherry). We would take up where Jenny and I had left off and become inseparable for the next four or five years. Sherry was an incredibly flexible (all three splits to be exact) individual, which made her really good at a lot of gymnastic related things, as one could imagine. Thinking back on it now, I don't actually remember ever talking to her about whether or not she had taken lessons before this or just decided to go out for the gymnastics team; either way I was very glad she was there. On the team I became a first-level spotter (someone who helps spot/hold a person as they're learning tricks).

I had learned this skill when I took gymnastics lessons at one of the local grade school gyms, and our teacher just happened to be an ex-USA gymnast who had actually made it to the Olympic trials. She had unfortunately gotten injured and was unable to make it on the Olympic team. Needless to say, what was a huge loss for her ended up being a huge blessing for us. She taught us all how to spot each other and taught us how to execute a trick with perfect form, which would stay with us throughout our seasons of competition. She was also a beautiful dancer and had taught us a lot about how to be graceful. She even helped us choreograph some of our floor routines for high school.

The sport I went out for in the spring was track and field. I ended up doing shot put, discus, and three relays. I was actually

CHAPTER SIX

probably much better at track than I was at gymnastics, but I didn't have very good coaching in either sport, so that didn't help me too much. I was a diligent worker and dedicated myself to sports, which helped me to keep a check on my drinking and partying habits. Sherry did not participate in track and field, which led me to make new friends. However, Sherry remained my closest friend and was always present whenever we did things together.

As my high school years continued, and the struggles and stressors that go with being a teenage girl, things at home became difficult. I fought with my parents on a regular basis, as well as my siblings. While I was a very difficult child, stubborn and willful, my parents also had a lot of their own baggage, which affected the way they handled and raised me. I know my other siblings went through a lot of their struggles too, but my dad's anger seemed to be geared a lot more toward my older brother and me.

Now that I'm an adult, I can look back and see patterns of behavior and problems on both sides of the equation, but when you're a child you see your parents as omnipotent, and if they don't verbalize their mistakes, it can lead a child to self-blame. My parents were most likely not capable of seeing their shortcomings, and were as broken as I am, so it left us in a tangle. Either way, my dad and I had screaming matches quite often, and I received a good deal of his work stress, especially since I pushed his buttons all the time.

As you read this story, remember these are my memories of the events, and my feelings as I was going through them. Naturally, in life, there are always shades of gray, but when you're a child, everything is black and white. And the black and white of it was I thought my parents disliked me immensely,

THE SUFFERINGS OF A TEENAGER

hated my friends, and basically disapproved of who I was as a person. Add to that the idea I thought my parents saw me as intellectually challenged, and you can imagine how I felt as a teenager. As for my siblings, it seemed as though they felt the same way as my parents did. While I know now they love me, at that time that was even in question. It just felt like every time I came home somebody was mad at me for something.

So I tried to be gone as much as possible, which wasn't that hard because I ended up forming a lot of friendships and had a pretty good inner circle to go do activities with, party, etc. Whenever I was home, I was always on the phone. That was my way of trying to avoid conflict.

I was very glad to have a big family unit, both immediate and extended. The great thing about having a big family is even if you're not getting along with one or two people there's usually someone you can get along with. When I was a young girl, that was my brother closest in age to me; when I was a teenager, it was my oldest brother; and when I became an adult, it was various aunts and uncles I developed close relationships with. I fought so much with my middle brother—cuz he was exactly like me—that we never really socialized when we were young. He was the only other one in the family who had a lot of friends and socialized all the time. He wasn't home very much.

When I was a teenager my younger sister (Lisa) and I spent a lot of time together because we had the same friend group and because we were the only ones left in the home. She had a fun personality, was very gifted in sports, and loved to dance. She was three years younger than me, and it wasn't the best idea to have her with me when I got older. Now that I look back on that time in my life, I really never understood why my parents pushed that situation so hard. I mean, practically speaking, I understand

CHAPTER SIX

they wanted someone to watch out for Lisa, but I was in a much older age group, and the stuff we were exposed to—and some of my friends involved in—was not something a young teenager should experience. It was a choice of me staying home all the time and not hanging out with friends or taking my younger sister everywhere with me. Unfortunately, I chose the latter.

As for my older sister (Anne) we were separated in age by three brothers and really never spent much time together when I was young. I mean of course we lived in the same house and when I was little shared a room, but we really didn't get to know each other until we were older. There was only six years between us, but with three siblings in between, it's crazy how far apart that seems. She is a really kind, loving, and supportive person. She cares very much for the people around her and carried on the torch for my mom as peacekeeper and surrogate mom. Sadly, though, I didn't feel like she had a fondness for me. I just always felt like I disappointed her.

As a whole, my family could be a very tough bunch to be around. We were all very opinionated and unfortunately liked to make our opinions known—some of us more than others. I fell into that same category, but mine was not so much being opinionated in regards to scholarly things as it was about how to treat people and how to act kindly. My family had a tendency to call people stupid a lot, and it aggravated me because it didn't matter if somebody was technically stupid because their life had meaning and value because our Lord created them. At least that was the black and white I understood.

We were pretty cruel with our words and short with one another. It was kind of strange, but my parents never seemed to intervene when we would lash each other with a wicked tongue. As a child I never understood that because it contradicted what

THE SUFFERINGS OF A TEENAGER

was expected out of us in the real world. If we had ever talked disrespectfully to any of our teachers or a priest, we would have received spankings, and yet when it came to our treatment of each other in the home it appeared there was a separate set of rules. Years later, when I was raising my children, my mom admitted to me she wished my dad and she hadn't let us talk to one another that way. Clearly she had regrets.

Not surprisingly, I contributed to this sometimes volatile interplay with my siblings. The problem was from my perspective I always felt a lot of guilt over what I said and whose feelings I hurt, but I didn't let it show because I didn't want to appear weak. I was very sensitive and got my feelings hurt quite easily but tried to cover it up so I wouldn't get mocked. I was an empath, you see, and we are wired differently than the rest of the world. The best way to describe an empath is comparing us to a light switch. It's like the light switch gets turned on the minute you are around other people, and you can never turn it off. You feel everyone's pain, suffering, and sadness without being able to filter it out. Years later I had a niece that suffered from the same ailment, if you will, and she described things the same way.

She said, "Whenever I'm around people, I feel everything they feel, and I cannot stop the sensory overload." I'm not sure that my parents understood this, but in my effort to hide my feelings, the only thing that ever got expressed was anger. Anger was the emotion that was allowed in our home; crying, sadness, or sensitivity was not. Anger, it seemed, "won the day." My friends were the only ones I didn't experience this with.

CHAPTER SIX

HIGH SCHOOL CONTINUES

So as a high school student, I participated in the usual amount of partying, drinking, and admittedly a bit of marijuana intake. Since I didn't want to jeopardize any of my sports I did very little partaking in these types of comforts, but I wasn't a teetotaler either. I believe that it was my body's extreme sensitivity to drugs and alcohol that kept me from becoming an addict. I do believe without that I would have easily slipped into that role. Sometimes sensitivity can be a good thing.

While I was growing up I witnessed hypocrisy in the church and the schools attended, which made me question those in charge of my formation. Despite this, I believed in some of the teachings of my Catholic faith and tried to hold on to those. For example, I desired to be chaste and pure until marriage. I need to do a shout out to my parents in this regard because they raised me in the faith and laid that foundation. From the time I was Baptized, and later Confirmed, those marks upon my soul would forever tug me back into the direction of Jesus Christ in the Catholic Church he founded. I was not very knowledgeable in the teachings of the church and did not realize how to make use of the sacraments to strengthen me. I left the church for quite a while until finally the Eucharist brought me home. Until that happened, however, a lot more came down the road.

So one of the pressures many young girls experience is the desire to look good, be beautiful, and most of all be skinny. I unfortunately grew up in the generation of fashion models and cover girls being the example of what we all needed to look like. I was in no way, shape, or form built like that, so it didn't do well for my body image. Add to that most of my friends were either duplicate builds for the fashion models or cute and petite. My broad shoulders and huskier build did not fit in. My poor body image coupled with my struggles at home (and the seeming lack of male interest), and you have a formula for disaster. My eating disorder started fairly subtly with just an occasional meal being rejected in the toilet and a growing awareness of calorie counts in the foods I ate. As time went on, the disorder got more dis-ordered.

I became obsessed with trying to look a certain way and would refuse to eat food for a couple of days at a time. I would get very, very hungry and then eat everything in sight, which would then mean I had to do something about it before it hit my stomach and got absorbed into every fat cell of my body. I was always into sports and exercise, so that just became a place of addiction. I would exercise for hours during the day, and as I got older, and things unfortunately got worse in my life, I actually started to wake up in the middle of the night and do aerobics for two hours. I am not proud of this, and I'm certainly embarrassed to admit this was happening, but it was my reality and part of my tapestry.

Continuing through high school I leaned heavily on my friends and their support. My best friend Sherry was with me on this journey to remain pure and chaste, but a few weeks before graduation, and at the end of our senior year, she decided she wanted to end that streak. I begged her not to and told her she would be making a big mistake. In her words, she didn't want to graduate from high school as a virgin. So at one of our senior parties, she took it upon herself to find a willing candidate—as if that's hard—and hustled off to his car to complete the task. She came back in and seemed to have visibly changed. She claimed to have been glad she'd done it, but her eyes told a different story. From that point on, I was the only virgin left in our circle of friends, and sadly that wasn't a badge of honor. Defeated as I

CHAPTER SIX

was, my Guardian Angel was on my shoulder giving me a hug and letting me know God was still watching over me.

GRADUATION AND THE STORY OF GEORGE

So much to my surprise I finally made it through high school and graduated. Over the three years of high school my parents and I had many debates about whether or not I was going to college. Now you have to understand my parents grew up during a time when college was not easily accessible for everyone. My mom went to college for about a year and then met my dad and, much to her chagrin, once she got married, never went back and finished. It was always the plan that after she had all of us kids and raised us, she would return to school and get her bachelor's degree. By the time we all left home, I think her appetite for learning, or maybe going back to school, wasn't there anymore. So she was never able to finish.

As for me, I was your typical rebellious teenager that hated school and thought college was stupid. I had no interest in going to college, and my dad had no interest in housing a defiant eighteen-year-old who refused to make anything of her life. So a few months after I graduated, I got myself a full-time job and moved out with my cousin. The three years that followed were incredibly fun and also incredibly painful. Now doesn't that just sound normal?

THE STORY OF GEORGE

During the time I lived with my cousin, in addition to being incredibly unstable, I was also full of life and always had a zest for spontaneity and excitement. So to add to that excitement,

THE STORY OF GEORGE

one day, lurking outside my front door, was this beautiful tomcat about the size of a small mountain lion cub. The tomcat was probably just about as wild. It appeared to be a stray as it had no collar or tags, and I spent several weeks trying to find its owner. No one claimed him, so he was mine. I, like any wonderful and intelligent young lady alive in the '80s, had fallen madly in love with George Michael from the pop group Wham. So the logical thing to do was to name this beautiful beast of a cat "George." Oh George, sweet, sweet George, was such a wonderful creature except . . . that . . . he was not.

He took an exceptional liking to our sofa and found it a remarkably perfect scratch pad. If you picked him up the wrong way, he lashed out at you and tried to claw your eyes out, and if he just wasn't in the mood, you couldn't get him to do anything you wanted. In other words, he was rebellious, angry, and aggressive, which was the mirror image of his new owner. It was love at first sight.

On one beautiful occasion, I came in the door only to find he had somehow nabbed a bird and brought it into the apartment. I'm not sure exactly when he got out or how he brought it back, but it was there and ready to greet us. As I ran through the house, jumping on top of my bed and trying to catch the bird before the cat ate it, my cousin walked in. I started screaming, "The cat got a bird, the cat got a bird," which, after slowly trying to process what I said, my cousin had to immediately dodge the incoming bird. He quickly started running around the apartment trying to help me round the poor creature up before he was consumed by the jaws of life—a.k.a. . . . George.

I still don't know how we captured that creature, but once we did and raced it outside, we were freed from the danger. My cousin and I fell to the ground laughing our heads off, and it is

CHAPTER SIX

still to this day one of the funniest memories I have embedded in this empty head of mine. Whenever I feel a little sad, all I have to do is remember George the tomcat and Jerry the bird. It was a nice opportunity to relieve some of the stress my Guardian Angel was experiencing from guarding me and allow him to enjoy some laughter as well.

CHAPTER SEVEN

MORE DARK DAYS AHEAD

The following story is where the most damage was done to my soul and psyche. I can't remember exactly how old I was, as I've blocked that out, but I do remember it was sometime after I graduated from high school and before I moved out to Seattle Washington. It was between the age of nineteen and twenty-one. My sister Lisa and I continued to spend a lot of time together. One day, when we were out shopping, we ran into an old friend of my brother's. We hadn't seen him in a while as my brother and he didn't hang out much anymore, so it was a welcomed surprise. We will call him Bill for the sake of the story.

Bill had frequented our doorstep many times when my brother was in high school. They played football together and naturally formed a bond over that. He was popular and well-liked by everybody and seemed very fond of my family. After talking to him at the store for a little while, we decided it would be very cool to have him come over and hang out and watch movies. I need to remind you my sister and I were both very naive and it never seemed to occur to us that this was not an inappropriate thing to do when we were the only two siblings living at the home,

CHAPTER SEVEN

we were female, and our parents weren't going to be home. Nonetheless, made the party plans and arrangements.

Now what should have been a red flag for us was the guy didn't even have a car or transportation to get to our house, but like the naive person I was, and overly trusting, I drove out to his house to pick him up. I don't remember the details very much, but after picking him up, we grabbed a movie, some food, and headed back to our parent's house.

When we got there, we started eating and drinking alcohol. Odd as it may be, I did not partake of the alcohol. That is to say I was the only sober one in the room within a couple of hours. I was trying to keep an eye on my younger sister (I realize at this point it begs the question of why was I even letting her drink—but I didn't think it was a big deal since I was there to watch her and we were at our house—again very naive) since she had ingested quite a bit of alcohol and was tipsy. I remember cutting her off at some point along the way to which she did not respond well. Either way, I knew she needed it, so I set up the bed for her and attempted to get her to go to sleep. That was a nightmare in and of itself as she kept jumping out of bed and running around the house and trying to get more alcohol, and Bill kept coming into the room laughing and getting her more riled up. It was like dealing with two very large children. Believe it or not, this man was three years older than I was, but you wouldn't have been able to tell. So after about an hour of fighting with both of them, I finally got them into their respective rooms and, I thought, asleep.

When all was said and done, I headed to the downstairs bedroom to go to sleep. I had just dozed off when I felt a warm presence in the bed next to me. I was still very much asleep and processing what I thought was a dream and trying to make sense of it. I remember feeling this very emotional weight on my heart; in my state of delirium, I knew that what was happening was very bad. I still wasn't quite awake, and I immediately felt somebody very strong and forceful press up against me and get even closer every second. When I finally woke up and realized what was happening, I started pushing him away and told him not to do it. His response was to press harder against me, and I pushed and cried and begged him not to do it. He held me in place, and within a blink of an eye, he finished the task he had set out to do. He was out of the bed in a split second, and I just remember rolling over in the bed, grabbing the blanket, and crying myself to sleep.

The next morning, when I woke up, my sister was in the room. It took a second for me to remember the night before, and I immediately panicked. I said is Bill still in the house, and she said no that she thought he left in the middle of the night. I got out of bed and looked down at it with pain. My sister looked directly at me knowing what had just happened, and as I started to tear up, she helped me take the sheets off the bed and prepare to wash them. I begged her to please never tell anyone what just happened. She promised me she wouldn't, and she didn't. My sister and I have had a lot of ups and downs, but that moment was probably one of the most tender and kind moments she had shown me. I will always appreciate that.

Once I was able to pull myself together, I proceeded forward with my life, deciding never to look back on this moment. However this moment definitely looked forward to me and permanently impacted my future and some of the decisions I made. While I realize some of you reading this may think I should have gone to the police, I instinctively knew better. I kept this to myself, and in the end, I was grateful that I had. It turns out that in my life I have had friendships with many women who have

CHAPTER SEVEN

gone through this same ordeal, and in many cases even worse, but none of them had any luck going the legal route. They ended up with no protection and just became revictimized by the system. I think I must have instinctively known this and known to protect myself by keeping my mouth shut. So many women suffer this same fate, and it's not right, but I haven't seen it change yet.

Oh sweet Guardian Angel, I now know how bad you must have felt for me. Thank you for trying to protect me even in that moment.

THE GROWING PAINS OF ADULTHOOD

I continued with my struggles of not feeling loved, not knowing my place in life, my attractiveness, and most of all my weight. I worked hard to keep from gaining weight over the years, and this period was even more difficult. When I was competing in gymnastics in high school, especially my senior year, I stuck to a very strict diet and a very intense exercise regimen. I desperately wanted to go to state in at least one event, if not all around, and I thought if I just worked hard enough and trained hard enough, I could do it.

What I lacked, however, was a particular set of skills, and in large part good coaching—for that matter any kind of coaching. None of this deterred me of course, and it became an obsession like so many other things in my life. As I've looked back in my past during that time, I can recognize how entirely insane I was. I think at the most I was taking in 1,500 to 2,000 calories a day, and training three hours a day—six days a week. You don't have to be a genius to realize that is going to take its toll on your body eventually.

I was probably over worried about my weight because some of my family members were overweight, as well as having been gifted with a slow metabolism. Now how's that for bad luck:

poor genetics, not a lot of natural skill in the sport I loved, and an obsession to achieve my goals at any cost—even my health. It didn't help that my friends were very thin, very popular, and very pretty. In addition, they happened to be very nice and kind people, which made it even worse.

Needless to say, I carried my insecurity into adulthood. If you combine that with my sexual assault, it wouldn't be much of a surprise to discover I had a full-blown eating disorder in my early twenties. I struggled with this disorder for the next ten years, and it was a long ten years. I know my life is like a textbook example of all the things that can plague a teen's life and negatively affect everything in adulthood, but this did not feel like a textbook. This was the loneliest period of my life, even though I was surrounded by lots of friends and family. What I discovered later, however, is the real reason I was lonely was because I thought God hated me and had turned his back on me. I was lonely because I thought my best friend, Jesus Christ, was disgusted with me and didn't want to have a relationship with me.

As if I didn't have enough going on I decided I would land myself in a hospital as well. Again I'm not sure of the order of these events as they are all jumbled up in my head, but I ended up getting very sick one day at work. It had started the night before and I had severe abdominal cramps, and felt very sick to my stomach. I was pretty miserable at work, and making sure everybody knew it. I complained to my boss so he finally sent me to the nurse that we had on staff. She gave me some pepto-bismol and suggested I go home. My boss was not too happy with this, understandably so as I missed a lot of work, but he let me leave.

I was racing to catch the bus and once I got on board I spent the next 40 minutes trying to keep myself from hurling. When I got home I hopped in a hot bath to try and settle myself down.

CHAPTER SEVEN

As I continued to bathe the pain got worse and more localized. I finally called my mom and asked her what side of my appendix was on. She told me the right side but that she thought it was highly unlikely I was having an appendicitis. I asked her if she could come pick me up and take me to hospital because I was in that much pain. She raced over to get me and found me shaving my legs in the bathtub. She asked me what the heck I was doing and I said I'm pretty sure I'm going to the hospital tonight and my legs are really hairy, and I don't want anyone to see that. She shook her head, got me out of the bathtub, and raced me to the doctor's office and then to the hospital. Within about 2 hours they were prepping me for surgery for an appendectomy. The highlight to all of this was that the nurse saw my legs and said "Your legs are so smooth," making all of the rest of this worth while.

I was broken in every way a person could be broken: physically, mentally, and psychologically. My relationship with my family was at best broken as well, and I didn't share much about what was going on in my personal life because I was afraid they would have abandoned me. This feeling wasn't completely unwarranted as my parents had a very difficult time raising me and, at least from my perspective, kept a good distance from me emotionally because they couldn't handle me. My parents didn't know how to handle an overly emotional child, so they kind of kept their distance until I grew too loud and hostile, and they had to engage. Naturally those engagements involved spankings, arguments, screaming, and yelling matches.

Since I have five siblings, there were a myriad of experiences we were all going through, and I realize now we were all just trying to survive, but at the time I thought it was them against me. The reason being they never seemed able to greet me with any enthusiasm and joy. It was more akin to: "Why did you slam the door?" "Why did you eat all the crackers?" "Why do you always do so bad in school?" They always complained about me being on the phone as well—however, this was a legitimate complaint because I was ALWAYS on the phone.

CHAPTER EIGHT

ON THE MOVE

As time progressed, I had a lot of ups and downs with my health that has continued throughout the rest of my life, unfortunately. I had a lot of trouble with men at this time in my life, and ultimately felt used. Upon reflection, I realized my self-esteem being what it was, coupled with the sexual abuses, made me a prime target to be used. Internally I was ashamed of what I thought I had done (not fighting back when he attacked me and letting him into my house in the first place), and I thought I was damaged goods. So I didn't care anymore about my chastity and purity (since it had been taken from me), and I went wherever the wind blew me. Wedged in the middle of two men who were both just using me, I reached a breaking point and decided it was time to move.

Since I worked for a newspaper, I decided to apply for some jobs at the newspapers in Australia. I got a good amount of feedback, but they required I pay for my own plane ticket to come out for an interview. While I desperately wanted to go, I did not have that kind of money saved up, so I had to put the dream on the back burner and look for another place to move.

ON THE MOVE

A few months prior to this, I had gone to a wedding for my cousin in Washington State. I was only there for about two days, but I absolutely loved the location and the beauty all around there. So I decided this was as good a place as any to pack up my belongings and make my new home. I told my boss I quit, told my parents I was moving, and told my roommate (my cousin) I was moving to Seattle, Washington. I asked if he was interested in driving me out there. Naturally, he was game, as always.

I was so ill prepared for a move like this. I had little to no savings, no car of my own, and no job to go to or apartment to stay in. Luckily I still had my cousins living out there, so I could shack up with them for a short while. It was a very steep learning curve, and while I don't regret it, there are smarter ways I could have gone about it. The problem was I was just angry, sad, and ready to make a change in my life.

Looking back on that move now as a parent myself, I can't imagine what it must have been like for my parents. They must have been so scared to have me move so far away they couldn't help me or be there in the event I needed it. This was exactly what I thought I needed, however, because I was ready to cut ties and try to make my way in life. If only I hadn't done it when I was so angry and spent some time in serious prayer, it might have gone better.

My boss at work was not very happy I was leaving as he was fond of me and didn't want to lose me as an employee. I didn't care because he had hurt me as well. It's a long story and involved, but the gist of it is he had a crush on me—maybe it was something more—and he strung me along, making me believe he loved me when in all reality he had a relationship going with another woman, and he ended up getting her pregnant. The worst part of the whole thing was I had been out with him on a Friday

CHAPTER EIGHT

night, and he kept trying to tell me something. He would start to say it, and then he would pause. I asked him what he was trying to say and told him to just say it, but he never did.

That following Monday I showed up to work and some of my coworkers told me to congratulate him because he had just gotten married. I walked over to him at his desk, grabbed his left hand, saw the ring on his finger, and proceeded to stomp out. Naturally, he came after me trying to talk, but I wasn't having it. The reality was the woman he had gotten pregnant, and ended up marrying, was a very sweet and kind woman. She deserved better than that, and so did I. Needless to say, years later I saw them and they seemed to be making a go of it. I thought that was a good thing as she at the very least deserved that.

So as you can see, I was definitely good and ready to go: me, my belongings, my Guardian Angel, and my bitter and angry attitude. I don't think Seattle was ready for me, nor do I think I was ready for Seattle. Either way, I packed everything I owned into the back of my dad's pickup truck, and my cousin and I headed out on our long drive to the Pacific Northwest.

PNW, HERE I COME

My cousin (Dave) and I had a very fun and exciting drive up to Seattle. We stopped to see the salmon ladders, we visited many sites along the way, and we ate at some great roadside diners. On one occasion, we had a very good breakfast at one of the local diners where they served, amongst other breakfast food items, some muffins. Now there's nothing very unique about muffins for breakfast, and it hardly deserves mentioning, except for the story of the banana muffin.

At the time we were on this journey, I happened to be fairly disgusted with the taste, texture, and flavor of bananas. So as we sampled various foods, Dave said I can't quite figure out what ingredient is in this muffin. I figured I could help him in this quest, so I grabbed it and took a bite, and no sooner did I chomp down when I realized "Oh crap, it's banana!" My cousin started laughing so hard I thought he was going to cry. He said he'd never in his life seen anyone so repulsed by a food. He also said he couldn't believe I was that sensitive to bananas because I barely tasted the muffin before I expelled it from my mouth. He just smiled and said, "I guess you don't like bananas."

We had some other funny interactions. For instance, I asked my cousin what direction we were headed as we drove to my new home in Seattle Washington. That's right; I was leaving Colorado and driving to Washington and didn't even know what direction it was. I just turned and said, "Geography has never been my strong suit—what can I tell you!" My cousin, who was always in the mood for a good laugh, chuckled, shook his head, and said, "What am I going to do with you?"

We eventually made it to our location in spite of my poor mapping skills. We arrived at a house on one of the islands belonging to my other cousin (Henry). These two cousins were actually brothers, the one who drove me to Washington and was my roommate for three years and the one who got married and lived in Washington. So needless to say the trip out there was an opportunity for them to get together, as well as move my butt and belongings out to the Pacific Northwest.

My cousin Dave stayed for a few days before he decided to make the long trek back home. If you haven't figured it out by now, we drove together in one truck, and he left in that same truck. So what that tells you is in all of my not-so-superior planning, I didn't think it was important to purchase a vehicle

CHAPTER EIGHT

before I moved. For that matter, I didn't think it was important to have a job or a place to live. I thought I could get all that I needed once I arrived, which would prove to be a very huge mistake. You know the old saying live and learn, but sometimes learning is very painful.

So I lived with my cousin Henry for a short while as I prepared to find a place to live in Seattle. Since I had never lived that direction, I did not realize the distance between the island and Seattle would be so great, but it was about an hour to an hour and a half drive one way. There was the option of taking a ferry across and then driving down to Seattle or driving up and around and down south to Seattle. Either direction involved some complication. What made matters worse was my big-time plan involved working and living in Seattle.

I realized the first thing I needed to take care of was getting a car. So one day, out and traveling around the island, lo and behold in front of me was this beautiful, gargantuan Ford vehicle for a measly $500. Oh yes, this car had to be mine. So I went into the store, talked to the owners, and drove away in my beautiful vehicle.

Once I had the vehicle in my possession, the next plan was to travel to Seattle and conquer the newspaper business—*Seattle Times*, here I come. I figured, since I was driving down there anyway, I may as well find myself an apartment. So I set out for what I was sure was going to be a very successful outing. Little did I know how popular a place Seattle was and equally how unimpressed the *Seattle Times* would be with an employee such as myself.

These adventures, if you would like to call them that, were the reason my Guardian Angel drew the short straw when it came to choosing who he was to guard. It's like that scene in the

Matrix when he has a choice to take the blue or the red pill, and he chooses the red pill—the one that leads you straight to reality. Later on, Neo wishes he had taken the blue pill; don't we all?

SEATTLE IS MINE

The first day I traveled down to Seattle I had a very busy schedule and a great deal of work to get done. I had the *Seattle Times* newspaper to go to, which would involve applying for numerous positions, as well as trying to find a good location for an apartment. I started by going to the *Seattle Times* and waiting in the lobby for a good deal of time before someone came out, greeted me, and essentially gave me the boot. Remember the former boss I told you I worked for back in Denver? Well, he had a contact at the *Seattle Times*, and I thought that would make me a shoo-in to get any kind of job. I just needed something to come in at the ground floor and work my way up. However, when his colleague came to greet me, he essentially said we have no positions for you. He gave me the good old speech about how he was sorry, but he didn't have any job opportunities at this time, blah, blah, blah! I wish that had been the last time I talked to him.

After finishing that "job interview," I decided it was time to start apartment searching. I went all over looking for a place to live. I didn't know this at the time (because I didn't do any research ahead of time [classic me style]), but there was only a 4 percent vacancy rate for apartments in all of Downtown Seattle and surrounding areas. In other words, it meant no apartments were available, especially in my price range and not in a good location.

By this point in time, it started to get pretty late, and I knew I would have to start this whole process all over again the next

CHAPTER EIGHT

day, so I decided to stay overnight. The problem was I didn't have very much money—just enough for a down payment on an apartment—and since I didn't have a job yet, I wasn't willing to spend money on a hotel. So in this young girl's stupid head, the next best possible solution was to sleep in my car and save a few bucks. I found a nice quiet neighborhood to pull into, and I started the car to get it warmed up and dozed off and continued this process all night long—wash, rinse, repeat. It was a very cold night and a very long one as well, but I made it through.

I was able to find myself a decent apartment just north of the University of Washington campus. I had no furniture, no bedding, and no dishes, but that would be a problem for another time. I managed to have just enough money to get into the place, so the next mountain to conquer would be the job. I went back to the drawing board and started applying for any newspaper jobs I came across, and lo and behold an opportunity presented itself. A position at a little newspaper called the *Bellevue Journal*. It was roughly thirty-thousand circulation (my newspaper in Colorado was three-hundred thousand circulation) and covered the areas of Mercer Island, Bellevue, Kirkland, and a few others.

I don't remember much in the way of details involving my getting everything moved in, but I did make it happen. After I got the apartment, I headed back up to Whidbey Island to let my cousins know and to pack up my belongings. I think they loaded up their vehicles and followed me down to my new location. I had so little in the way of belongings it did not take very long to unload all my stuff. I showed him around the area and explained the new job. After that was done, they headed home, and I proceeded to sleep in my very lonely new apartment for the first time by myself. The loneliness was a feeling I was getting quite used to.

One of the most ridiculous things that has ever happened to me happened in that apartment. As I mentioned before, I did not have any dishes to speak of, let alone any money to buy any. I was not even able to buy any food because of my limited budget. So on one occasion, when I had gone to the store and bought a couple of items, I came home with a beautiful shiny can of Hi-C. Back in that day, Hi-C was sold in large tin cans. These tin cans required a can opener to puncture a hole in the top of it and release the heavenly fluid. I did not have a can opener, an item that probably cost about $0.25 at the time, so I broke down in tears and called my parents once again.

When you live alone in an apartment with no family around, no friends nearby, and a city you are unfamiliar with, your parents are the people you're going to call, even if you're mad at them. I never realized at the time, being a fairly self-centered young adult, how much this must have hurt my parents emotionally. I was 1,500 miles away, struggling immensely, and they were not able to do anything about it. But this is the way I stacked the deck, so it was on me to figure it out. About a week later, the most beautiful gift arrived in my mailbox. It was small, silver, made of metal, and could puncture a hole in the top of a tin can. Yes, my mother and father sent me the most glorious care package, which included the tool that not only could help me dig my way out of prison but would also allow me to guzzle that most refreshing drink I had sitting in the refrigerator. Here's to you, Mom and Dad. And hey, Guardian Angel, if you're not too busy, can you bring them both a frosty glass of Hi-C from me?

CHAPTER EIGHT

SEATTLE NOT QUITE MINE

So I got to work at my new job and started getting the lay of the land. If I haven't mentioned this before, you must know how incredibly late I was to my job and everywhere during that time. I was late to work, social events, late to wake up, late to go to sleep.... You get the picture. So this job was no exception, and I found myself getting in trouble regularly for being late. That to me, however, was a reasonable expectation for a boss to have—show up on time. So the fact my boss was often mad at me made sense in light of this little idiosyncrasy of mine.

As time went on and I started to learn the job, I found it to be quite easy. I had worked for a much larger newspaper before, so all in all this kind of made sense. Because it was easy for me to pick up on, I decided to start cross-training and learning other jobs. So as it turned out the vice president of the department had also decided I should start cross-training, which was helpful, so I wasn't bored all the time. Unbeknownst to me, he saw something special in me, and he knew he could use that as a benefit to the company.

Because I started cross-training, and in essence learning other people's jobs, that didn't go over well. Most of the office was filled with women, and they were not taking too kindly to an outside female threatening their territory. Meanwhile, living my life unaware of this fact, I continued to do what I had always done and make friends. Or at least I was trying to make friends, but they weren't having it. Luckily, however I bonded with two of my coworkers, one female and one male, and from that point forward we spent a lot of time together. There were so many fun moments we shared.

On one such occasion, we decided to go out and party a bit.

We were all jammed up in the front seat of a truck preparing to drink a bottle of cheap rum. I remember holding up the bottle and saying, "Do you know what this bottle represents? This, my friends, causes a little-known disease I would like to refer to as 'the love syndrome.'"

They both looked at me with tipsy and perplexed eyes and said, "What are you talking about?"

I smiled and said, "By the time we finish this bottle, we will love each other more than three people have ever loved each other in the history of mankind."

They both started laughing hysterically. I will be darned if that is not exactly what happened within two hours of finishing the bottle. We kept telling each other how much we loved each other, how much we meant to each other, and overall, how great friends we were. Just as a side note, shortly after I lost my job, I never heard from them again, which shows you how short-lived the bonds are when you're drinking buddies.

So as time went on working at this small newspaper, I started to get proficient at the job and really began to like it. That's when problems started to arise with my direct supervisor and some of my coworkers. Every time I came into the office, she seemed to have a complaint against me. My supervisor would ask me why I was late, why I hadn't done dispatch records, why I hadn't followed up with phone calls when I needed to, whatever they could drum up. I went to explain to her that I hadn't made these mistakes, and I didn't know why she thought I had. I tried to explain to her how I did my job and my process during working hours. She wouldn't even listen to me and just kept accusing me.

On one particular morning as she was reading me the "riot act," I asked her who was lodging these complaints against me, and she refused to answer. I explained to her that she needed to

CHAPTER EIGHT

tell me who my accusers were since she was taking their information as gospel. This must have struck a nerve with her because she got angry at me and told me I wasn't doing the job. I may have had a lot of problems in a lot of other aspects of my life, but I was not screwing up the job, and I told her that. I even told her she could put me up against any of the other employees and test our skills, but she was unwilling to do that. It seemed like her only goal was to make my life as miserable as possible. I never understood why she had such a vendetta against me, but I did eventually find out who was making the reports. It was a couple of my female coworkers, and months later I found out they were just jealous of me. They actually told me this.

While my work struggles were happening, I also heard back from the gentleman that worked at the *Seattle* Times—my former boss's colleague. He asked me to dinner on the pretense he had a position available for me at the newspaper. We talked about the job, had a nice dinner, and then he drove me home. He walked me up to the apartment because he wanted to make sure I was safe and opened the door for me. He started giggling about my lack of furniture, made some off-the-cuff comment, and shuffled his way into the apartment. I started to feel kind of uncomfortable, and in short order he started to come on to me. He started grabbing me and pulling me closer to him. I told him to stop what he was doing, but he kept forcing himself on me.

He responded by saying, "You knew this is what I wanted, and you want it too."

All of a sudden I realized I was completely alone in the apartment with an older man, and if he wanted to do anything to me, he could. I finally exploded and told him to get away from me and get the hell out of my house. I was angry enough at this point, and making enough noise, that I guess he decided it would be best to just leave. He walked out the door, and I quickly locked it behind him and started to shake. I cried myself to sleep that night and never told another soul what had happened.

I continued working at the *Bellevue Journal* for a while, but things just got worse for me with my boss and coworkers. I finally submitted to the bullying and quit my job. I walked off the job one day after telling my supervisor she had made my life hellish. I think that was the only time I saw her appear to feel bad. Nonetheless she was seemingly more than glad to take my resignation. I was incredibly distraught, confused, and angry. I had no one to really talk to about it and help me process all that had happened, which forced me to just internalize it all.

Sadly, now I struggled immensely with my eating disorder. Because I didn't have much money for food, I would go for a couple of days without eating, and then if I got the chance, I would overeat, and I would make myself sick. As if moving to a new state with no support system, no friends or family nearby, and being broke wasn't enough—now this. It is not too surprising I struggled with my eating disorder as emotional and psychological stress are the root causes of the disorder itself. The issue was I didn't have anyone I could trust to talk to about the eating disorder; I was immensely embarrassed I acted in this manner; and finally, I had grown to hate myself and thought everyone hated me as well—including and most importantly God.

If only there was more information about eating disorders at that time and a general understanding of what causes it—I might not have been so incredibly sick. For those of you who are not aware, eating disorders are connected to feelings of shortcomings, inadequacy, and the sense of feeling like a failure. People can suffer from an eating disorder for several reasons but first and foremost extreme insecurity and low self-worth.

CHAPTER EIGHT

So, after I quit my job and got home from work, I started crying uncontrollably. I was sobbing and shaking and absolutely feeling hopeless—even suicidal. It was the strangest experience as I couldn't seem to stop. I can't even remember how long I was in the state or how many hours I may have cried, but I do remember this: I received a phone call from the vice president of the circulation department that night. When he called me, I did not know who it was, was in such a bad mental state I couldn't pull myself out of it to carry on a conversation, so I must have sounded horrible on the phone.

When I answered the phone, he announced himself and started to talk to me about the work I had done at the newspaper. He told me I was doing a really good job, and he was confused as to why I had left. I couldn't believe the vice president was on the phone with me, and yet, somehow his own manager hadn't even bothered to tell him why I had left and what had happened. I was such a wreck I don't much remember what I said, but I think I told him that every time I came into work, I was accused of mistakes and wrongdoings I hadn't done and was never given the opportunity to defend myself or prove my worth.

He was a very kind man and told me he wanted to get this department moving in a different direction, and he thought I could help do that. He told me he needed my knowledge and experience to help move the newspaper in the direction he wanted. You know those moments in your life, especially when you are young, when you wish you could take a deep breath, calm yourself down, and allow yourself to be open to a new idea? I wasn't there yet unfortunately, and I'd like to think that if I had someone to bounce ideas off of that I might have accepted his offer. After all, he was going to make it right for me and fix the situation with my supervisor. Can you just imagine how sweet that would have been to walk back in the door with the vice president on my side? It would have been great to see her squirm in her seat, but alas, I was too immature and broken, and in the moment was in the middle of a nervous breakdown, and therefore unable to take the life preserver he was throwing to me.

After I lost my job, things started to unravel. I had a car that needed new brakes, and I didn't have any money to fix it, so I left it at the junkyard and tried to get around on public transportation. It didn't go very well at times, that's for sure, and I ended up in some very scary circumstances. During the time I lived in Seattle, there were some notorious serial killers there, not the least of which was Ted Bundy. It is a miracle I did not get picked up by one of them as I took up hitchhiking, periodically, when public transportation did not work out. One of the times I got picked up, as I hopped in the car, I realized there was no door handle on the passenger side door, but it was too late because the door was already shut, and we were moving. I tried rolling down the window, but there wasn't a handle for that either, so I started getting angry and told him to pull over and let me out. I must have pitched enough of a fit as he quickly pulled over and opened the door from the outside to let me out. Up until that point, I had lived rather recklessly because I kind of had a death wish, but in that moment, I realized there are more terrifying ways of dying even I was afraid of.

My Guardian Angel was holding my hand in that situation, for sure. I think he whispered in my ear to get angry and aggressive to free myself from what may possibly have been a very horrible event. I can look back in my past and see all these moments in my life where God and his Angels watched over me and protected me from my foolishness. I am so grateful to God for all

CHAPTER EIGHT

his love and mercy, and most importantly my Guardian Angel for sticking with me.

HOMELESS IN SEATTLE

After all the events—getting harassed by my supervisor and eventually leaving my job, receiving sexual advances from a married man, living alone in a city without any friends or family (my doing), and struggling with an eating disorder—I eventually lost my apartment as well. I was evicted because I didn't have any money to pay the rent, and I didn't have a job. I could have applied for another job, but I was not in a good state of mind and to be honest was quite fragile.

The next step was to go investigate some mental health facilities in Seattle to see if there were any treatment programs for my disorder. After multiple phone calls, and a lot of time and energy, I finally got an appointment to see somebody at one of the treatment centers. It is important to understand that when you are looking for mental health assistance, it is a very personal and invasive process. I basically had to expose everything about myself, my personal life, and my history to complete strangers, all in an effort to get the help I needed. That is not an easy thing to do.

I finished all the documents they had given me and went in to talk to my assigned social worker. We talked for a little while, and when he finished interviewing me, here's what he told me. He basically told me that I didn't qualify for in-house treatment because I was not "sick" enough to fit the criteria to be admitted to their thirty-day program. That's right, in the middle of all my struggles, I hadn't demonstrated enough mental health illness. How's that for assistance? I was tearing apart at the seams and about as depressed and hopeless as a person could be, but I was not sick enough to receive care

After crying a lot, and talking with this gentleman for a while, he said something that was actually very helpful to me. He said, "I recommend that you go back home, move in with somebody that you know and trust, and get yourself a job and try to get yourself more stabilized." He said, "After you've done that, you will be in a better situation to go and get some therapy and help dig yourself out of the place that you're in." He said that he didn't think even the in-house treatment would help because I really wasn't as unstable as I may have felt. He said, "I think that you have the strength to do this, and you will be better off once you are independent and functioning on your own." Weird as this may sound, he was the first one to really give me any hope.

Shortly after that, I went to my cousin's house on the island and one day decided to go down to the beach. When I went down to the beach, I decided to climb onto one of the large rocks and sit quietly as I watched the waves crash into the neighboring rocks. It was mesmerizing and somewhat hypnotic and utterly peaceful.

It was then I realized I needed God. I was so afraid to talk to him and so embarrassed and ashamed of my behavior that I didn't think he would even have the time for me. I remember closing my eyes and telling him, "I am so sorry for everything I've ever done to hurt you." It wasn't but a few seconds later I got my own personal miracle and message from God.

It was a typical Washington day, the skies were cloudy, and it had been raining, but in that moment, some of the clouds parted, and a ray of sunlight beamed down on me and the rock I sat on. It instantly filled me with joy, and I could almost hear God telling me how much he loved me and how long he had been waiting for me to come back to him. He wrapped his arms around me and

CHAPTER EIGHT

told me how much I meant to him. I promise you, to this day, I have never felt the kind of love and forgiveness I received in that moment. I instantly knew I was his and had always belonged to him, and I would never find true happiness again unless I stayed close to him for the rest of my life. I feel that way even today.

I think that's why I'm such a fierce defender of the church and our Lord. Because when you have been in the abyss and been rescued from it, you know who your savior is. God is and has always been my one true, faithful, loving, and kind Father, and I know he will always be there for me, even after I die.

Before this occurred, however, I had completely pulled away from the church and from God. During the time I lived out in Washington, I had started to explore various churches. Some of the time I went with my cousin to the church he attended, and other times I would go and just randomly attend a church that sounded interesting to me.

While I found the people in these churches to be very open and welcoming, the structure of the service was very foreign to me and never felt quite comfortable. After my recent encounter with God on the beach, I decided it was time to visit a Catholic Church again and try to see what it was I was missing having grown up in that faith. I was carrying a very heavy burden from all the bad things I had done in my past, as well as the abuses done to me. Up until then, I had no idea how to release myself from that burden, but for the first time in years, I decided it was time to go to confession.

It was the hardest confession I have ever made but the best thing for my soul. When I finished confession, I cannot begin to tell you the relief and freedom I felt from asking God's forgiveness and being released from the weight of it all and feeling God's love and mercy all over me. That was enough to bring me back to the church. I started making my slow and gradual return to the faith, and as time went on, I finally realized it was the Eucharist (true presence of Jesus) calling to me all along.

So I started trying to put the pieces of my life back together again. When I had left the social workers' office, I started looking for a place to live. It was only by coincidence I ran into one of my old co-workers from the newspaper in the mall one day. She was there with her little boy, and as soon as he saw me, he called me by name and came running over to me. I had spent time with her and her son when I first tried to get to know people at the newspaper. As it turns out, I was pretty sure she was one of the ones who had officially "stabbed me in the back," so I wasn't exactly happy to see her; however, for the sake of her son and decorum, I pretended as if everything was okay.

The encounter went very well, and we started visiting for a little bit and walking around the mall. After a few hours had passed, she inquired about where I was living and what I was up to. I shared a little bit of my struggles and tragedies and explained to her I didn't really have a place to live but had been staying in a motel for a couple of nights through the church. It was at this point she admitted to me she was behind my getting chased off the job. I asked her why she did that to me when I had only tried to be her friend, and she said she just jealous of me, and she didn't want me doing better than her. She cried a little bit and told me how very sorry she was. What can I say? I'm a sucker for a good cry, so I hugged her and told her it was going to be fine, and then I wasn't mad at her anymore.

As it turned out, she needed a nanny to watch her son while she went to work during the day. So she suggested I move in with her family and stay there until I could get on my feet, in exchange for taking care of her son. This was a no-brainer as I really loved her kid, and living in a house with a family sounded wonderful at this

CHAPTER EIGHT

stage in my life. Naturally she brought me over to meet her parents, and we hit it off immediately. I moved in with them and started cleaning the house, making meals, and babysitting her son. It was the very least I could do for them after giving me a place to stay.

It wasn't very long with this new arrangement when I got a call from my dad back in Colorado. He wanted to tell me what was going on with my mom. When I answered the phone, I knew something was wrong and asked him "What happened to mom?"

He said, "How did you know?"

I said, "Because I knew when I left Colorado that she was having health struggles, and they were not going to go away."

I had suggested they go and see another doctor, but my mom and dad got very reactive to this comment and said they'd been with this doctor for twenty-plus years and were not going anywhere. There was nothing I could do, and I had a sense it could be a serious matter down the road.

It was during this conversation my dad asked me if I would come home. My mom had suffered a heart attack, and he asked me if I could come back home and try to help her. I agreed to do this and proceeded to pack up my belongings in boxes and ship them home on a train. In the meantime, my dad bought me a plane ticket back to Colorado, and I went home to see my mom.

THE SLOW ROAD TO RECOVERY

Once I returned home to Colorado, I immediately went over to the hospital to see my mom. It was a very sad and scary sight to see her struggling so much and none of us being able to do anything to help her. I don't remember much in the next few days and weeks that followed, but I knew my mom was not doing well, and it was going to take her a long time to recover. These are pivotal moments in our lives when we recognize our own mortality, and it was scary to watch my mom facing hers.

I moved back into my childhood home with the understanding I was going to be helping my dad take care of my mom. Not too surprisingly, however, my dad and I did not manage to keep our fighting to a minimum, which would eventually overshadow my mom's healthcare needs. I wish I'd had the maturity to be able to separate my feelings of anger and animosity toward my dad to take care of my mom. After all that was my responsibility, and more than that, my God-given duty, but alas, I was stubborn, childish, angry, and hurt, and I could not manage my emotions very well.

On top of everything else going on in my life, the move back to Colorado, the eating disorder, my mom's heart attack, I was also hemorrhaging money from a hospital bill I had acquired in Colorado before I moved. You will probably remember the story of my almost-ruptured appendix, when my mom found me in the bathtub shaving my legs. Well that surgery, and four days in the hospital cost me a few thousand dollars that I did not have. It was roughly the price of a newer economy car, and my time in Seattle did not get me any closer to paying it off. So even though I communicated with the hospital about my bill regularly, I couldn't pay the bill, so they eventually turned me over to collections. I was so incredibly stressed at this point I didn't know what to do. Luckily my sister-in-law walked me through the process, and I was able to arrange payments with the collection agency. If I paid my bill in the agreed upon payment installments, then they wouldn't put it on my credit report. It paid off in the long run as I was able to slowly pay the balance off. This kept my credit score from tanking.

After that situation resolved itself, the focus came back to how best to take care of my mom. Although I was not very close to my parents, when I was out in Washington, I leaned on them

CHAPTER EIGHT

emotionally, and I felt like they really tried to come through for me. So, as I was sitting here watching my mom, seeing how easily I could lose her, I was very distraught. I felt guilty for all the emotional phone calls I made to them while I was in Seattle and how much that must have impacted her health. I think I internally blamed myself for her heart attack. One of my siblings agreed with me. Naturally this crushed me and made me regret having come home. All I wanted to do was be there for my mom, love her, and take care of her, but it wasn't going to be that easy.

After mom got home from the hospital, she started building back her strength. Things seemed to be going okay, and as she started to improve, I was able to feel a little less guilty. That of course would come to a quick end. What started happening was my dad and I started arguing once again. We fought all the time, and this was causing my mom stress. I had made some new friends when I moved back home, and my dad didn't like them, and we always fought about it.

One night, when I headed out of the house to go visit my friends, my dad told me to stay home as it was too late at night for me to be going out. You know the old saying nothing good ever happens after 1:00 a.m. in the morning? That's a saying for a reason, and even though my dad was right, I didn't want to be home. So I told him it was my life, and I could do what I wanted. He made an implication I was going to meet up with a guy, which wasn't even close to the truth. The way in which he presented it was degrading, and I just couldn't handle it, so I told him if that's what he thought of me, then I should move out. I told him I would have my bags packed the next day and I would be leaving, and that is what I did. I left the house, something my poor mom did not want to happen, and proceeded to couch surf for a while until I could find a friend to move in with.

CHAPTER NINE

OUTDOOR ELECTRICAL SIGNS

While we've been dabbling in a lot of sad stories and wallowing in some self-pity, I think it's time to have a little fun. Although my life had a lot of difficulties, it did not have a shortage of crazy and fun experiences. My next line of work was one of those.

Now if I haven't told you this before, I'll tell you now—I am a sucker for infomercials and people selling products online. This job opportunity was no different. My poor mom and dad must have been scratching their heads in complete bewilderment with me because I never did anything normal or mainstream. After all of the financial struggles I experienced, you would have thought I would have come home, buckled down, and got myself a good job. Instead, however, I decided I wanted to go the entrepreneurial route.

There was an advertisement in the newspaper for a job that would pay a very high monthly salary for individuals with an outgoing personality and good people skills. This sounded like the right kind of job for me and my skill set. Of course, this job fell under the category of being a commission-only job, but I wasn't going to let that stop me because I was going to make

CHAPTER NINE

my millions somehow—someway. So I showed up to the office building under the impression I was being interviewed for a job that would become quite lucrative. Basically, however, there was no official interview. Instead, they were willing to take any poor sucker that would jump at the chance to work this difficult job, so it turned into "training." I immediately jumped on board and started memorizing a script and prepared for the great unknown.

The concept behind this job is rather simple: go into small businesses, ask to speak to the owner, and then pitch him or her with a fifteen-page memorized speech about how an outdoor electrical business sign would make them lots of money. Oh sure, at the outset common sense would tell you that's a ridiculous philosophy, but this was a belief system we held on to, nonetheless. I don't know if that's because we were so desperate to make money or if we thought spending a couple thousand dollars on a business sign was a good investment. Nonetheless, a group of us proceeded to advance ourselves and go to the next training session, which would eventually lead us to the great and lucrative unknown.

We spent a few days learning our scripts as management prepared to take us out on the road with our new gig. I think we probably would have been more successful had we been roadies versus salespeople. We had no experience in business and were very green, but what the heck, let's tell business owners how they can make money. Of course, we considered ourselves attractive and quite intelligent, so naturally we thought everyone would see us through the same eyes. As you're reading this, you've probably figured out that was not the case.

After we finished our training, we were told they were going to take the group of us up to a town in South Dakota. For purposes of complete understanding, you must know not only did I not have any money to my name, I was living with my parents, but I also didn't even own a car. I had to ride up with one of the managers as we set out for our giant conquest.

It was a good, long drive and an opportunity to get to know that manager a little better, which I would have thought would have caused me to form a bit of a relationship with him, but it did not. When we arrived at our location and got checked into our not-so-fancy motel rooms, I came out and started doing an impromptu meet and greet. It was during that meet and greet I met a beautiful young lady who would later become a good friend of mine. She drove separately and arrived later than the rest of us as she had some other stuff to do. When she walked in the door, I do believe every guy in the room had to pick his jaw back up off the ground. As I said before, she was beautiful and very charismatic as well, and every guy wanted to date her. I proceeded to walk up to her, introduce myself, and shake her hand. From that point in time, we became very bonded.

I had also formed a good relationship with another coworker, who was the craziest character I think I've ever met. He had a very unique name (Nam) to go with his unique personality, and he was outgoing, outspoken, and very charismatic. It was a good thing he had such a good personality because it made up for all the annoying things he did. For instance, he followed sports fanatically and loved to bet on games and studied statistics closely. While we were in the process of learning our new job and getting to know each other, Nam placed a lot of sports bets with a lot of our coworkers, and he swept up. I think he won every bet, and these guys continued to bet against him. I just shook my head and told them to get smart. He asked me if I wanted to place any bets, and I laughed in his face. I told him I'd bet him on the sport of gymnastics to which I felt I would be much better at

CHAPTER NINE

gauging. He looked at me baffled and confused, shook his head, and said, "That's the stupidest thing I've ever heard!" We both laughed and proceeded to go spend some of those earnings on dinner. We brought my new girlfriend with us.

For the purposes of this paper, let's just call them Nam and Summer. The way the job worked was to go into small businesses, ask to see the owner, and if we were lucky enough, they would come out and talk to us. It was at this point we would break into our very well-practiced, very rehearsed, fifteen-page script. Let me assure you it is not easy to make a script that size sound natural, and I'm not sure we did, but we sure had a lot of confidence and didn't back away from the challenge. It was very exciting as we formed teams of two, sometimes three, and proceeded to compete with one another.

On one occasion I was grouped with Nam to do our sales pitch. We went into a couple of businesses without much luck, and then by magic we ended up talking to one of the owners. As soon as we arrived, Nam looked back at me and said, "Let me do the talking and you do the drawing," as he aggressively slipped the notepad under my arm and handed me the pen. I tried to tell him this was a very bad idea as I had less than zero drawing skills. When I was in high school my art teacher said to me, "I've never met somebody who tries as hard as you but can't manage to draw the simplest of pictures." I begged him to let me do the talking, but he said, "No, no," and shook me off.

So I backed off and let him take the reins. I could not have been more disappointed in that choice as not only were my drawing skills not up to par but he had not memorized the script and didn't have it organized in any manner whatsoever. Nam's manner of talking was likened to a well-dressed, used car salesman who talks at the speed of an auctioneer. He would get going and talk so fast nobody could even understand what he said. To add insult to injury he was of Arabic descent walking into a small-town business in a Podunk town in South Dakota. If you tried to come up with an odder combination, I don't think you would be able to. Naturally none of this stopped him as he was blissfully unaware of the confused look both owners had on their faces. Periodically I would try to intervene with a particular and legible statement, to which Nam would shush me and proceed to ramble on.

The highlight of this whole escapade was the moment Nam turned to me and asked me for the sketch I had done. I was supposed to be drawing a sketch of what their business sign might look like. Of course we didn't rely only on our ability to sketch as we had some more professional images we could use. On this occasion, however, we had neither of those two tools—professional image or a sketch artist. When Nam grabbed the notebook from my lap to show the customer, upon seeing it, he made the most foul and hideous face, looked at me with complete confusion, and threw the notebook back down on my lap. He then turned to the client and said we can show you a better sketch later. As you can imagine, we were not successful in closing this client. Surprisingly, he was interested in the product, but he had a very sick daughter, and his medical bills were too expensive, so he didn't have any money to buy anything. A fact that just irritated Nam but made me very sad.

After we left the store and went outside, I started laughing so hard I began to cry. Nam was just looking at me as though I had lost my mind, which only made me laugh harder. He said, "What are you laughing about?" I proceeded to show him the face that he made when he looked at my "attempt" at drawing the business sign. I tried to duplicate the look someone gets

CHAPTER NINE

when something smells putrid, and they can't get it to clear their nostrils. Nam said, as he was laughing, I was the most horrible sketch artist he had ever seen. He couldn't believe I could be so bad at drawing. He said I have no right to attempt any kind of drawing again. The more he talked, the harder I laughed, which eventually got him to laugh so hard we both bent over holding our stomachs laughing/crying. I will never forget that moment as it is forever frozen in my mind. It was a very happy time.

As time went on, Nam and Summer decided to date. By this point in time, the three of us had become quite close as friends. It was during this process of building our friendship when I had the blowout with my dad, so I was desperately scrambling to find a place to live and to get a real job. Our time of working at trying to sell outdoor electrical business signs, while extremely enjoyable, had come to an end. The three of us decided to quit and go about finding a real job. When I moved out of my parents' house, I contacted Nam and Summer and told them the situation. I couch surfed for a couple of nights, and then Nam said, "I've got somebody that would be a good roommate for you." He introduced me to his ex-wife, Sylvia, and we hit it off. To be honest with you, she hit it off well with Summer in addition, and we all spent a good deal of time together.

After Sylvia and I got to know each other, we moved into an apartment. It was a great experience, and we grew very close, very quickly, and decided to move to Virginia together, which is a story for another day, or the next chapter as it were. I worked a couple of different jobs during that time but was still irresponsible. I do not know for sure why I was so flighty and ungrounded. When things got difficult, I tended to run. It was a signature of mine from my youth—but why did I do it? Was it my insecurities or my emotional injuries, I do not know. After I quit my last job, however, Sylvia and I decided it was time to move. I let my parents know I was going to be changing states once again, a fact I'm sure they weren't too happy to hear, but my mom and dad were beginning to realize I wasn't going to stay around.

Before I moved to Virginia, I started having health struggles again. My brother was overseas fighting in the Gulf War, and I was watching the news regularly and worrying about him nonstop. This was a sign I really did love him, even if he made me crazy.

I ended up in the ER a couple of times with severe abdominal pain (my parents were the ones who usually drove me there). The doctors could never figure out what was causing this pain, so they gave my illness a rather ubiquitous name, spastic colon / irritable bowel syndrome, and sent me packing. One of the times they sent me home with medication, I had a crazy allergic reaction. I was riding a bus home from work and started having a massive anxiety attack. I felt the urge to climb out of the window and jump off the bus. I stopped taking the medication immediately and was left without anything to relieve my pain. On another trip to the ER, however, a doctor prescribed Belladonna for me and that seemed to do the trick. I proceeded to use it for years to come.

VIRGINIA, SYLVIA, HANDSOME MARINES

So Sylvia and I decided we were going to pack up our stuff and move to Alexandria, Virginia. She had a couple of friends living out there, and they had a spare room in the basement we could share. We weren't both going to be able to go there together, so Sylvia went ahead of us to get situated, get a job, and prepare for me to come. In the meantime, I stayed to finish out the lease on our apartment, and I took care of her cat (Gigi).

CHAPTER NINE

About two months later I shipped my stuff out and headed to the great state of Virginia. I had never even been there, so I didn't really know what to expect, but I always had a sense of adventure and welcomed the new frontier. Within a couple of weeks we had our first issue. We had a shared townhome we lived in with a couple of other girls, and it was attached to another townhome. Both of these homes had basements. One day when we were calling the cat for dinner we realized she was gone. Since she was new to the area, we started to get worried because she didn't really know her way around yet. We went out looking for her, calling her by name, but couldn't find her right away. After searching all over the house and the grounds outside, I heard a very quiet meow from underneath the steps to the basement.

I called Sylvia over and found Gigi underneath a stairwell leading to the basements. I couldn't quite reach her and didn't want to stick my hand out to grab her as I could see her eyes, and she looked very scared. We eventually coaxed her out only to discover she was covered in spray paint and looked very sad. I was so angry because I knew someone had done this to her. We took her to the vet, and as they were looking over her, they discovered she had been shot with BBs from a BB gun. As the veterinarian was extracting the BBs, he found one that had been lodged in her forehead. When he took it out, he said if it had been any further in, it would have killed her. I've never seen any vet as angry as he was. He filed a report in the event we found out who had done it.

We went home and discovered it was most likely the tenant in the townhome attached to ours. It wasn't hard to figure out as we went over to their house, under the pretense of something else, and when they took us down in the basement, we saw the same color spray paint and a BB gun. Since there wasn't a way to prove it we couldn't do anything legally, but we made it very clear to him we knew he had done it, and we would be keeping an eye on him. I was ready to deck the guy right then and there, but Sylvia kept me calm.

We had so many adventures while living in Virginia and really enjoyed ourselves. Our roommates were wonderful Catholic women, and we enjoyed each other's company. The woman who owned the townhome unfortunately had a very busy job that took her away most of the time, so we didn't get to visit with her often. She was a very kind person and a great role model. When I first got to Virginia, we signed up for a softball team so we could meet people. We had a great time on the field and off. They, however, were as wild as I was, so it didn't help me mature, but I never regretted the time we spent together. The members of the softball team got together for each other's birthdays, dinners, and barbecues, etc. One of the most exciting and memorable times I ever had was getting invited to the Preakness Stakes in Maryland. Naturally I went with the softball team as they were my connection to the inner circle, so to speak.

We got tickets for the inner circle at the Preakness Stakes, where we hung out on the grass, ate, drank, danced, and sang. Everybody on the team, barring myself, was pretty well hammered halfway through the races, but I was obsessed with seeing the thoroughbreds. You see the inner circle in this case was the cheap seats—the grassy knoll in the middle of the field—and a green screen was on the chain link fence, preventing us from seeing any of the horse racing. It was, to a large degree, a very frustrating experience for me. Because while I was at Preakness Stakes, I couldn't watch the Preakness Stakes. All my friends were enjoying each other, getting drunk, and having a great time. I honestly went there with the delusional idea I would actually get to see some horse racing, but that was not the case. Here I

CHAPTER NINE

was at one of the biggest events in thoroughbred racing, and I couldn't see anything. Nonetheless the few races I could see, while pinning my face up against the fence, I extremely enjoyed. I could only imagine how exciting it must have been from the grandstands. Oh well, I was just lucky to have been there and can add it to my bucket list.

In addition to the other stories, there was our fabulous trip to New York City. Well, I had multiple trips to New York; the one to Manhattan—which Sylvia planned for us—was most amazing. We also traveled to Upstate New York a good deal to see my family that lived in Oneida, New York. I consider this a pretty great gift from God because I got to spend so much time with my aunt and uncle there, which I would not have ever been able to do had I stayed in Colorado or Washington. We had so much fun with them, and they adopted my friend Sylvia as one of their own.

So the trip to Manhattan was a birthday surprise for me from Sylvia. She didn't tell me where we were going or what we were doing, which made it even more exciting. As we headed into Manhattan, it became very clear to me we were going to do some of the activities we had been wanting to do for a while. She had booked us a hotel for two nights and got us tickets to a show off Broadway, which just happened to be *Les Miserables*. As you can imagine, the show was fabulous, and for a young twenty-three-year-old it was so exciting to be in New York City. We went to see Radio City Music Hall and Tower Records and were of the understanding one of my favorite recording artists—Melissa Etheridge—was recording that weekend we were there. Although we tried to get in to see her, it was of no use but exciting nonetheless. We went into the Empire State Building, saw the Statue of Liberty, ate some New York-style pizza, talked it up with anyone willing to engage, and overall just enjoyed the heck out of ourselves. It was an amazing birthday present—Sylvia was always very good and thoughtful when it came to birthdays—and one I'll never forget.

One of the funniest trips on our way up to visit my aunt and uncle in Upstate New York involved a toll road, two broke girls, and a missed exit. If anyone has driven that stretch between Alexandria, Virginia up to Oneida, New York, you know there's a lot of toll roads, or at least there was back then. As I mentioned before, we didn't have a lot of money because the cost of living was so high, so we tried to travel frugally. Well needless to say, on one occasion, in the middle of winter, I accidentally missed our exit and went too far. If I were to go to the next exit, which was a few miles up the road, we would have had to pay an extra toll to turn around and come back. So I, being the genius I was (and my unwillingness to pay an extra toll), decided to try to turn around in the median and save myself a few bucks. A few bucks were not saved—that is for sure.

It was hard to determine how deep the median was because there was so much snow on it, so I proceeded to use the truck, and an unwilling passenger, to test it out. Halfway through we got stuck in a ditch and could not get ourselves out with any amount of pushing. So yes, that is correct, in an effort to save a couple of dollars, I now cost us $75 in towing costs. That is how I do math for those of you who don't know me. Exasperated and disappointed in myself, I got out of the truck and sat on top of the hood while waiting for the tow truck, lit up a cigarette—there was nothing left to do. That is the kind of stuff my friend, and my Guardian Angel, got stuck with all the time. Sadly, for my Guardian Angel, he didn't get a new assignment, and sadly for me, I didn't avoid my toll. Somewhere in the recesses of my photos is a picture of me on the truck, in the middle of the median,

CHAPTER NINE

smoking my cigarette. To this day, it's one of my husband's favorite photos.

When I moved out to Virginia, I decided to work for a temp agency to make money quickly and get myself acclimated. I took on quite a few jobs, one of which was at the real estate assessment office in a very rich area in Virginia. That job was about as stressful as you get. I would go into work at 8:00 in the morning and not be finish till about 9:00 or 10:00 at night. It got to the point I recognized there would be no way one individual alone could get all the work done.

I must have been doing a pretty good job as the director of the department called me into his office to talk to me about it. I had an extremely difficult boss who became an impediment to my progress, and he knew she was. The director asked me what I thought about her and about getting the job done. I was honest with him and told him she was making it very difficult because she wanted me to report my status to her every thirty minutes. In addition, I told him the amount of work required to do my job could not be done by just one person—it would require at least two. He agreed with me and proceeded to inform me my supervisor had been in and out of numerous departments, and this was pretty much her last chance. I didn't stay at the job much longer and went to another assignment. I did find out later they hired two more people to replace me, and my supervisor was let go. I wish they had done that when I was there.

The next job I took was at Quantico Marine Corps Base. Now the job itself was completely monotonous as we were typing in field manuals to a database all day long. The location, however, being surrounded by Marines, was quite delightful considering I was twenty-three years old and single. I got to know one of the supervisors really well, and she later invited me to their department barbecue around the end of the summer. Sylvia and I were very excited to go, as one can imagine.

When we arrived at the event, they had some volleyball, football, baseball, and a variety of sports, as well as paddle boards and canoes down by the lake. After mingling with the supervisor for a while, Sylvia and I decided to go try our hand at the canoes, which was quite an adventure. Sylvia was not a strong swimmer—not at all—and was scared to be in the canoe. I was—a strong swimmer—and a bit of a jerk who kept scaring her. The net result is we tipped over, fell in the water, and got drenched. I made sure she was okay as we were close to the shore anyway and proceeded to fall onto the ground laughing. Yes, it is a recurring theme with me that I find humor in things that are not very enjoyable for other people. I have a twisted sense of humor.

As the day went on, we decided to go and play volleyball. Sylvia was not very athletic because she didn't really grow up doing sports, but I didn't let that deter her. I was always willing to show her how to do things as I couldn't resist any opportunity to play sports. As we were playing volleyball, we spotted a couple of particularly good-looking men on the opposing team. As the game went on, there were some looks, some flirtatious interactions, and lots of laughing and sand being kicked everywhere.

When it was almost dark and about time to go, our friend (a.k.a., our supervisor) came over to inform us these two gentlemen were interested in getting our numbers. The thin 5'8" athletic volleyball player was totally into Sylvia. He had these incredible light-green eyes and a brilliant smile. It was an easy connection to make. The gentleman interested in me was about 6'2", 215 lbs., and very muscular. He was super introverted and super quiet, which worked wonders for me because I had no problem pulling people out of their shells.

CHAPTER NINE

VIRGINIA, SYLVIA, HANDSOME MARINES CONT. . . .

They asked us out on a date, so we made plans for the next evening. I don't remember where we met for the date or where we even went out to eat, but what I do remember was this fabulous experience out on a dock where I proceeded to negatively impact my sweet Sylvia's vision for a few days. It was a horrible thing for me to have done, but the drunk version of me—in usual style—found it hilarious. We were sitting out on the dock with our two new "friends" talking and getting to know each other. At one point in time, Sylvia said to me please be careful because my glasses are sitting right there. She told me she didn't want me to knock them into the lake. I got super sarcastic with her and said, "What the hell glasses are you talking about, and who the hell are you to tell me what the hell to do."

Well in all my animation I managed to literally kick the glasses off the dock and into the water. With an absolute panicked instinct, I almost jumped into the water before my gentleman friend pulled me back. Thank goodness he did because the intoxicated version of me would not have done so well in the water. I was actually still pretty drunk, so I started to laugh until I realized what I had done. It was at that point in time I felt very bad and apologized over and over to Sylvia. We had to go and get her a new pair of glasses, and I of course would need to pay for them, which meant she was blind until that happened.

Shortly after our first dates, we met back up with the supervisor from Quantico, her husband, and a few of their friends. She took me aside later and said, "I can't believe you and Jay are still going out." I looked at her confused and asked why. She said because he had never gone on a second date with anyone. She smiled and said he must really like me. Which I was thrilled to find out as I found him to be very easy to talk to, very intelligent, and definitely not bad on the eyes. We continued dating these fine gentlemen for a couple of months.

As time went on, I started to fall for this Marine of mine. He had big plans for his future and no shortage of smarts, and he was very protective of me and patient. As I look back on my state of mind at the time, my wild behavior, and my drinking, I wonder if I chased him off. I was still a mental and emotional wreck. I hadn't worked through my problems yet and was drowning them either in alcohol or evasive behavior. As luck would have it—bad luck in my case—Jay had decided not to reenlist. His service was coming to an end, and he was moving back to his hometown. That hometown was only about three hours away, but I was pretty sure he was not going to stay in touch with me.

When we got closer to his moving date, I started to tell him how much I had enjoyed being around him and how much I cared for him. I also apologized for being such a mess and so out of control. I guess I was preparing to say goodbye forever. Much to my surprise, however, he asked for my address and wrote down the home phone number because he wanted to stay in touch with me. I told him not to give me any false hope. I thought it would just be better to break up and be done with it, but he insisted he still wanted to date. So we parted ways, and I hung onto the hope that I would see him again.

I don't think anybody can be too surprised to discover that he never called me again. He never even wrote a letter explaining why or saying goodbye. While I understand he moved back home, started going to college, and probably met somebody else, I just wished he would have told me. For that matter I wished he had never promised to stay in touch because it's always easier to deal with a goodbye than the hope of a relationship in the future. Quite honestly, he broke my heart.

CHAPTER NINE

Sylvia and I decided we should get our own apartment and move out of the house. Unfortunately this meant I would have to work three jobs to pay the bills, a task I was willing to take on. So I took on a motor route, which is an adult paper route, worked as a switchboard operator for a company during the day, and then a couple of evenings a week we worked at a private residence sorting files in the basement. I had to get up at 3:00 in the morning to work the route and then come home, change clothes, and go to my day job, which was located nine miles from my house and took an hour in traffic to get there. I was late to both jobs quite frequently as I was horrible at time management, and the drive for both jobs weren't easy. I took on a third job later, which would eventually lead me back to Colorado, go to college, and get my degree.

We decided to get a high-rise apartment in Alexandria and lived on the seventh floor. We loved the apartment and had so much fun there. Little did we know at the time what a dangerous area we lived in. We were able to deduce this because of the multiple gunshots we heard going off at night. For whatever reason, this didn't deter us as we continued in our blissful ignorance. One of the things I found convenient was we were located right off the Metro, so we could get to places pretty cheaply and easily when we needed to. We just couldn't get to our jobs using the Metro, so that made things a bit more complicated.

I recognize how confusing this may be for those of you reading this as when I left Washington I finally returned to my Catholic faith and began my healing, yet while I'm in Virginia, I still seem to be unraveling. As I mentioned before, it was a long process of growing in my faith and submitting myself entirely to God. In addition, I had some self-help work to do, and I wasn't there yet. It was hard to do, and I needed to mature.

VIRGINIA, SYLVIA, HANDSOME MARINES CONT. . . .

We moved into our apartment and had some additional adventures. To begin with, we decided we wanted to have a real Christmas tree, so we went to a lot to buy one. Since we were broke, buying a Christmas tree was an expensive endeavor. Once we picked out the Christmas tree, we loaded the truck and headed home. We put the tree into the elevator, and when we got to our floor, drug it down the hallway to our apartment. As soon as we came in the door, we tried to set up the tree. There was a missing piece to this puzzle, however, and that was called a tree stand. We had no way to stand it erect, or for that matter, water it. We did, however, have some twine, so I decided to jury-rig it by tying the base of it to the legs of the couch and coffee table. It looked ridiculous and obviously didn't work. We were reluctant to spend any more money but realized we would need a tree stand if we wanted to make this work, so we bought a tree stand.

The best part of the story is what happened after Christmas was over. The tree was very dried out and pine needles were falling off of it at a rapid rate. We decided we would load it up in the elevator and take it downstairs, but it was making a huge mess down the hallway. We decided to bring it back into the apartment. When we got back, I was immediately struck with a genius idea. We had a big outdoor patio, so I opened the sliding glass door and proceeded to throw the Christmas tree over the edge (we did make sure no one was below us when we did it). Much to my amazement, and joy, that darn Christmas tree landed upright next to three other trees and looked like it had returned right where it belonged. Since we didn't really have a way to haul it off, we decided to leave it there. Every time we walked past it we laughed.

Another one of my crazy incidents had to do with locking the keys in the apartment. Sylvia and I had a couple friends over

CHAPTER NINE

for dinner and decided we were going to go outside for a walk. It was similar to an episode of the TV show *Friends* when Monica and Rachel each thought the other one had the keys. Sylvia and I looked at each other as we went to close and lock the door and both said, "Got the keys?" We left, went outside to take our walk, and when we came back, we both realized neither person had the keys. She was mad at me because she thought I said I had the keys, and I was mad at her for the same reason.

So I stood back and looked at the outside of the apartment building we lived in. I was calculating whether or not I could climb the outside balconies to get up to our apartment. Each of the balconies extended out from the wall of the building a couple of feet, which would make for great footing if I needed to climb up. In addition, we were both pretty sure we had left the sliding glass door open, so that would make it easy to get in. Naturally all of this process was happening in my head, and instead of vocalizing it I just started my ascent. There was a group of men on the bottom balcony drinking and having a good time who decided to step out on the lawn and watch this event happen. I started shimming up each of the balconies until I made it to the top and was met with the sound of applause. Too bad they didn't have a "Ninja Warrior" competition when I was growing up because I might have won it. I was able to get into the apartment, grab the keys, and come downstairs to let my roommate and our friends in.

I'm not going to lie to you. I was very impressed with myself and naturally assumed Sylvia would be as well. To my surprise she was angry and fit to be tied by the time I got to her. I was a little bit confused as I thought she would appreciate my immense problem-solving skills. I didn't, however, calculate the fact I had drank alcohol that night and could have easily slipped

VIRGINIA, SYLVIA, HANDSOME MARINES CONT. . . .

and fallen to my death. A point she was very quick to express to me. Once again, I found myself in the position of apologizing profusely to Sylvia and trying to make amends. I appeared to be on a path to destroy every good relationship I had. This was subconsciously self-sabotage. God was the only one that could endure all the mess I was making out of my life, but for now I was lucky Sylvia still was.

With me around there was no shortage of crazy experiences and relationships. As time went on, however, I started to feel very aimless and without much of a purpose. I continued struggling with depression and loneliness, which I think was very evident by the amount of partying I did—and self-medicating. It was strange, because I never could handle my alcohol well and was a "lightweight," but for some reason I kept doing it. Luckily my body could not handle drugs at all, so it kept me safe from those dangers. I knew I needed a change, but I didn't know what that change would be until a very special night when my roommate and I went to our evening job.

This job I mentioned earlier was in the basement of somebody's house. As it turned out this gentleman was a high-level lawyer in DC, and in the basement of his house were lots of boxes containing files strewn all over the floor. He needed all of them sorted, organized, and put back in order in the boxes. It was a very large task, so there were three of us working on it, and it was very mindless, so lots of opportunity to talk.

The third person that came to work on the files with us was the wife of one of our former coworkers. She was a very sweet person and very shy. She had a baby she brought with her to work because she didn't have anyone to take care of him. The baby was a sweet kid as well and very easygoing, so it made our time together peaceful.

CHAPTER NINE

One evening in particular I started asking her some questions about her life and her background (a not uncommon approach for me to take when meeting a new person). She wasn't particularly interested in talking about herself or very forthcoming in our initial conversations, but for some reason this night was different. As we began to talk and I started to ask more questions, it seemed to bust open the dam. She started sharing a lot of her personal experiences—which was an extraordinarily difficult past—and how she had come to marry the man she was currently with. It was a very emotional night, and when she finished her story, I politely asked her if I could give her a hug. We both stood up and embraced one another. That's when she looked at me and said, "I've never told anyone that stuff, some of it not even to my husband." She also said, "I think you need to be a therapist. You are very easy to talk to and you've made me feel safe—only my husband has ever been able to do that for me."

For the first time in several years, I started really thinking about going to school and getting my bachelor's degree in psychology. The more I talked with Sylvia, the more we decided it was time to make a move back home to my family so that we could both enter school and have a good support system around us. A few months later, we decided to move back to Colorado, and Sylvia in the meantime decided to track down Jay so we could visit him before we moved. I had no idea why he agreed to this, but they made the plan without my knowledge. When Sylvia told me she had contacted him, and he wanted us to come and visit, I was very shocked. To be honest I was ticked off at first, and then shocked. I told her she had no right to do that without my permission, to which she responded, "Well you were never going to do it."

I said, "I know; that's the whole point—it wasn't for me to

do; it was for him—and if he wanted to see me, he could have contacted me, and he didn't, which means he doesn't." I must have still had some feelings for him though because I agreed to go, which is very uncharacteristic of me.

I think the real reason Sylvia contacted Jay was because she didn't like my current "boyfriend" and wanted him out of the picture. I wasn't that interested in my current boyfriend either—as he was very smothering and seemed overly obsessed with me—so I had no intention of continuing to date him. A fact I had stressed to Sylvia before, but I don't think she believed it. If I remember correctly, I had already broken up with him once, and he wasn't getting the message. I even told him I was dating other people, and that didn't seem to deter him. Reflecting upon it, she may have seen something I didn't and figured the best cure for a man unwilling to accept a breakup is a big, strong superhero that strikes fear into the hearts of those around him.

Well, whatever the reason, when the time finally arrived, we went to visit Jay, and it was even worse than I thought it would be. He wasn't there when we arrived, and his roommates didn't seem to know anything about us coming. I recognize college roommates—not being informed of a visitor coming—is not exactly a dead ringer we weren't welcome, but it sure did add to that overall feeling. I don't remember how long we hung out before he got home, but it seemed like a while, and it was very awkward.

So how do you think Jay greeted us when he came in the door? He ran over to both of us, embraced us, and told us how much he missed seeing us, and then he picked us up and twirled us around. Okay, now that we have the Disney version out of the way, here's what actually happened.

Jay came in the door, said hello, and then proceeded to be silent for the next few minutes. I mentioned before he was

CHAPTER NINE

naturally introverted, but this took it to a whole new level, and as if the last two hours weren't awkward enough, now we had this. He almost acted like he didn't even know us. After about five minutes, he asked us if we would like to go on a tour of the town.

"Yes, yes, yes, please take us for a drive and get us the hell out of this house." That was what was in my head, but what came out was a simple, "Yes." The drive and "tour" were rather emotionless, robotic, and quite boring. At this point it was abundantly clear to me he had no interest in me whatsoever, so the longer this charade continued, the more uncomfortable it made me feel. I thought to myself once again this was not my idea, and the two of you, Sylvia and Jay, arranged the whole thing, so why is he acting so weird? This made me look like I was an obsessive ex-girlfriend, crashing in unexpectedly and trying to win him back.

We finished the awkward tour and came back to the house. "Yay, I'm back in a college bachelor pad, with a bunch of dudes I don't know, and no conversation being had," again, all in my head. I proceeded to watch the clock tick by very slowly until it was time to go to bed. This would have been a perfect opportunity to have exited my torture chamber and gone back to my private little cell (a.k.a., the car), but Sylvia had arranged for us to stay the night in this lovely frat house. I think at that point I could have killed her, buried the body literally where no one would find it, and headed home. Instead, I went to bed in a room of the house, with absolutely no one we knew or trusted except for Jay (and Lord knows where he was at this point), and were expected to sleep—well I assure you that didn't happen.

We woke up early the next morning and started getting ready. Jay came into the room to check on us, and I think he was surprised we were already packed and ready to go. He seemed a little friendlier than the previous day, but I wasn't staying around

VIRGINIA, SYLVIA, HANDSOME MARINES CONT. . . .

to try and find out why. We said our quick goodbyes, thanked his roommates for letting us stay there (as it turned out they were stellar dudes), hopped in the car, and drove away as fast as possible. I think I left some tire tracks on the way out. This ended up being one of the most painful experiences I've ever had, although the world in all its kindness afforded me many more painful experiences in the future.

Sylvia was so upset and kept apologizing over and over on the way home. She said, "I never thought it was going to go that way. He seemed so excited to see you when I talked to him."

I just simply turned to her and said, "Sometimes these things are just better left alone." After that we made our journey back to the apartment.

We had many adventures during our time living in Virginia, and we were both very glad to have been there and met so many good friends and had so many good experiences. Having said that, however, it was time for us to move on. We packed up our belongings, loaded up the truck with everything we wanted to bring, sold everything else, and then hit the road. It was a three-day drive back to Colorado, and we stopped along the way to see some of the sites. Prior to moving, we reached out to my brother and sister-in-law living in Colorado Springs and asked them to put us up for a while until we got ourselves situated with jobs.

I hadn't taken the SAT or ACT exams when I was in high school because I had convinced myself I would never go to college. Now, here I was, eight years later, studying for the ACT. God must surely have been laughing. Mine and Sylvia's goal was to try to enter the commuter campus located in the area, which was a satellite campus for the University of Colorado at Colorado Springs. We were a little bit older than your average university student, so we thought this might be a good fit.

CHAPTER TEN

ROOMMATES, A FAMILY, GIGI THE CAT, AND APPLICATIONS TO COLLEGE

After a long drive and sleep exhaustion, we arrived at my brother's house. He had a room for Sylvia and I to share, and the accommodation was quite comfortable. Add to that two of my nieces were there, which made for a very exciting package. My brother, in the meantime, had also brought on another tenant. We made fast friends with this gentleman and quickly found ourselves hanging together a lot. He was trying to figure out his next steps for a career and a family, as he had already finished school.

As soon as we arrived, I went to the library and got myself an ACT study guide and got to work. It had been quite a few years since I'd been in school, and my skills were rusty. In addition, I was never very good at mathematics, so it was a steep learning curve. I didn't let this deter me as once I made up my mind to do something I just did it. I tried on a few occasions to work with my dad on math, but I didn't really understand it, and he wasn't very patient, so the two of us didn't blend so well (same old, same old). Sylvia was studying as well, but she had always done well in school, so she didn't find this as hard to do.

ROOMMATES, A FAMILY, GIGI THE CAT

We both picked up some part-time jobs and tried to pay a little bit of rent to my brother. It was very little, so to make up the difference, he worked it out in manual labor. On various occasions we tore apart his bathroom, dug trenches around the yard, and put up a fence, as well as a myriad of other things. It seemed like a good trade at the time. Once I started school, I would wake up early in the morning and go get my nieces out of bed, change their clothes, and feed them a quick breakfast. That way when my sister-in-law came downstairs, she had a decent start to the morning. While this may have been another way to help pay rent, it was more of a benefit for me as I *loved* being around my nieces.

The time finally arrived for me to take my ACT test. I completed the test and walked away not feeling very confident. I was unsure if I would pass math, but I was hoping the English, writing, and comprehension would make up for the lack of math skills. I started working and kept myself busy while waiting for the results. I had applied to school at Arizona State University, as well as the University of Colorado, since those were the two schools my friend and I were looking into.

Eventually the results came in, and I managed to score well enough to get into both schools. As anticipated, my math portion of the test was abysmal, but the English, writing, and comprehension, were high enough to pull the average up and qualify me for entrance into both universities. I spent some time deciding what school I wanted to attend and finally landed at the University of Colorado. Much to my surprise, Sylvia (clearly my best friend by this point in time) decided she wanted to go to ASU. Sadly, there was going to be a separation for us in the near future. A fact neither one of us wanted to spend much time thinking about.

We both continued working at our jobs and finishing up

CHAPTER TEN

the application process for our various universities. In our free time we hung out with my family and our other roommate, Joe. We had a lot of family around, which ensured a lot of activities were to be had, including volleyball whenever an opportunity presented itself. We loved playing volleyball and formed various teams later. We also played in a lot of volleyball tournaments; all in all those were some of my favorite memories.

By contrast, one of the saddest memories for Sylvia and I was her cat "Gigi." You remember the earlier story of how she was tortured by our neighbor in Virginia and what a difficult time that was for us. Naturally the three of us have become very attached and now a tough decision was to be made. My brother and sister-in-law did not want any animals living in their house, so we had to go find a home for our beloved cat. We posted her for sale in the newspaper and eventually got a call on her. We spent some time getting to know them and decided it would be a good fit. When the time came to say goodbye, the two of us cried ourselves into a puddle. It became very apparent we wouldn't be able to take her to her new home and part ways. So Joe—out of the kindness of his heart (and most likely being annoyed with our overly emotional and dramatic female responses) offered to take Gigi to her new home.

I was initially working part-time at a Mexican food delivery place close to where I lived. When I started the job, there were a few employees on their way out. I ran into them a couple of times, and we conversed briefly. I was a tad bit older than most of the people working there, so I felt like a little bit of a mother hen. One of the young girls working there attached to me fairly quickly. In addition, a young man with stunning blue eyes and a tall gangly build also caught my eye. He wasn't very friendly or talkative, so I just dismissed it as being young and immature. I couldn't have been farther from the truth. Little did I know we would cross paths in the future.

I worked at this job for a couple of months and started going to school as well. The job didn't last much longer as I got robbed one of the nights, which put a quick kibosh on the whole thing. The story goes something like this: the owner of said fast food restaurant was what you might call "cheap," so he didn't feel any need to put steel drop boxes inside the restaurant for us to deposit our large quantities of money. In other words, he didn't seem particularly concerned with protecting us or making our job easier if doing so came with a high price tag. So we carried our cash bags with us in our vehicles.

The situation was I was driving a vehicle that wasn't very easy to get into or lock and unlock. So me being as silly as I was, ran up to a house to drop off their delivery and left my vehicle unlocked. It was only a couple of minutes, and when I came back, the cash was gone. I didn't remember for sure how much money was in there, but we had receipts to add it all up. When all was said and done, it was around $300. I was paying for school now and borrowing a car from my parents, so I didn't have $30 extra, let alone $300. The owner of the company wanted me to pay the whole $300 back, which made a lot of my coworkers angry, and I wasn't too happy either. He kept pushing the point, so I quit. By law he was required to give me my last paycheck, and he told me he was going to take the money out of that, but once again he couldn't legally do it, so I took the check and ended our relationship.

As I was struggling to adapt to the new school schedule, and now in search of a new job, I was overwhelmed. I was still having some health problems, and it made my day-to-day kind of difficult. At this point in time, I was actively engaged in my church

CHAPTER TEN

and in my faith. Naturally I was still working through a lot, but I could feel myself growing closer to God. Sylvia and I attended Mass regularly and spent a lot of time talking and praying with my brother and sister-in-law.

Truth be told, it was a real blessing to live with them. They were so kind to have brought me into their house and show me the path to a more anchored faith. Sadly, I would temporarily damage that relationship as well. It is an understatement to say my physical problems weren't the only problem I had. I continued to battle with depression, bulimia, and feelings of inadequacy. I didn't like who I was, although I am nothing if not a brilliant actor when it comes to hiding my feelings from the world. The only people that really knew what was happening were my best friend, Sylvia, and later down the road my soulmate/husband. My sweet Guardian Angel never left my side, but I wasn't fully aware of that.

THE COLLEGE EXPERIENCE

After I left my job at the Mexican restaurant, I headed once again into a job search. I went from business to business dropping off resumes and filling out applications. Much to my luck, on one such occasion, I went into a department store and to the back offices. I applied for the job they had posted, and it just so happened the human resource manager was there. She came out from around the desk and asked if I had a few minutes to talk to her. "Of course I do," I replied, and we talked for quite a while and immediately made a connection. I was offered the job on the spot and arranged to start the following morning.

The job paid well and looked to be pretty promising. I really enjoyed working with the staff at my new job and formed a

THE COLLEGE EXPERIENCE

friendship with the human resource manager. For some reason unbeknownst to me, she trusted me. So when she and her husband traveled, they paid me to housesit for them. Considering how nice the house was, that it was a quiet place for me to do my schoolwork and be alone, and it came with additional pay, I was on board. I even housesat for her parents on one occasion, which came with an even more beautiful house and all the rest of the stuff.

The human resource manager, Jane, could see how fast I picked up on tasks and how efficient I could be. I was quick at learning jobs and able to take on a lot of tasks at once (I think it has a lot to do with my ability to multitask, which is a trait that has come in handy for raising a family and running a home), which gave me the confidence to try new things. I worked there for a while as well until I had an encounter with one of the other employees. I assure you it did not go well.

Have any of you ever been given multiple job assignments and duties without multiple pay? If so, you'll understand what happened. Some of my coworkers were not exactly hardworking, and I received a lot of their tasks because they weren't getting them done on time. On one such day, I was working three jobs at the same time because someone called in sick, and the other person refused to help from one of the other departments. While I was busy dealing with one of the customers at the front counter, a manager from a different department came up to me and called me out in front of the employees and the customers. She was mad because I wasn't doing the task she wanted done, but I was super busy and prioritizing the job tasks. Number one on that job task was taking care of the customer, which is what I was doing when she called me out.

After that was over, I met up with the manager that had

CHAPTER TEN

berated me and gave her a piece of my mind. I then threw down the pencil and said I quit. I headed home, and shortly after that Jane called me and asked me to come back and work. She told me I wasn't in the wrong and that she had reprimanded the manager. I should have gone back because she was so good to me, but I had this idea in my head that I couldn't let go of.

The whole time I was growing up, my dad seemed super stressed with his job. He was always complaining about management, the hard work, and how "stupid" people were. He would come home from work and hide in his office all night long except to eat dinner. So, I, as a teenager, made up my mind I would never let a manager or business owner push me around, and I refused to stay in jobs where I felt disrespected. Here I was once again in a similar situation to what happened at the newspaper in Washington. Had I grown up enough by then to realize this? The answer is no, so out on the job hunt I returned. Even now I'm shaking my head at my foolishness.

The next time around was much easier because I was able to get myself a work-study job at the University of Colorado at Colorado Springs (UCCS). Luckily, because I had taken so long to enter college, I was completely emancipated from my parents and could qualify for work study based on my very low income. I didn't even know what it was when it was offered to me. For those that don't know, it's a job on campus you get paid for, and they also pay your tuition. It was such a blessing because it paid for the next three years of school for me. I began in the safety office on campus, but it didn't last long; this time for a good reason. The safety manager was a wonderful man, but his assistant secretary had some serious issues. So the chancellor, who worked across the hall from us, interacted with me quite often and asked her secretary to steal me away.

I loved working in the chancellor's office because my boss was fabulous. She was so easy-going, a great trainer and instructor, and an incredibly decent human being. I worked there for the next two years and never wanted to leave. Now I would never lead you astray when it comes to how difficult the chancellor was to work with, but it just shows you that when you have good coworkers, you can really deal with most anything. I am going to be kind and not list the nicknames we had for the chancellor, but suffice to say she was tough as nails and very scary. For some reason she liked me and trusted me, and that made my life easier.

It was a pretty great gig I had there because not only was I getting paid to work but I was also able to do schoolwork in my free time. Granted there wasn't a lot of free time, but even if I needed to write a paper or use the computer for anything else, I was free to come back at any time and make use of the office equipment. I think they also let me use the printer paper, which was quite generous considering how many papers I wrote over the course of my employment there.

Now, as I mentioned previously, the chancellor was a very intimidating individual. If you've ever seen the movie *The Devil Wears Prada*, she was very similar to the main character Miranda Priestly. If you can visualize that scene where she comes flying through the office, throws her coat on the secretary's desk, and rattles off about ten tasks, that was our day in and day out. Luckily for me, I wasn't her direct assistant, so my interactions were less intense. Nonetheless it was like preparing for combat daily.

There were three of us working in the offices for the chancellor, and we made a pretty good support system for one another. We also made a support system for the rest of the university staff and professors. We developed different code words and signals to

CHAPTER TEN

let people know when she was in her office and/or on campus. It was quite funny and entertaining to see so many adults so afraid of one skinny, disorganized, and seemingly detached woman, but she was a force to be reckoned with. She injected fear into us mere mortals working in close contact with her. Secretly it kind of impressed me to see that much authority, but I like people too much to ever be that aggressive.

As I mentioned before, she seemed to like me, and it made surviving in the chancellor's office that much easier. It was a really great job for me to have in terms of gaining experience and taking on some very difficult tasks. My boss, who I will call Kate, trusted me with a lot of those difficult tasks. I had opportunities to plan large events on campus. One year I oversaw a silent auction. The auction had been done many times before, but Kate was very impressed with the outcome from my year of running it. She said I got more donations than she ever had when she ran the project. Granted it's a very big compliment, but completely in my wheelhouse. Talking to people is the easiest thing for me to do, so asking if they can donate to the university was a simple job. I was also in charge of helping plan the commencement exercises every year. As many of you know, commencement is a large undertaking, and there's a lot that goes into the planning of it, which was another job I really enjoyed doing.

About the time I started at the chancellor's office, it was about my second semester after starting school. Since I had one semester under my belt, I had a pretty good handle on where everything was located and the setup of the university. I had started meeting some other students, and I quickly became attached to some of the professors as well. I guess you could say that is the benefit of being an older college student; the professors aren't that much older than you are.

THE COLLEGE EXPERIENCE

I really loved going to school there, loved the professors, loved the campus, and loved learning. This came as a complete shock to me considering how much I disliked . . . despised . . . and avoided doing schoolwork when I was growing up. My birth family can attest to this as they had a front-row seat to my rebellion. I think I had a natural inkling to learn, but I asked a lot of questions, and people did not like that. I also didn't really enjoy the curriculum and structure we had in grade school. In my opinion, there's nothing that curbs learning faster than being told what you must read, write, listen to, and do versus being free to explore the things you're interested in.

So that's what made college different because I had the freedom to choose what courses I wanted to take and explore those subjects in depth. Of course we had required general ed classes, and those weren't always so fun, but you got through that to get to the good stuff. I absolutely loved my psychology classes. I had a lot of fabulous professors and could not get enough of the deep dive into people's psychological processes—more specifically when those processes broke down and disorder and dysfunction set in. I have always been a little bit dark in my thinking as I tend toward what things make an individual behave in an unstable way or even, in extreme cases, commit heinous acts. This is a combination, in my opinion, of nature versus nurture and good versus bad. Trying to determine how much of it is just somebody's natural inclination toward something, versus a learned behavior from someone in that person's inner circle, is part of what gets flushed out when seeking to understand that individual. The part the field of psychology doesn't like to investigate is the spiritual battle of the soul going on underneath the visible layer of said individual. I have found that if you dismiss this aspect, you will never have a complete picture of the who and the why of that person.

CHAPTER TEN

My next favorite subject was philosophy, and I lucked out there too. I had great professors in this field and managed to make a few friendships with them along the way. As time continued, I grew in love with the field of philosophy. I later decided to minor in it. When I look back now at the time spent at UCCS, I miss those intellectual debates and discussions. Those discussions just don't seem to happen too much in our everyday life, so those were very treasured times for me.

THE COLLEGE EXPERIENCE CONT. . . .

Shortly before I entered college, I met with an advisor to map out the next four years. I remember coming into the office, sitting down with the advisor, and saying, "I want in and out in four years; tell me how I can do that." I laugh now because I remember thinking I could not bear the thought of dragging it out past those four years as in my mind I had a whole lot more school to do. I was always intending on getting my PhD, so I had eight years of schooling to look forward to.

My advisor smiled at me and said, "Here's what you would need to do." She said take a full course load each fall/spring semester (twelve to fifteen credit hours), and then a full course load over the summer (six credit hours) to graduate in four years. I guess it never occurred to me I would be working year-round when I started this program, but it didn't deter me in the least. I said, "Okay let's get at it," so we started looking at coursework, general-ed credits, electives, and upper-level psychology and philosophy courses. We did a pretty general outlay of what it would look like for me, and I just went about filling in the classes. I was so headstrong and determined to finish in those four years that I never even allowed myself to drop a class or change classes

THE COLLEGE EXPERIENCE CONT. . . .

when it didn't look like it would be a good fit. There was only one class that left a negative mark on my record because of my stubbornness, and that was economics. It was because of this I ended up feeling a little bit of what shall we say . . . hatred toward that discipline.

After the first semester, I started to feel at home on campus. I met a few people in some of my classes and several at the gym. They were great people to hang out with, but surprisingly I spent most of my time hanging out with the people I had met at my Mexican food delivery job. We went to country bars and dance clubs quite often and enjoyed hanging out at pool halls as well. If I wasn't busy doing schoolwork, or my job, I was out with my friends socializing. I always had a desire to meet new people, and I loved getting to know someone in depth. The people I hung out with the most had very interesting lives but extremely difficult, and therefore struggled to make good life decisions. It created quite a tangled web in their lives, and I got caught up in that web as well, unknowingly.

The story goes like this: The employees from the Mexican restaurant were surprisingly very interested in the new kid on the block, a.k.a. . . . me, and invited me along everywhere they went. I was roughly about five years older than most of the people in this friend group, and as such, I kind of operated in the capacity of being an older sister or an aunt, if you will. I mentioned earlier I was included in the group, and in some odd way maybe even needed. They confided in me on a regular basis about their personal struggles. One of the young ladies I got to know (Eva) seemed to struggle a lot in her personal life. She had a beautiful young boy, James, who was just a small toddler when I met him and whom I got very attached to in short order.

Eva and I spent a lot of time together talking and hanging

CHAPTER TEN

out and clubbing when she had a babysitter to do so. James's father was not in the picture at this time, so she was a single parent. On one of the nights we decided to go out, she introduced me to a woman by the name of Sherry. We had a good time the first night we hung out, which I think surprised Sherry as she seemed very skeptical of women. On another occasion, when we decided to go hit the bars again, I came over to her house to pick her up.

Unbeknownst to me, a young man was at her house babysitting her adorable son, Connor. I recognized this "babysitter" immediately from crossing paths at the Mexican restaurant—and if I'm being honest, I remembered his stunning blue eyes and beautiful eyelashes. Secretly (and not so secretly) I thought he was very handsome. I didn't think of him in dating terms as he was much too young for me. So when I was at the house, I tried to strike up a conversation with this fine gentleman while waiting for Sherry to come out and was met with resistance. It's not often I can't strike up a conversation with somebody, even the most introverted of persons, but in this case, it wasn't going to happen. His name was Thomas (Tom), and he was very introverted and shy, which I thought was the reason he didn't talk to me, but later I found out even more.

The evening started out strangely and got even stranger. We got to the country bar and met up with her other friends. Unfortunately, I had a little weirdness of my own going on. One of the young men I worked with (Derek) had shown interest in me, and although I wasn't much interested in him, he was very persistent. We started hanging out together, and it created a very odd situation. I guess you could say we "dated" during that time, but what I really was trying to do was to help him get some direction in his life. He came from a very dysfunctional background (surprise, surprise) and didn't seem to know how to get

THE COLLEGE EXPERIENCE CONT. . . .

himself out of the life he was living and on to a better path. Yes, I foolishly thought I was the one that could help him do that (ever heard of a savior complex?). As time went on, however, I realized it wasn't going to work, so I was detaching myself, which wouldn't happen easily.

While at the bar, I was confused with Sherry at this point because of the Tom situation. Here he was home with her little baby boy, and she was out at a bar drinking, dancing, and partying. I didn't want to jump to any conclusions, so I assumed maybe she was home a lot and this was her one night to go out and relax. I found out later that was not the case. She was flirting with a lot of guys at the bar and didn't act in such a way as to make one think she was taken. The next thing I'm going to say will make me sound like a horrible human being, but I tried to get her to connect with Derek in hopes I could pair them up and untangle myself from the situation. I thought that would be better for both Tom and I, but it was largely selfish.

I was not successful in my matchmaking, so I had to be more assertive in my efforts to end this thing with Derek. Basically, I told him I didn't want to see him anymore except in a friend capacity, but that I had no interest in dating him. That information was met with a rather odd reaction as he proceeded to open the door to my car, which was moving at the time, and jump out. In all honesty, it took a minute for me to process and do the right thing. As I started to pull over, for one moment I hesitated and thought maybe I should just keep driving (not kidding, I almost drove off), but charity took over the better part of me, and I turned around and went back to pick him up. Surprisingly he was not very injured, some road rash and a large dose of humility was all he incurred. I took him back to his house, dropped him off, and told him we wouldn't go out again. I think at that point he

CHAPTER TEN

probably realized that stunt had sealed the deal, and he finally let me go.

It wasn't but a short while after this crazy weekend I ended up in a really good phone conversation with Tom. I called Sherry to talk to her about something, and the next thing you know, Tom and I were on the phone together talking about music, movies, our families, and everything else. I think we were on the phone for about an hour, and then Tom, in a very panicked voice, said, "Oh boy I've got to get off the phone because Sherry is getting mad at me."

I said, "Mad at what?"

He said, "She doesn't like me to talk to other women." That is when I started to realize why he was so awkward with me when I came over to the house to pick her up. I think at that point I mentioned something about how she seemed to have no trouble talking to other men when we were at the club. He said "goodbye" and jumped off the phone.

The next time I saw Tom was at a movie theater with some of my other friends. He came running up to me while I was standing in line with a friend and said he needed to ask me a question. He said some of his friends told him Sherry was flirting with the guys at the club the night we went out, and he asked if that was true. I said to him, "I really don't want to be in the middle of what's going on with you two."

He said, "I'm not asking you to. I just get the feeling that you would be honest, and I need to know if what my friends said is true." He said, "You don't need to worry cuz I've already broken up with her, but I just want to know." I just kind of nodded my head yes, and he thanked me and walked off.

We had exchanged phone numbers before this, so he and I continued to talk on the phone and get to know each other. We

THE COLLEGE EXPERIENCE CONT. . . .

also ended up going to a lot of clubs and pool halls together and hung out with a large group of friends we had. In this friend group were some other gentlemen I was close to as well. For the sake of clarity, I want you to know that at this stage in my life, I decided I wasn't going to have a serious boyfriend because it would interfere with my schooling and plans for the future. What's that old saying? "If you want a good laugh, just tell God your plans?" It was not going to play out the way I thought.

CHAPTER ELEVEN

THE TERMINATOR, THE SLEEZY CAR MECHANIC, THE BIRTHDAY PARTY

This oddly has got to be one of my favorite stories as it points to my chronic bad luck, lack of proper planning, and insane experiences. Life continued, with me still living with my brother and sister-in-law and working and going to school. I was starting to feel happier and as though I had more direction in my life. I think you could say I finally had a purpose. My purpose at this time was to get my bachelor's degree and move to North Carolina for a PhD program in psychology.

On the side, I continued to enjoy myself and whatever free time I had available to me. My parents bailed me out by loaning me cars on several occasions: firstly, because I was so irresponsible, and secondly, because I refused to accept monetary help from them in any capacity, so they supported me where they could. I was very stubborn and felt as though the mistakes I made were my own and no one else's, which is why, even when I was in dire straits (I had no food at all in my refrigerator and wouldn't ask for help), I wouldn't call and ask them, or anyone, for help. Oddly enough, I was willing to borrow vehicles from them, and at this

THE TERMINATOR, THE SLEEZY CAR MECHANIC

time I was borrowing their truck. It was kind of them to lend it to me. As the expression goes "No good deed goes unpunished."

One morning when I was heading out to school I walked over to my truck and saw the side window had been shot out. There was glass everywhere, and it was very clear it had been vandalized; although, nothing had been stolen inside. I found out at a later occasion some young punks would randomly decide to go shoot the windows out of vehicles in the neighborhood. They alternated by targeting different colored vehicles, red one night, blue another, etc.

As one can imagine, I still wasn't in a flush monetary situation, which equates to I had no money to replace the window, so it would have to wait for a week or two until my paycheck came in. In the meantime, my brother and I did the best we could to tape up a piece of plastic in the window to protect against the elements.

Sometime after we taped up the truck, I was driving out of the neighborhood when a newsworthy event occurred. I remembered being at a stop sign, checking both directions to make sure it was clear, and then pulling out. It was literally like being in slow motion as I remember this overwhelming feeling as I pulled into the intersection that something was not right. The next thing I know, I remember coming to and facing east in westbound traffic, staring at the front of a school bus. It took my brain a couple of minutes to realize I had been in a car accident. Once I realized that, I instantly processed the fact children were on the bus, and in a panic, I tried to get myself out of the truck.

I didn't understand until later the reason I could not open the driver's side door was because it was bowed in as that is where the impact hit when the bus struck me. I somehow comprehended I needed to go out the passenger side and then ran

CHAPTER ELEVEN

over to the bus and in a panic started yelling, "Are the kids okay? Are the kids okay?" The bus driver said everyone here is fine, but you are the one that's bleeding. She made me get onto the bus and sit down. I looked back at the kids and told them I was sorry and asked if any of them had gotten thrown.

She said, "No, we all had our seatbelts on." I was surprised as a lot of the buses didn't have seatbelts at that time, so I was grateful for that.

It wasn't but a short while after that an ambulance showed up, the police, and if I remember correctly, a news helicopter. The EMTs started evaluating me and immediately put me in a neck brace and on a gurney. I was so angry as I just knew I didn't have any neck or back injuries, and I also knew I looked ridiculous. I was even well enough to recognize the EMTs were cute, so how bad could I be really? The most embarrassing thing of all was some news reporters ended up at the scene of the accident, and I ended up on the news looking horrible for the whole world to see. I even made some off-the-cuff comment about it being a slow news day if they were covering this "event."

I went to the hospital and wasn't there very long when they finished up my evaluation. They took that annoying neck brace off and allowed me to sit up, which made a big difference. I don't think I knew the extent of the cuts and scratches I had all over me until I got home. I was definitely looking a little worse for the wear. I think one of the saddest moments I had was when Tom called me and was angry. Obviously, he'd seen me on the news, and he did not understand for the life of him why I hadn't called him when I got back to the house. He felt like he just wasn't important enough to me for me to have followed up. I tried to explain to him I was just embarrassed at what had happened, that I had caused the accident, and that I ended up on the news

THE TERMINATOR, THE SLEEZY CAR MECHANIC

looking as bad as I was. I think by the end of the conversation, he felt a little bit better. We talked for quite a while that night and laughed away some of the tension.

It was a miracle I had lived through that car accident. I recognized later how lucky I was not to have had any serious injuries after being t-boned by a school bus in a 40 mile an hour speed zone. It triggered this memory for me of a scene in one of the *Terminator* movies. In the scene he ends up in a massive car accident with a semi, and when you think he's dead, the camera zooms in on the terminator's metal foot, and he starts walking out of the wreckage. That was literally how I felt after being smashed in by a school bus and not even breaking a bone. Proving once again how timeless is the line "I'll be back."

As if my luck wasn't bad enough, I had to experience some more humility. I felt so bad for destroying my dad's truck, and even though it wasn't my fault that the window had gotten shot out, I still felt guilty. It was in that guilt that I decided to get the truck fixed as cheaply as possible so as to return it to my dad in working condition. Anytime I've shot for finding a cheap way to do things it has definitely backfired, and this was no exception.

I talked to my very good friend Jake (who would later be a short-term love interest) and asked him if he knew a mechanic that could do the repairs for me and save me some money. He connected me with a friend of his, and we went about making the arrangements. The idea was he would get a new cab for the truck and replace the old one. This of course is a very complicated process, and while it may sound easy to do, it is not easy in action. Which is a fact I wish this jerk of a mechanic had known. It was in the shop for a few months, and every time I contacted him, he had one excuse after another.

I had given him some money on the front end to pay for

CHAPTER ELEVEN

some of the repairs and be able to purchase the replacement cab. I finally got tired of this little game of cat and mouse and decided to call him on his bluff. I said I was coming to get it in a week, and he had to have it done. The week passed, and when I arrived at the repair shop, the truck wasn't working. Although there was a new cab on it, the lights were not hooked up, and the electricity was not done. Tom came and helped me drive it to a trustworthy mechanic he knew who managed to get the lights to work but said the whole electrical system was a mess. I wanted to get it up to my dad's and fix it up there, so we drove it during the day and dropped it off at my dad's house.

When we got some more of the electrical problems fixed and I went to get it licensed, we realized there was no VIN number. That's right; this jerk put on a new cab and never replaced the VIN number. I'm pretty sure he got this cab illegally as he turned out to be a very sketchy person. So now I was really screwed because the truck wasn't fully functioning, and I couldn't even get it registered for my dad. I told my dad I would get him back all the money I paid for the truck and that we would figure something out. I told him I was going to sue this guy. My dad said, "What's done is done; don't waste your time because you'll never see a penny of it." All I could think is "challenge accepted." I felt horrible about the situation I left my dad in, and I was determined to make this guy's life hell until he paid me back.

So that is what I did. I took him to a small claims court. He didn't bother to show up, and the judge told me I should have sued to the limit of the court, and he would have granted it to me. I told the judge I was just trying to be honest and only get back what I had paid. The judge told me my time, loss of vehicle, and all the stress he put me through was also worth money. All in all, I think it's safe to say the judge was pretty ticked off. So I won

THE TERMINATOR, THE SLEEZY CAR MECHANIC

my case in court and set about collecting the money. Nobody ever tells you how hard it is to collect money from a criminal.

I started by garnishing his wages at the job he was working. After a while, he quit that job and disappeared. I ran into him again and found out where he was working and garnished his wages yet again. He responded by quitting that job and disappeared for even longer at this point, but once again we tracked him down and finally collected the rest of the garnished wages. I found out where his new job was, proceeded to call the business, and ask if he was working there to get confirmation, and upon receiving confirmation called the sheriff to serve him with a bench warrant.

As a surprise to me, there were multiple bench warrants in his name, so he asked me which one I was referring to. I gave him the information and then suggested he may as well serve him all the bench warrants since I had already done the legwork to find him. I would have given anything to have been a fly on the wall when they showed up to his work to serve the papers. He paid the balance he owed me, and I never saw him again, thank goodness.

The sad part of the whole situation was my dad's truck was useless to him as he could not get it registered anywhere without the VIN number. I investigated taking it to another shop and trying to get the cab replaced again, but it was very pricey, and at this point, my dad had just given up. I felt so bad as the truck was in great condition when he loaned it to me, and I managed to destroy it. I had a lot of these issues in my life: plagued by bad luck, unable to keep a job, broke and unsuccessful. I constantly told myself I was a loser, an idiot, irresponsible, fat, ugly, you name it. I beat myself up and never seemed to have a kind thing to say to myself. In addition to that, I was prideful, stubborn, willful, and scared. I knew I needed to change. I had been in and

CHAPTER ELEVEN

out of therapists as I could afford it, but now I needed to ramp things up in the self-help world or else I was confident I would never make anything of myself or be a good wife, or mother, (which were always things I desired—well, the mom part—I was scared to be a wife). I decided to ramp up the self-help work and address the issues bothering me. I'll give you a hint: some of those things plaguing me were a plague—demonic in nature.

I was recovering from the car accident and my friends were there to help me. At this point in time, Eva was dating one of the guys in the group (Tom's roommate), and to our surprise she ended up getting pregnant. He was not ready to have a child, and that situation did not go very well. It was a lot of drama I didn't want to be a part of but somehow got thrown in the middle of. I quickly removed myself from the middle of it and made it clear to both parties they would have to figure things out on their own. I must have made my point clear because they didn't involve me anymore.

As if that wasn't enough drama, we decided we'd add some more. On one of the nights we had gone out, Tom decided to come out of his shell and talk to me. It was really kind of awkward and really kind of funny the way he approached the situation. If I remember correctly, we were out shooting pool and decided to go eat at a breakfast place—which wasn't an uncommon thing for us to do. As you already know, Tom was introverted (on my initial impression I thought he was stuck up), and he had a hard time talking to me. One night he had ingested a large quantity of beer which gave him that very well-known gift of "liquid courage." So when we got to the restaurant, he decided to sit next to me, pull out one of the laminated menus, and block us from everyone else at the table. He started talking a lot and got irritated every time somebody tried to talk to me or ask a question. It was quite funny

THE TERMINATOR, THE SLEEZY CAR MECHANIC

and contrary to how I normally work; I didn't get mad at him for being such a dingbat and just laughed it off.

As you know from earlier, I didn't have a vehicle and needed to get back home, so Tom offered to drive me. However, because of his high level of intoxication, I needed to do the driving. He gave me the keys, and I drove him back to his apartment. When we got to his apartment, we sat in the car and talked for a couple of hours, after which, realizing the conversation was going to continue, we went inside. We literally talked the rest of the night, and when the sun came up, I decided after being gone all night that it was time for me to head home. We shared a lot and deeply bonded through these conversations and seemed to share a lot of the same value system. He was very intelligent, more so than even most of the men I knew, and seemed to come from a solid home. These were all positive attributes; the only thing that was bothersome to me was our age difference, and that bothered me.

We headed out to the car and started our trek home. We were both exhausted after not sleeping all night, and I was in a bit of a zombie state. I remember gazing out the window feeling kind of melancholic when I heard Tom mumbling about something. I wasn't sure what he was mumbling—because in all honesty I wasn't really paying attention—but recognized the fact he was waiting for a response from me. I pulled myself out of my mental stupor and turned to him and said, "I'm sorry, what was that?"

To which he responded, "I would really like to date you; would you like to date me?" I instantly went into panic mode—you know the kind of panic that makes you frantically search for the eject button in the cockpit of a plane?

I turned to him and said, "Why would we do that?" He seemed confused he had to explain why but proceeded to do so, expressing all our similarities in our viewpoints, our background,

CHAPTER ELEVEN

and our interests. Everything he said was true and logical, but in my mind, he was too young, hadn't had enough life experiences, and might get in the way of my plans for the future. I don't think I was very kind, but I said I just didn't think it was a good idea. I told him I had friendship to offer him, but that was all.

Much to my surprise, he said, "Okay, let's just be friends," which utterly shocked me. I guess he was playing the long game.

Looking back on all the drama I created in my life and the drama thrust upon me, it is a wonder he wanted to remain friends at all. I can't say I know for sure what it is like to live around me and the very large wake I produce, but for some odd reason, he and others were willing to do it. Another layer got added to this drama. There was another male friend of ours (Jake) that I found out later was interested in me. He was part of this large friend group we had going, and he was a very cool person. I went to the bars and clubs with him and his friend Louis on a very regular basis, and occasionally, we combined Tom's group and Jake's group.

As time went on, Louis decided Jake and I should date, and he got it in his head to make that happen. After a while, Jake finally approached me about the possibility of dating. Maybe his timing was right, or maybe it had to do with him being older, I don't know, but I decided to say yes. He asked me out right before I was heading out on a trip. Tom was driving me to the airport for my trip, and we decided to stop and get something to eat. It was at that time I told him Jake had asked me out, and I had said yes. To his credit, Tom remained very calm but looked at me very confused. I think he asked me why I was okay going out with Jake and not him. I'm not sure of my answer, but I'm guessing it went something like this—he's older, more established, and we've known each other for a while. I'm pretty sure Tom could see through the BS, but I certainly couldn't at this point.

THE TERMINATOR, THE SLEEZY CAR MECHANIC

Jake was a very kind person, very polite, and gentlemanly. He had a good job, was also smart and handsome, and was easy to talk to. We went out on our first date, which was kind of awkward because we had been friends for quite a while by this time but decided to get to know each other more personally. We finished the date and made plans for yet another and then said good night. I think we went out on a few dates over the course of two weeks, and then that was it. Neither he nor I felt any chemistry, so it was time to call it off. I had to be the very bad guy and do the breaking up, but we both agreed it was a good idea. I thought he was in the same place I was, or at least that's what he expressed, but his later reaction proved to be different.

If I look as flaky when it came to dating, as I was in my day-to-day life, that's only because I was. Truthfully, I feared everyone and everything. I was scared to fail at school, in my career, and most of all in life. I covered that fear with cocktails and entertainment, but it was rooted deep inside of me. There were some insidious creatures riding on my negative thoughts and helping to convince me I was useless and probably shouldn't be alive. Had I known that, I could have addressed them directly and worked to fight against them and not myself, but I didn't. In my mid to late 40's I finally realized demons are always hanging around to get us humans when we're down. When we're at our lowest, they're quick to swoop in and convince us our worst nightmares are true: nobody loves us—least of all God—and we will never amount to anything. I'm here to tell you there is nothing further from the truth. We are amazing, every one of us, and have a purpose in life, a purpose we were created to fulfill. So don't give up on yourself because the negative whispers in your head are not true.

Well, despite the "mutual breakup," Jake had big plans for

CHAPTER ELEVEN

my birthday, so he rented a limo to drive us up to Denver, eat dinner at a very nice restaurant, and then come back to the Springs and shoot pool, etc. All of this sounded like a fabulous evening except for one small problem; Tom was not invited to any of it, but the rest of the friend group was. As one can imagine, he was not very happy about this, nor was I, as I thought everything was kosher between the two of them. Obviously, Jake saw Tom as a threat and blamed him for our breakup.

Tom was very upset, and when he talked to me, he said, "I wanted to spend time with you on your birthday, and now Jake is icing me out because of you." He said, "I don't think the breakup was as mutual as you think it was."

He wasn't wrong, but there wasn't much I could do as plans had already been made, and I tried to get him to let Tom come, but it was a definitive no. I wasn't going to ruin the plans he made, so I went along with it. It was quite frankly a wonderful and over-the-top birthday party. We had a blast driving up to Denver, eating fancy food, drinking, and entertaining ourselves. We enjoyed pretending to be sophisticated enough to eat at a five-star restaurant. Once dinner was finished, we drove back down to the Springs, enjoyed some more spirits, and ended up at our favorite pool hall. In the meantime they invited my childhood friends from Denver, as well as Tom and some of my local friends, to the party at the pool hall, where we all shot pool, drank, and visited.

After a little while, we decided it was time to leave the pool hall and head to a dance club. This was always my choice for entertainment. I loved to dance, and it was always so much fun to hang out with a good group of friends and bring in a new birthday year. We went to the club and started dancing and sobering up—well, somewhat sobering up. Jake was interested in another young lady who had come in the limo with us, and she continued to hang out with us the rest of the time, which was a positive for him. She was very pretty and charismatic, and to be honest, quite a few of the guys liked her. I was drunk, by then, and as the evening came to an end, we all started to go our separate ways. Tom and I, however, did not separate and instead headed over to his friend's house with a small group from the party. We stayed at his friend's house and once again talked through the night. The next day was much more difficult recovery wise as I had a pretty good hangover to work through. Tom drove me back home in the morning, and I returned to my usual life. However, from this point forward, nothing was going to be as usual.

COMMITMENTS, MORE SCHOOL, GLIMPSE INTO THE FUTURE

A few days after my glorious birthday party, things kind of returned to normal. I dove right back into school, my job, and continued to work very hard. Tom and I became inseparable, and romantic, which led him to step forward once again and ask for a commitment. I started in with my usual concerns and a long list of reasons why it wouldn't work, but he wasn't having it. He just looked at me and said, "We spend all of our free time together and are together on campus as well, so what difference does it make really? Why can't you just try it out for a while and see how it goes?" Whether it was just good sound logic or my growing feelings for him that I was doing my best to bury deep inside my heart, I agreed to his "unreasonable plan." He was very excited I finally agreed, and at some point, in the next few weeks, we proceeded to go and meet his family.

His parents liked me, and we received their seal of approval. Whether that was due to their dislike for his last girlfriend or just

CHAPTER ELEVEN

good timing, who's to say, but it seemed to flow well. We visited with them, ate dinner, listened to music, and got to know one another. We met his brother somewhere along the way as well, but I don't remember the timing on that per se as he was going to college up in Denver at the time and was in and out of their house visiting. We started dating right around the time of his brother's graduation from high school, so Tom brought me as his "date" to the graduation. The graduation itself was special, and then we headed back to his parents' house for the reception. All their extended family traveled out for this graduation, and I, as a newly ordained girlfriend, got thrown quickly into the fire. Talk about a bit overwhelming. Luckily for me I had come from a large family myself and was used to visiting with a lot of different people. I would say overall the weekend went well.

As for school, my classes were going very well and I was holding a very high GPA in my major and minor. The only thing that brought my overall GPA down was some of the natural science classes I had to take. In one class, Physics 101, the highest grade I could manage was a C+. I had a fabulous teacher for that class who went above and beyond to help me do well on my tests. The tests were multiple choice, and I did horrible on multiple choice tests. I understand why this was the case now that I've gotten older, but at the time, I just couldn't comprehend why other people could get such good grades on these types of tests, and I struggled so hard.

You see when you're naturally a very abstract thinker, as I am, you see only things in gray not in black and white. I would constantly infer things from the multiple-choice questions. I didn't know how to read the question as a straightforward question and thought they were always a clue to something else. So in my professor's efforts to help me he said if I was ever unsure of

COMMITMENTS, MORE SCHOOL, GLIMPSE INTO THE FUTURE

a multiple-choice question that I could write a small explanation on the side explaining why I concluded what I did, and he would at least give me partial credit if it made sense and followed a logical format. He did exactly that and gave me credit for those answers I provided. Even with that I still couldn't get above a C+. He smiled and said it was the hardest-earned C+ he'd ever seen.

I spent a great deal of time on campus and got to know most of the teachers and a lot of students. When I met Tom, who up until this time was the smartest guy I had ever gone out with (and still holds that title), he was carrying a very low GPA and was close to his way out of college. You see it wasn't that he didn't have the brains or the talent to do great in school; it was just that he had a hard time dealing with the hypocrisy of some of the professors, did not like being told what he should and should not learn, and thought there was better ways to spend his time. It was a combination of school not being challenging enough for him, he not having a good goal for what he wanted to do with his life, and ultimately needing motivation to get him to buckle down and do the work.

Apparently, I was motivation for Tom, and it helped him get back on track, although I never pushed him or forced him to do anything he didn't want. I basically explained to him that what he wanted to do in his life, and with his life, was his choice, but that I had goals and dreams of my own. I explained to him I had wasted a lot of years trying to figure out what I wanted to be when I grew up, and I was finally on the right God-given track for me, but that track was going to take about eight years. If I'm guessing correctly, I think Tom realized that if he wanted to be with me, and continue to date me, then he needed to figure out what he wanted to do with his own life. He decided to stay in school and chose a major he was interested in.

CHAPTER ELEVEN

As our relationship continued into the next month, I informed Tom I couldn't let the relationship go much further until I knew how well he traveled. You see I was pretty much obsessed with the idea of traveling and seeing the world, and I couldn't be with anybody that didn't have that same vision. From the time I was little I was always fascinated by this big, beautiful world God had created. I would look at pictures of the landscapes, wildlife, and nature in all these other countries, as well as the people that lived there, and I was absolutely obsessed with seeing it all. I felt like it was not very considerate to God, and all that he created, not to go and experience it. In addition to this, I wanted a person that was flexible and easy-going when they traveled and could adapt to any situation that presented itself. I wanted somebody that was low maintenance when they traveled, and I hoped he would be the one.

Tom was on board with all of this as he himself had made plans to move to another state after graduating from college. He loved the idea of traveling and seemed up for the test. We had the perfect opportunity present itself the next month. I was going out to ASU to go visit my friend Sylvia, since I hadn't had an opportunity to see her since she had moved. I asked him if he wanted to go along for the ride, and he was all in. So we packed up our very few belongings and made the long drive down to Tempe. I don't remember much on the front side of the trip except that it was a very enjoyable and easy drive. I was a smoker at this stage in my life, and Tom seemed to adapt to that. The funny thing I found out later was he had sworn to himself that he would never date a smoker because his mom smoked so much when he was growing up. Never say never, right?

Sylvia was so excited to have us there and to see me again. She took us on a tour of the campus, and my biggest highlight was the outdoor Olympic-size swimming pool and the gigantic gymnasium. I was an exercise junkie, so this was like heaven to me. I don't remember if I got to work out in the facility. I think you had to be a student, but either way it was a great tour and an amazing campus.

Things got really weird that night when we went to a party with Sylvia and her friends. Let's just say her friends . . . well . . . their doors swung in both directions. Tom and I were pretty much as straightforward as they come (if you get my meaning) and found the whole ritual to be extremely uncomfortable. At one point in time, I think Tom and I had both been hit on multiple times by the same person. It was getting more and more uncomfortable, so we asked Sylvia if we could leave and headed out of there. She apologized profusely and said she didn't know this group of people, but they were just friends of a friend of hers—you know how that goes! We told her it was fine, but she seemed embarrassed—and we were embarrassed as well.

That night when we got back to the apartment, I wasn't feeling well, so I mistakenly took some Nyquil and proceeded to try out for the NBA. Now most people when they take Nyquil experience some lethargy and a reduction in cold symptoms. I, however, had the opposite reaction, and it caused me to become wide awake and suffer from the jitters. I was so antsy I could not contain myself in the apartment and kept fidgeting. I turned to them both and said I needed to go play basketball if there was a nearby court. Of course there was a court nearby. We were located near a college campus. I went out and shot hoops for an hour or two with Tom and Sylvia. Eventually the liquid form of speed (a.k.a., Nyquil), left my system, and I was able to go back to the apartment and sleep. I know I've mentioned before that I have trouble with medication, and this is just an example of the

CHAPTER ELEVEN

many experiences I've had when taking said medication. Despite all of it, Tom still seemed interested in dating me. Foolish boy!

It was the end of our visit with Sylvia, so we packed up our belongings, loaded up in the car, and Sylvia and I said a tearful goodbye to each other. She whispered to me she really liked Tom, that she thought I had a good one there, and then she said her goodbyes to him as well. On our way home, Tom and I were jabbering away with each other, and I remember looking out the window, daydreaming as I had done before with him, when he asked me a very loaded question (he likes to do that).

He said, "How do you feel about me?"

This was an extremely loaded question, and I was kind of ticked off he asked it. I was very quiet for a while and sat and thought. You see, these questions are a trap. If you say that you think of that person as a friend or good buddy, and they have real feelings for you, that can jeopardize the situation. If, on the other hand, you say you have serious feelings and that individual does not, you just give away your position.

After what seemed like an eternity, I finally turned to him and said, "Well I feel like if you left me at this point, a piece of me would be missing (to this day I still don't know why that came out of my mouth)." He got super quiet and didn't say a word. Internally I thought to myself, "How dare you make me vulnerable like this?"

Then all a sudden he took off his sunglasses and looked at me with a tear in his eye and said, "I feel the same way."

"Whew, I got through that one relatively unscathed," I thought to myself.

Shortly after this brief, but intense, talk, we stopped for some fast food. A debate still exists between the two of us as to whether we stopped at Taco Bell or McDonald's, but either way,

COMMITMENTS, MORE SCHOOL, GLIMPSE INTO THE FUTURE

the result is the same. After going to the counter and getting our food, the two of us sat down and started talking about "us." We started talking about how well we got along, how comfortable we were with each other, how well we traveled together, and that we had a seemingly shared moral compass. It was at this time that Tom said to me, "You know I could see us getting married."

As I bit into my burrito, or hamburger (depending on which fast food joint you're going with), I said, "Yeah, me too."

Then he looked at me and said, "Do you want to get married?"

I said, "Yeah, I think I do," and we decided to get engaged. For those who know us, you know how fitting this proposal was over a non-romantic, fast-food dinner, but I guess when you know, you know.

After eating dinner and getting ourselves engaged, we decided to head home. I don't know if it was the stress of the question-and-answer session I had with Tom regarding my feelings for him or the weird and inappropriate conversations he had at my friend's party or just the long travel days, but I ended up getting very sick. It started with a slight headache, which grew into a massive migraine on our drive home. I remember being in a lot of pain and moaning a lot when finally I asked him to pull over. I got out of the car and proceeded to empty the contents of my stomach on the side of the road. Once I completed the task, I felt good enough to finish the drive. It was a long few hours to get home, and we both went our separate ways once we landed back in Colorado Springs. All I remember was crawling into bed with the joy of knowing I was engaged and the fear of wondering whether that headache would lead me to another week of feeling miserable. From the time I was little, every illness was a concern in the back of my mind: will I get better, and what was coming next?

CHAPTER ELEVEN

The Sweet Guardian Angel of mine was/is always at my side, watching over me, and making sure I was okay. I feel confident he put a good word into the big man upstairs about Tom and me as he probably thought he would be a good protector for me. Let's be honest; it is always God arranging things—but our sweet Guardian Angels do a lot of the grunt work.

BEING ENGAGED, SCHOOL PLANS FOR TOM, THE ACTUAL WEDDING

After we returned from our trip to Arizona, we realized it was time to go and break the "good news" to his family and to mine. Let's just say his family didn't seem to take it so well. I mean, in all fairness, we made this decision on a whim, with no plan, and I wasn't even wearing an engagement ring. The truth of the matter is that engagement ring wouldn't come until a much later date. I guess we assumed everybody would be flying as high from the news of our engagement as we were, but that was not the case.

We went to Tom's parents' house and sat down with them to share the story. The first reaction was shock, which was no big surprise, but the next reaction was a little bit unexpected. His mom said you can't be engaged if you don't have a ring, which made us both laugh until we realized she was serious. We both told her we didn't have the money right then to buy an engagement ring, and the wedding would be off in the distance anyway. Much to my surprise, she didn't seem very happy about this arrangement. I don't remember much of a reaction out of his dad except to say he didn't seem as dismayed. As for his brother, luckily, he was very excited. He said he thought we would make a good couple, and he would be excited to have me as a sister-in-law. We left that night a little bit confused about parts of the evening but optimistic about our future.

So when it came to informing my family of the engagement, it was a much different reaction. They all seemed very positive about the match up. This was not at all surprising to me considering how fond they seemed to be of Tom already. This fondness of Tom deserves explanation. You see, my family was very into sports and lived and breathed football, baseball, volleyball, gymnastics, and most of all, the Olympics. Four of the six of us kids were, what shall I say, relatively obsessed with the idea of being famous sports figures, and Tom seemed more naturally athletic than all of us.

When we were young, we all took on various sporting activities. I played basketball, volleyball, and softball as did the rest of my siblings, along with pickup games of football which the whole family partook in. As was mentioned earlier, gymnastics was my favorite sport, but it is a very small number of the population that could ever make it to the Olympics in gymnastics. Gymnastics only allows for four to six gymnasts per team in each country—and that's what I decided I wanted to set my sights on. Either way, whether it was football or gymnastics, none of us rose to the top of our chosen sport. So what we did was treat all our volleyball games and tournaments like an Olympic competition. Oh, our poor friends must have hated us. We probably sucked the fun right out of it!

So what does this have to do with Tom, you may ask? Well as I mentioned before he was a very intelligent person, had a good set of morals, and was easy to talk to. What I didn't tell you, however, is that he was a super jock. He was naturally very athletic, could jump very high, and had great speed. What this meant was when he came to play volleyball with us he could always dive

CHAPTER ELEVEN

and return those balls that nobody else could get. He also was amazing at the net because of his ability to jump and block spikes from the opposing team. In addition, because he could jump so high, and was ambidextrous, he could hit with either his right or left hand. Let's just say he was a force to be reckoned with.

So my family was very happy to have a "ringer" on our side, which would hopefully give us an advantage against the other teams. While I would like to say we all had the loftiest goals for each other when it came to choosing spouses—that wouldn't be 100 percent honest. Tom was accepted, and officially in by default, because of his athletic prowess. I know there was more to it than that, but it is funny how much weight that held. When we went to Denver to let everybody know we were engaged, they were ecstatic.

There was, however, a different level of respect my mother and father had for him. To begin with, as I had mentioned earlier, my dad was very intelligent and very well read. These two things connected my dad and Tom, and it made his approval easy because of that, and I assure you no one gets my dad's approval very easily. As for my mom, she seemed very attached to Tom and thought he was very sweet and kind, so her approval was also forthcoming.

As time went on, we started making our wedding plans. We decided to get married at the end of my junior year, which would leave us the last year in school together as a married couple. I figured I could finish up my senior year, even if I was married, and made it very clear I wouldn't get married unless that happened. As for Tom, he was having some struggles when it came to school. He had declared computer science as his major, but as it turned out, he really did not like the classes, and I do mean really. Considering he had five back-to-back computer science classes the first semester of his junior year, things were not going well. He was very unhappy and uncertain of what to do. So the two of us sat down and discussed options. Basically, what it came down to was if he didn't want to get a computer science degree, he would have to choose another major, and that would mean more time in school.

I asked him point blank, "What do you want to do?" I wanted to know what his interests were and try to see if we could get him going in a different direction. He said he thought about law and for a while was kind of interested in that path. So I asked him about a political science degree. He said he thought about doing that as he enjoyed those classes when he took them. So we pulled out the catalog and looked into what it would take and how long it would take for him to finish a political science degree. It would mean an additional two years, and he wasn't sure if he could even transfer classes at this late date (we were pretty far into the semester). I had a pretty good friendship with one of the political science professors, so I told Tom I would ask him if he could transfer into some of his classes. The professor said as long as he could catch up on the work, he would accept the transfer. We made the necessary arrangements, Tom got busy on makeup work, and he proceeded to change his major. Funny thing is the professor ended up being an usher at our wedding. It's interesting the friendships that you make.

While I'm not exactly proud to say this, Tom and I decided to move in together before we got married. I had made a mess of things toward the end of the time I lived with my brother and sister-in-law, and they were forced to kick me out; I left them no choice. We did, however, repair the relationship—which means I had to apologize for what I had done. I moved in with a friend of mine from school, and that worked for a while until she moved

CHAPTER ELEVEN

her boyfriend in as well, and they never kept quiet, and I couldn't get my schoolwork done.

After that Tom and I decided to move in with a very good friend of his—Brett. This guy owned a house at the ripe old age of nineteen and was renting out the rooms to his friends. We became one of those tenants. He had known Tom since they were kids, and he was just a solid person and reliable friend and overall a great human being. Everything was great for a while, but Brett's friend and I started fighting, and it eventually got so out of control we ended up moving out. We were mad at Brett for not doing what he said he'd do and holding all the tenants to the same standard with house chores. We were still mad when our wedding came around, so we didn't invite Brett. That was the stupidest thing we've ever done. Since you're reading this now, don't ever leave somebody out of an important event just because you're having a silly fight. You'll live in regret forever—we still do.

We continued plugging away at our classes, playing sports, and working out whenever possible, planning the wedding, and spending time with both of our families. As one can imagine, there's a lot of difficulty getting all these things done and keeping our sanity. I was still struggling with my irritable bowel syndrome (IBS) and had a few attacks that rendered me immobile for a day. I also ended up in the hospital a couple of times because the pain was so intense, and I had no medications or treatments that would lower the intensity of pain. I was feeling rather helpless. I was going to see a chiropractor regularly, and he told me he was suspicious I had gallbladder issues.

I was seeing a chiropractor because I had gotten t-boned by another car when I was turning left onto a major road. I was hit on the same side of the car (the left side) as when I was hit by the school bus. I was driving Tom's car, and it stalled on me in the middle of the intersection, and because the door handle was broken, I had no way of getting out. Luckily, I just suffered some whiplash and didn't end up breaking any bones or incurring any major injuries, once again with the help of my Guardian Angel. It was a very scary situation, but I was recovering nicely thanks to Tom's suggestion for me to see a chiropractor. The chiropractor was the only one that had even suggested I could be struggling with gallbladder issues or, for that matter, believed me and Tom.

I ended up going to a number of doctors before and during the time I dated Tom trying to figure out what was happening. Over the course of the years, before and following, I probably saw twenty different specialists and none of them managed to make a solid diagnosis. This got me, and my fiancé, to start doing our own research, and when all was said and done, I fit every symptom of gallbladder disease. The problem moving forward, however, was trying to find a doctor that believed me. That was not an easy task, and it led Tom and I to look into holistic medicine and opened my mind to a whole new pathway for treatment and healing. The pathway that nature provides. At one point, I actually asked Tom if he still wanted to marry me. I told him I could be sick for the rest of my life and asked him if he was sure he'd want to carry that burden. Oddly enough the guy said yes. What was he thinking?

We planned our wedding in June at the end of our junior year. The wedding was beautiful and at the same time a complete disaster. It was one of those weddings where if something could go wrong, it did go wrong. Luckily for him and me, the only thing that really mattered to us was getting married and not so much the wedding, which I think helped us when things started to unravel.

To begin with the wedding was supposed to be a Mass, not

CHAPTER ELEVEN

just a nuptial service, but the Deacon forgot to tell our priest, so we only ended up with a short ceremony. I had picked out music for the Mass and hired a vocalist, but as it turned out, she was only able to do two pieces of the music. One of my bridesmaids had her mother making her bridesmaid dress for her, and the day of the wedding, she still wasn't finished. I called my seamstress to see if she could finish it for us, and she said she could if we got it there quickly. We went over to her mother's house to get the dress, and her mother started physically attacking her, grabbed her arms, and started to shake her. My sister had to run into the apartment and get my friend out of there before her mom did any more damage. My friend was bruised and emotionally distraught, but she pulled herself together and made it work for the sake of the wedding.

It rained cats and dogs the night of the wedding, and a lot of people got drenched leaving the ceremony and heading to the reception. I wanted to have an evening wedding, and I also wanted to have children be able to attend the wedding, and the combination was a bad thing. These kids were so spent by the end of the night and so were their poor parents. I didn't think about how hard late nights are for little kids, and I should have been more respectful of that—which is a regret that I hold to this day. Our DJ quit the day before the wedding and didn't bother to call, so we asked our friend to bring his equipment to the reception hall, along with all the CDs he had, and he did the best he could to DJ our wedding. In addition to everything else, we ran out of food, although the caterers had the full count before the wedding started. It was one ridiculous disaster after another, but neither one of us really cared, because after two years of waiting to get married, we were finally married. The rest was all just icing on the cake, if you will. All in all, I guess it worked out as my

SURPRISE, SURPRISE; GRADUATION; AND WHAT COMES NEXT

husband and I have now been married for twenty-eight years and been together for thirty, and I don't think either one of us has plans to go anywhere.

SURPRISE, SURPRISE; GRADUATION; AND WHAT COMES NEXT

The wedding ended up being wonderful despite all the difficulties, but the honeymoon was even better—aren't they all? We decided we wanted to go to Cancun for our honeymoon and decided the best option was an all-inclusive resort. It was so beautiful and everything we wanted. As is the case with all-inclusive resorts, everything is included in the initial price. That means any of the food we ate, the alcohol and drinks we consumed, and the five or so espressos my husband drank after dinner every night was also included. We had a gorgeous swimming pool with a swim-up bar, and the beach was right next to it.

We swam at the pool some of the time, but we preferred to go out to the ocean and swim in the waves and play on the beach. After all, you can swim in a pool anytime. The worst part of this whole situation was I got sunburnt the first day. I was very surprised by this as I had already gotten a pretty good tan before the wedding and had a nice base built up. What I did not know is the closer to the equator you are, the more likely you are to get sunburnt if you're out in the sun for too long. Needless to say, it was a pretty good sunburn, and it hurt most of the time we were there, but that didn't stop us from having fun.

We enjoyed the rest of the week at the resort and then headed home, getting used to being Mr. and Mrs. Once we got married, we had to get our own apartment, because we had roommates beforehand and decided the grown-up thing to do was to get our

CHAPTER ELEVEN

own place. I started a new job as well since I wasn't going to be able to work over the summer. They needed someone else to take over my position in the chancellor's office, so I reached out to a friend, and she became my replacement and made a perfect fit. I only stayed in my new job for a few months because that wasn't a good fit. I decided after that to go look again on campus for a job and see if there were any openings for work study.

I ended up getting a job in the foundation office with a really good group of people. It was out of this office that fundraising for the university was facilitated. In addition, this was the office that wrote and prepared the speeches the chancellor gave at various events. It was a really good fit for me, and I was grateful to have it to finish up my final year of college. I had worked with the gentleman running the foundation office when I was working in the chancellor's office, so he already knew my work ethic and didn't need to vet me. I was grateful for the position.

So while all of this was going on a big surprise was waiting for us in the future. Amongst all my health struggles, a new symptom presented itself. On top of everything else, I was now having trouble keeping my vitamins down in the morning, which was not a good thing. We were both starting to get worried because we didn't know what was going on. As time progressed, we realized that I might actually be pregnant. I think this came as a very big shock to both of us (even though of course we knew there was a possibility it could happen) because we never imagined it would happen that fast. Our best guesstimate was I had gotten pregnant a month to a month and a half after the wedding. Talk about rapid response.

I was sick as hell throughout my pregnancy, which made for a very long forty weeks. Obviously I still had two semesters of school to finish up in order to complete my bachelor's degree.

SURPRISE, SURPRISE; GRADUATION; AND WHAT COMES NEXT

That definitely seemed like a pretty tall order: to be pregnant, carrying a full load at school, and carrying a full load in my abdomen. Tom and I talked about it, however, and we decided I would finish up and get my degree. We both agreed prior to me getting pregnant that when we started having kids, I would stay home and take care of them. This is definitely something we both wanted. It was because of this I knew I would not want to try and go back and finish up my bachelor's degree later once I started having my family. It never worked out for my mom, and I didn't want to risk being this close and not making it. In addition, secretly, I assumed once I had my kids and they started school, I would go back and get my PhD and go into private practice. I was unwilling to let go of that dream. God had different plans for me.

I went ahead and found myself an OBGYN. It was my first visit in his office, and I was just a couple months pregnant, and while in the exam room, I started having one of my attacks (we assumed it was my gallbladder). The doctor wasn't in the room when it first happened, but by the time he showed up, I was fully committed to the pain and laying in a fetal position on the ground. The doctor came into the exam room and said, "I need you to get up on bed so I can examine you."

Tom told him that he had to wait until the pain subsided for me to be able to do that. Eventually I got up, he examined me, and after everything was done, he said, "We cannot have you like this. When I'm taking care of my patients it's the mother as well as the baby that I'm taking care of, and we can't have you continue in this condition." It was because of this conversation, and his concern for my health, that he helped me find a solution to the problem after my child was born.

So as time progressed, so did my belly. I wasn't one of those cute first-time pregnant women that never showed until the last

CHAPTER ELEVEN

month or two. I was more about making a bold statement right out of the gate; I had a baby bump about four months out. In other words it was evident I was pregnant. I was very miserable throughout my pregnancy, and it made for a very long process. I had crazy amounts of morning sickness that was there on and off throughout my whole pregnancy. I had a great deal of ligament, back, and pelvic pain as well. In addition the campus was built onto the side of a bluff, so it was very hilly, which made getting around pretty painful, and I was always running errands and delivering documents in various locations. It wasn't what I would call a pleasant experience. Looking back on it, I realize how many of my other health struggles probably added to making it a difficult pregnancy, and in addition my demanding school and work schedule was very stressful, which probably didn't help my sweet baby either.

I continued to have my eye on the prize, however, and I kept pushing through. As the pregnancy progressed, my IBS / gallbladder / spastic colon worsened as well. I was continuing to work out while pregnant, as the doctor said it would be okay to do, but the further along I got, the harder my recovery was. Because of the intestinal pain I experienced, the growing baby in my belly was making the pain way more intense. There were entire days I was left incapacitated because of these attacks. It was because of this my chiropractor suggested I stop working out and just do low impact activities. He was concerned that if it was a gallbladder problem, it might actually rupture. As time went on, I also started reacting poorly to more and more foods—don't even get me going on onions, which almost became the death of me. By the time I was ready for delivery, I was only able to eat yogurt and pretzels without getting sick.

About two weeks before my due date, I had an episode that

SURPRISE, SURPRISE; GRADUATION; AND WHAT COMES NEXT

sent me to the hospital. I decided to drink a soda on that particular day, which was very unusual for me as I wasn't a soda drinker by nature, but it just sounded good at the time. I was very good about taking care of myself, eating right, and drinking lots of water, so having a soda one day out of a month didn't seem like that big of a deal. I started having painful contractions (Braxton Hicks, I found out later), and the intensity made me have to go to the hospital. When I arrived, they ran some preliminary tests and got me hooked up to an IV. As it turned out, I was dehydrated, and that's what was causing the pain.

The nurse felt it necessary to start lecturing me about the evils of drinking soda. I was confused number one by her intensity and number two by the fact it was only one soda. I explained to her I didn't even normally drink caffeine, and I just felt like having some that day. It took a while for me to get to the bottom of what she was upset about. She basically said the type of soda I drank had a very high content of sodium, causing dehydration and in turn Braxton Hicks contractions. After multiple lectures about the evils of soda, she left the room for a break. When she came back from her break, however, I smelled something on her. To her surprise, I turned to her and asked, "Did you just go out and take a smoke break?"

She looked at me with surprise and hesitantly responded, "Yes."

I then proceeded to give her a lecture on the extreme evils of nicotine and how bad it is for a nurse working in healthcare to be smoking cigarettes. She got my point, laughed at me, and said, "You are right." We both smiled at one another, and she agreed to try and stop smoking, and I agreed to not drink anymore soda while pregnant.

After leaving the hospital, it was strongly suggested by the doctor I stop working until the baby was born. He only left me

CHAPTER ELEVEN

two options: either I quit school or quit my job, but either way, it was taking its toll on my body, and he said labor would be very difficult if I didn't get some rest. I proceeded to quit my job and try to get some rest before the baby came. This still wasn't easy as I had my finals to prepare for and graduation around the corner.

Two weeks after that hospital visit, I finally went into labor, and it was every bit as difficult as he said it would be. I started labor, and when we thought it had progressed enough, we headed to the hospital. Once there, I proceeded to walk the halls for a number of hours when finally I came back to the room looking for a reprieve. It was at this time the doctor suggested breaking my water. He did so, and it launched my contractions into warp speed. Well the speed and pain were warp level, the quickness of the delivery was very far off. It took another eight hours of white knuckling and gripping my chair until my son decided to make an appearance. Oddly enough, when that little creature came out, all the animosity I felt toward him in the last twenty-four hours just drifted away. I looked at his face and fell completely in love, and truth be told, so did his dad. It took me an entire day to launch that small little baby out of the comfort of his little home, but it was worth it.

Because of this little excursion, I missed one of my presentations in one of my classes—a fact the professor was not very happy about. Other than that, I had gotten most of my finals done and just had a paper left to write. Luckily my professor that required the paper was very easy going and told me not to worry about getting it done. She said I had plenty of time. I just wish I could have taken that in and relaxed about it, but as my Guardian Angel will tell you, if I could do that, I wouldn't be me, now would I?

SURPRISE, SURPRISE; GRADUATION; AND WHAT COMES NEXT

So with the baby born, most of my school work completed, and adjusting to our new way of life, the only thing left to do was graduate. We had invited all of our families and a lot of other guests to the graduation. It was lining up to be a pretty fabulous event, and as luck would have it, it was going to be the first commencement exercise done outside, on one of the parking lots looking out over the bluff. Even though the chancellor had some crazy ideas along the way, this one was a pretty great one. In addition, Tom and I were invited to bring our newborn baby along as we walked across the stage. It was a very special day as I knew most, if not all, the professors who greeted me as I walked across the stage, and the chancellor herself came over to me and gave me a hug. To this day, I still laugh that my son graduated from college at two weeks old. Oddly enough, this never gets old for me.

So after everything was said and done, my husband's uncle presented us with an opportunity we couldn't resist. He had a tiny house available for us to rent on about half an acre if we wanted it (it was owned by his former in-laws, and they needed good renters). That was a no-brainer after living in apartments and having lots of roommates. We were ready for some quiet, and peaceful surroundings. Little did I know how quiet it would be, but it was a perfect size for a small family, and the price was definitely right as it was very cheap to rent. We started moving in shortly after graduation.

I definitely need to make it clear here how much we loved and adored his uncle. He was a very kind man, a very talented craftsman, handyman, and mechanic. Although he had all those gifts, the thing that stood out most was his huge heart and love for everyone. He was truly the kind of man that would give the shirt off his back to anyone who needed it, and he always took

CHAPTER ELEVEN

care of those around him in any way they needed it. Unfortunately he died way too early, and he has been greatly missed ever since. I wish we had gotten more time with him, and the world definitely would have benefited from having him on this planet a lot longer. He was a very special soul.

So we moved in, got ourselves situated, and then began the next journey of our lives. I was immediately thrust into the position of being a stay-at-home mom (by choice of course), and it came as a huge culture shock for me. Here I was as an extreme extrovert who loves interacting with people, going places, and doing lots of activities, and all at once it came to an abrupt halt. Not to mention the fact I lived a good distance from most of my friends, who were all busy with their own lives and didn't have time to come and visit very often. It was a very lonely period of time for me, and I would like to say I used that time to grow in my spirituality and pray more often, but that is not what happened. I slunk into a depression that took a while to get out of.

CHAPTER TWELVE

FAMILY LIFE BEGINS, HEALTH SOLUTIONS, OUR FAMILY STARTS TO GROW

So Tom and I started adapting to our post-college lives and started to have some new experiences. It was a kind of strange feeling for Tom as well as me to have finished college. You spend four years (in Tom's case six years) doing nothing but taking classes, studying, and working at your job, and then when you're finished, it's very anticlimactic. I didn't think about what it would feel like to be done with my bachelor's degree because it was just a stepping stone to the next part of my life, or so I thought. God had much better plans for me. For Tom, however, getting his bachelor's degree was the end of the line for him at that point in time. So then began the process of incorporating one's degree into an actual career.

As he was trying to figure out that part of things, I was still struggling with my health issues (a.k.a., intestinal problems). As I mentioned earlier, my OBGYN was a very good doctor and fully intended to take care of me, even after the baby was born. During my pregnancy, I was trying to find a good internal medicine doctor, one that looked outside the box and had good listening

CHAPTER TWELVE

skills. Upon referral from a friend of ours, we got connected with an incredible internal medicine doctor. When we went to the appointment, he actually sat down with us in an office and told us to tell him the whole story start to finish, of how long I'd been dealing with this problem and what symptoms I'd struggled with. He spent two hours just taking copious notes and listening. That in and of itself was a new experience for Tom and me as no doctor had ever spent that much time just listening.

After we finished talking with him, he said, "I'm pretty confident I know what the problem is, but I will do a quick exam before you go." He took vitals and then proceeded to check my abdomen and do the rebounding test (a test that they use to check if the gallbladder is inflamed). As was always the case with that test, I failed it yet again, but it gave him what he needed to know. He said, "I definitely think it is your gallbladder, and although I know you've gone through all these diagnostic tests already, I want to do one more." He said the goal of this test was not to get radiology information but rather to see if the contrast liquid used in the test created the same symptoms as when I had these attacks. He said if it did, that would tell him with a level of certainty that it was my gallbladder.

I set an appointment, went to the hospital, got prepped for the radiology test, and drank the contrast liquid. Not much to my surprise, I ended up having another attack during the radiology testing. The good news, however, was I now had a doctor that believed me, and he had the results he needed. When we got back in touch with the internal medicine doctor and went over the results, he said now comes the next difficulty. He said we needed to find a surgeon that would operate without any diagnostic proof. Meanwhile, my OBGYN had to sign off on all of this, and he did not hesitate to help me.

After lots of phone calls to various surgeons, I finally tracked down one that was more open-minded. I assure you if you think doctors are in the box thinkers, surgeons are even more in the box, so this was kind of a miracle. We set up an appointment with him, and he agreed to do the surgery, assuring us he had done lots of these surgeries without diagnostic proof, and every one of those individuals had a "bad gallbladder." We scheduled the surgery, our OBGYN signed off on it, and I took the necessary steps to prepare for Justin's care and feedings during and after my surgery. Justin was only three months old at this time, so he still needed a lot of care.

We got everything in place, and I went to the hospital. We were there with my parents (Tom's mom and dad took care of Justin during the surgery), and everything went according to plan. When the surgeon completed the surgery he came out to talk to the family. Apparently he told them my gallbladder was diseased and was so inflamed it was the size of his fist (the gallbladder is normally much smaller than this), and he said I was lucky that it hadn't ruptured during the pregnancy. I think that brought great comfort to my parents that the surgery was a success and nothing catastrophic had happened beforehand, as my mom was very concerned about me having surgery without actual proof of there being an issue.

I reacted very poorly to the anesthesia, so it took a long time for me to recover. I had surgery early in the morning and wasn't released till late at night. I still wasn't feeling better and couldn't keep anything down, but we decided it was better just to go home and deal with the nausea there. This was how my body always reacted to most types of medication, so I wasn't all that surprised. It just made recovery very difficult. To add insult to injury, the next step was even worse.

CHAPTER TWELVE

The plan was my husband would take care of Justin, including all of his feedings, so that I could go home and sleep and start the recovery process. The problem, however, was Justin would not take a bottle. I guess we should have tried this out ahead of time. So much to our stress, he pitched a giant fit and would not settle down. This of course caused my husband and I to start screaming and fighting with each other—normal high-stress child-rearing stories. I finally took Justin and laid him on my very sore and inflamed abdomen and nursed him. Once he was full, I was able to hand him off, and I went to sleep. Slowly but surely, I started recovering, and for the first time in my life, or at least that I could remember, I didn't have any abdominal pain.

As for my husband, moving into his future job, he had some stuff to figure out. He was working at a fast-food restaurant when we had our son Justin, and was still working there for about six months afterward. Luckily for us, the place where he was employed just happened to carry health insurance, which paid for most of the labor and delivery for our son and paid for my surgery as well (at least most of it). That was quite a blessing for us considering it was a part-time menial-level job, and one that you wouldn't expect to provide insurance. I guess you could call that the high-deductible year.

As time went on, we decided it was in our best interests to get Tom a "grown-up" job. So as it turned out I still had a lot of friends over at the university I had worked with, and one of those friends had a job opportunity. Her husband worked for a utility company, and there were some job openings. I asked if she could recommend my husband for the job, so her husband arranged the interview. Everything went well, and Tom got hired very quickly. The funny thing about it was he had to take a pay cut just to get a foot in the door at utilities. It was a hard pill to swallow because it was about $5 an hour less in pay. The difference was the new job provided lots of upward mobility, great health insurance, along with paid leave and sick days, and was a full-time position. It was going to be better in the long run.

Life started getting back to normal after my surgery, but I definitely found myself feeling the blues. It was difficult to go from a busy and active lifestyle to a more isolated stay-at-home lifestyle. During that time, and even now I would argue, there definitely seemed to be a division between stay-at-home moms and working moms. Those in support of the stay-at-home philosophy thought I wasn't trying hard enough and embracing that lifestyle. As for the working moms, they thought getting a job would be the answer to my woes. It seemed like the stay-at-home moms looked down on their working counterparts for not being home with their kids, and the working moms acted as if stay-at-home moms were wasting their lives and their talents. Neither side was doing right by one another. Although I was mixed up in all of this drama (as were all of the moms raising kids during that time period) there was a bigger problem going on with me, which was more than just the baby blues, and whether or not to get a job or stay at home. The actual problem wouldn't reveal itself until later.

While all these crazy changes were happening in our life, I was continuing to make small strides in my faith as well. By the time Tom and I had met, I was going to church on a regular basis and had made it abundantly clear to him I wouldn't get married unless he was okay with raising the kids Catholic. He had agreed to all of that when we got married but had himself stated he would never convert. I definitely wasn't far enough along in my faith, nor knowledgeable enough, to know what that would mean.

CHAPTER TWELVE

For whatever reason, however, I agreed not to hassle him about coming into the church.

Looking at it now it seemed a little bit naive, because it could have ended very poorly for both of us, but I just didn't know that. Looking back over the years, I can actually see how my life was the same as the gospel writings. In the scripture they talk about seeds falling on rock and not being able to grow and on the sand where they start to take root but can't plant deep, so they get blown away, and finally landing in good soil where they form very deep roots, which cannot be washed away. That in a nutshell was my faith journey in my marriage. Luckily, I think my Guardian Angel knew how much I loved God and that I would never compromise my faith and devotion to our Lord again. My guess is that is when he hatched his not-so-evil plan, but I'll never know for sure.

SWEET BABY TERROR, AND KIDDO NUMBER TWO

Now I haven't gone into very much detail about Justin, so I think this is the perfect time to do it. Each one of my kids deserves a special entry in the annals of my life, and starting at the top is the best way to go.

To begin with, he was about the cutest little boy you ever did see. In the hospital they kept asking me if he was a C-section baby to which I responded, "Hell no, I suffered through every one of those twenty-four hours." I did, however, ask for clarification on why they kept asking me that question. They said he had a perfect round head they don't usually see with natural deliveries. I guess that was a compliment. He also, interestingly enough, had very slanted eyes when he was born, which I just found to be so cute. When I was first examining my son, I noticed his toes because they looked just like his dad's. Tom has very crooked toes and so does our son. I laughed very hard when I saw this and said "There's no need for a paternity test." "The proof is in the toes."

Now Justin was a very wonderful and sweet baby, but he wasn't very easy, and he liked to make himself heard. He was a first-time son, and I was a first-time mom, and I think we fed off each other's stress levels. Needless to say, what this equated to was lots and lots of crying and lots and lots of screaming—and Justin did some too. For whatever reason, he could not be soothed easily, and nothing seemed to calm him once he started crying. My husband shared a memory with me just the other day. He said he remembered coming home from work one day and baby J, who was just a few months old, was in his car seat screaming, and I was sitting next to him rocking the car seat, crying and begging my husband to take him because I couldn't calm him down. We couldn't even put him in the car seat and go for a drive to calm him down because that seemed to make him more hysterical.

When our son was about six months old, I found out I was pregnant. At that time, I think I was about eight weeks pregnant. Believe it or not, Tom and I were both very excited. I had always wanted to have a good-sized family, and since I was quite a bit older when I got married, I knew it would be better to have the kids sooner rather than later. I was suffering again with severe morning sickness, which made it hard to take care of a fussy little baby. Nonetheless we kept plugging away and preparing for a new addition to our family.

A couple of weeks after I found out I was pregnant I volunteered to take my husband's friend to the hospital for surgery. He had broken his jaw, and it needed to be operated on. While I was there, I had to break away for a minute to use the restroom. I started cramping, and I went to the bathroom. I started to

CHAPTER TWELVE

bleed. I knew immediately what was happening and just started to panic. I tried to collect the tissue, but I didn't have anything to put it in. I was absolutely devastated, but I tried to pull myself together for the sake of our friend. When I came back over to see him before surgery, he knew something was wrong immediately. He asked me what was happening, but I didn't want to tell him. He insisted, so I told him I thought I had lost the baby, but that I just wanted to be there for him. It was obvious it took its toll on him as well. It was a very sad day for all of us.

My husband and I mourned the loss for quite a while, but luckily for us, God saw fit to bless us with another pregnancy. I was able to conceive about five months after that, and we once again looked forward to adding another child to our family. I was quite sick throughout this pregnancy as well and the accompanying accouterments, therefore it took me awhile to recognize the blessing of my fertility. When we try to stay close to God and remain faithful, he blesses us in so many ways, but we don't always see it. I already had one child, and although that pregnancy was very difficult, he was born happy and healthy, and here I was once again carrying another beautiful child.

The experience of giving birth to my beautiful daughter by contrast to my son's delivery was quite different and very peaceful. Before she was born, I actually took some Lamaze classes and learned breathing techniques—a suggestion I should have followed the first time around. The difference between carrying my son and my daughter, however, was I was not trying to graduate from college, fulfill all my school requirements, oh and yeah carrying a bloated gallbladder around in my abdomen while transporting a little human. I feel quite certain that made things easier as well, but that is just a hunch.

My daughter's delivery was very long as well but much

easier. I knew what to expect this time around, and I felt much more in control of each contraction as they came, even the hard ones. Now this sweet girl was the only one of my kids to come early, and I believe to this day it is because I walked that child out of me. I was very pregnant, and exhausted, while chasing my little son around, and I guess I just decided it was time for her to come. I proceeded to load Justin up in a stroller and started walking until I couldn't walk anymore. I do believe that walk consisted of about ten miles. So, lo and behold, after I was done with the walk, I went over to see a friend of mine, and she insisted I was going into labor. Luckily for me, she was not wrong.

After about eighteen short hours my baby made her appearance. I tried to tell the nurse I was about to have this baby, but she kept dawdling around. I finally insisted she get the doctor, but I had already delivered her by the time he came. I'll be honest with you; this seemed to be a reoccurring theme. Nonetheless, out came this beautiful baby girl we decided to name Faye. Once again I hit the jackpot and delivered a gorgeous child. She started nursing right away, and everything seemed so peaceful. It was definitely a blessing because I was starting to wonder if my second child would be more difficult than the first. This was already proving not to be the case.

We brought her home and she and Justin became the best of friends. He loved having a little sister, and we loved this new addition to our family. She was a very easy baby and didn't require much. She could sit in her diaper for hours without fussing, and as long as we fed her regularly, she was content. I had never seen an infant sleep as much as she did, and it came as quite a shock. One night, about two weeks out, we went to sleep and about eight hours later woke up in a panic. She hadn't woken us up to eat or change her diaper, and we thought she had died.

CHAPTER TWELVE

We rolled over to check on her, and there she was sleeping peacefully. After having a little baby that woke up every couple of hours to having a baby that sleeps eight straight hours in a row, we actually started to wonder if something was wrong with her.

As time progressed, they started playing with each other more and more. Justin would do the funniest thing: he would climb into her crib and lay on top of her—belly to belly, rock back and forth, and make her giggle. He loved doing it, and she loved it being done. They were so cute together, and we were so glad they were so happy. As Faye started to get older, she required more food but didn't manage to increase in weight. This made my pediatrician crazy because I guess he thought I was starving her. It became quite an ordeal every time I went to the doctor's office, so he started having me supplement and keep track of all the food she ate. Now if any of you have had two youngsters under the age of two, you know how difficult a task that would be. Regardless I managed to do it and kept track of all of her food.

When I arrived at the pediatrician's office the next time, with my food charting, he started to argue with me. He said there was no way she could eat that much food and be as thin as she was. I didn't know what to tell him other than the fact she seemed to be thriving. He somehow missed the fact she was smiling and laughing every time he interacted with her and never seemed distressed. I sometimes think doctors don't like to be wrong and for some reason feel like their patients are challenging them just by asking questions. I was doing neither of those things. I was just trying to take care of my children and be the best mom I could be. As one could imagine, I ended up switching pediatricians.

So Faye continued to grow and get cuter every day, and so did Justin. Now I know I'm a biased parent, but I would literally get stopped in the stores by people telling me how cute my kids were, so I'll consider that confirmation of my bias. Needless to say, things were going along charmingly well, cars needing to be fixed all the time and general chaos in our home. In a lot of ways, we were just like any other family, but there were some other difficulties that made our life stand out both in good ways and in bad.

GOOD STUFF, NOT SO GOOD STUFF, AND MORE KIDS

So one of the things that made life pretty difficult for us was we seemed to have a lot of family events with my extended family. As I mentioned before I had a large family, and we got together on most occasions. We celebrated birthdays together, which meant at least a birthday a month, as well as Thanksgiving, Christmas, and Easter. My family lived about an hour and a half away, so it was a little more difficult to see them on a regular basis. Tom's family, on the other hand, lived about ten minutes from us, so we saw them regularly, his parents that is, as his brother lived up in Denver where my family was.

Now with my family background, we were raised to spend a lot of time together. Family was very important to my parents, especially my mom, and they went out of their way to make sure we had relationships with one another and all of our extended family. My mom always insisted on doing whatever she could to keep relationships strong—although that did not always work in their life or in ours. Needless to say, I grew up with the idea you made time for family relationships (which also extended to my friendships as well).

Tom's family was definitely different from mine. While his immediate family tried to spend a lot of time together, they didn't seem to be very interconnected with their aunts, uncles,

CHAPTER TWELVE

and cousins. In fact, the only people I remember them visiting, in the early years of our marriage, were Tom's grandparents on his mother's side. On his mother's side, she grew up with four brothers and lots of extended family. She and the oldest brother, Steve, were from her mother's (Sally) first marriage—that I understood to be very tumultuous. When her mom remarried (Harry), her husband adopted them both, and then they had three sons of their own. I can honestly say I never saw any favoritism from Harry (Tom's grandfather). Harry and Sally also came to Colorado Springs a lot to visit Sue, John, Tom, and his brother (Tony). Tom's grandparents were also good about visiting all of their extended family so I don't know where the drop off happened when it came to Sue and John.

As for John he grew up in a much different situation. He was an only child, and he didn't have much family around. To this day I don't think we fully know the story of what happened with Tom's granddad (Alex) and why he wasn't close with his birth family. All I know is that when I came into the family there wasn't anyone to meet from John's family. I found this very surprising considering the environment I came from, being surrounded by lots of extended family. Sad thing is as the years went by, we realized just how many siblings grandad had. He had plenty of family around but chose not to spend time with them for whatever reason. This lack of connection with John's extended family might have been the reason John and Sue didn't visit people very often.

John and Sue met shortly after he returned from Vietnam. John did a year tour in Vietnam and saw a lot of action and fighting. He lost a lot of fellow soldiers during that time and he was definitely scarred by the experience as most of these men were. John had a hard time recovering from the impact of the war which may have affected him in the future. He met Sue a few months after he returned state side, and they went on a couple of dates and were married a couple of months later. They had 2 children and were married for 52 years—which is amazing and beautiul in my opinion.

There was a little bit of stress between my mother-in-law and I in regards to the time we spent with my family. She always said men spend their time with their wives' families and no longer with their own families. I didn't understand this as I had made so much effort to bring the kids around all the time. I used to take them to the bowling alley, get-togethers with their friends, and over to their house. I think sometimes when we're wounded, we rationalize things based on how we are feeling and not on what's happening, and maybe that was it for her. I don't think she liked the fact Tom got along so well with my family. I just wish we could have talked through it, but it was such a sensitive subject we never seemed to be able to do that.

As things progressed in our marriage a lot of our wounds took a prominent place in our relationship. We fought a lot in the first ten to fifteen years of our marriage, and I do believe it had a lot to do with unhealed trauma and complete and utter stubbornness. Now let me draw the picture for you so you can understand what we were battling. Tom's lineage was Norwegian and English. You could definitely get a feel for the English with his mom and her maternal family and their emphasis on proper etiquette and decorum. They also liked to to win arguments, which wasn't always easy to be around. On the other side of the family, the Norwegian side, which came from his father, was a lot of strong-willed stubbornness and a need to conquer everything in their path. They also liked to be in control all the time, which was also difficult to be around. When it came to my lineage, I had French, Slovenian, and Irish, and boy did I wear those countries well.

CHAPTER TWELVE

Tom and I would dig our heels in over everything and fight as if it was the last battle we'd ever have. Neither one of us seemed to want to compromise or concede, so that made life very difficult. I wasn't very close with my parents during this time, nor was Tom with his, or they might have been able to help us through this youthful pride, but alas, we just had to suffer our way through it. So what this meant for our relationship was we were seemingly at odds all the time. I have a visual for this now, which is that when people are married, and things are going badly, the tendency is to look at the spouse as if he or she is the cause of all our problems. We want to blame everything on each other. What we should be doing is standing side by side with our arms locked. We should unite and fight the outside world as it tries to penetrate and break up the marriage. We have the wrong mindset.

So what this meant was we carried our stubbornness into other relationships, which is what I'm sure caused a lot of the friction we had with Tom's parents and brother. This is much clearer now, much like looking through a rearview mirror after passing something. The view is much more accurate. Having said that, the other side of things is true as well. His family was equally as stubborn and unwilling to bend as we were. In addition, they never showed much interest in introspection, so it was difficult to talk to them and get them to recognize their own behavior in any situation. The combination caused a lot of fighting for all of us.

To make matters worse, although at the time we thought it was making matters better, his brother started dating another girl. Now in the world of his brother, this was not unusual. As I mentioned before, he was a very gregarious person, very social, and easy to like. The problem I had with him, however, was he liked to play around, and I was no fan of that as it involved a friend and a family member of mine. Needless to say, when he brought this new girl around, I didn't even want to learn her name because I knew she'd be out the door quickly. That was not the case, however, as he was—shall we say—quite smitten with this one.

We took to the new girl very easily as well and she and I ended up being good friends. The problem, however, came along when she started to recognize some of the family dynamics, and they weren't very flattering to Tom's parents or his brother (Tony). A little background is needed at this point. You see, his brother got in a very bad bicycle accident when they were young. I think Tony was about ten years old. He was riding his bicycle through a mobile home park. He and Tom were racing each other, and when they turned down one of the side streets, Tony ran into the side mirror of a vehicle stopped at a stop sign. The speed with which he was riding his bike caused a tremendous impact, and it laid the side of his head open.

Tom was very scared and stood next to his brother in shock. Somehow his parents were notified and came to the scene of the accident. By this time, the paramedics were also there, and it wasn't looking very good, so they had to transport him to a hospital by ambulance. The next few days and weeks were very "touch and go," and they weren't sure he was going to make it. As one can imagine, this is one of the most horrifying experiences a parent can go through, so I understand the worry and panic they must have experienced. Luckily he came through relatively intact, but Tom said he was never quite the same when it came to his behavior and overall attitude. Tom did try to tell his parents he noticed a personality shift, but they couldn't hear it because they were just happy to have their son back. I think Tom carried a lot of guilt over this incident and blamed himself for the accident and really had no one to talk to about it.

CHAPTER TWELVE

The reason I'm explaining this is because it goes right to the center of what I think was the issue Tom and his brother had with one another. You see, Tony was the favorite child by a long shot and virtually everyone outside the family could see it, except his parents. I think this favoritism developed out of that accident and the panic of almost losing Tony. The same thing happened in my family with my brother Richard. He had severe asthma that went undiagnosed for a long time, and because of poor medical treatments, my parents almost lost him. This caused my mother to be overly indulgent with my brother, and she definitely showed favoritism with him as well. In a nutshell, he could do no wrong, or at least that's how we saw it as kids. As an outside observer that is what it looks like happened in Tom's family, and unfortunately for Tom, he was on the wrong side of this favoritism.

So this is what Ashley (Tony's new girlfriend) observed early on, and when she mentioned it to Tom, it was the first time, outside of my observations of course, that someone noticed the favoritism and vocalized it. As time went on, Tony and Ashley got more serious and eventually got engaged. She and I had formed a very close friendship, and we spent a lot of time together. We also talked on the phone quite frequently. This ended up not being a very good situation as their marriage started having trouble early on, and Tom and I ended up in the middle of it. We will get to that in a minute.

On a funnier note, I remember one of the things Ashley and I griped about fairly regularly and that had to do with how Tom and Tony's family did holidays together. You see, the boys were definitely very athletic—Tony was a great swimmer, and Tom (as mentioned previously) was very good at ball sports. They both grew up playing football, basketball, and baseball whenever possible and loved to do activities. The change came, however, when holidays would arrive, and they loved to harness their inner-couch slug.

All three of the boys (Tom, Tony, and John) would eat insane amounts of food as their mother was a very good cook, and they loved to engage in their favorite pastime, eating until there was no room left in their abdomens. Well at least that's what it looked like from my perspective as I never had as much room in my stomach as they did. After they finished engaging in the sport of fork and knife Olympics, all they wanted to do was sit around the kitchen table talking, playing board games, and drinking enormous amounts of liquor—which was also not a favorite endeavor of mine, Ashley's, or Tom's for that matter. She and I wanted to go for walks, or play volleyball or tennis, or any other activity that would help us digest the uncomfortable amount of food we pushed through our mouths. The four of them just stared at us like we were nuts, but remember, I came from a family that played volleyball at every opportunity, so sitting around was very foreign to me, and I think Ashley as well since her family appeared to be like mine in that regard.

Ashley and Tony got married when Faye was just about eight months old. They asked our sweet baby boy to be the ring bearer, and oh what a disaster that was. For whatever reason, he froze up before it was time to walk down the aisle and refused to go. As many of you know, you can't push a two-year-old to do something they don't want to do, so we rolled with the punches and moved along. After they got married, things took a turn for the worse, and Tony and Ashley seemed to be fighting nonstop. As mentioned earlier, coming from that same situation in my own marriage, I just thought they needed to learn to communicate better, but that was not the case.

CHAPTER TWELVE

We had our own crisis hit when Tom and I started looking for a house to buy. We had outgrown that beautiful country home and needed some space and a place to call our own. We looked at roughly fifty houses before we narrowed in on the one we wanted. We were first-time buyers, so we didn't know anything about the process, and it was quite a learning experience. As we seemed to have quite a lot of bad luck, another one of those lucks passed our door.

One day when I was out with the kids, I came back to find my house broken into. I called my husband and then called the police, but there wasn't much they could do. The thieves left a giant footprint on our door as they kicked it in and proceeded to steal random things in our house. They didn't steal the laptop we had on the table, but they took a bunch of our CDs and DVDs and then some other non-crucial items. They didn't even take the TV, which we thought was really weird.

Needless to say, I was feeling very uncomfortable and didn't feel like I could stay at the house anymore, so we decided to put our stuff in storage and move out temporarily until we could close on our new house. My sister offered her house in Denver to us, but Tony and Ashley wanted us to come and stay with them. Little did we know that would be the end of the four of us. So we packed up our stuff, put it in the storage unit, and then moved to Denver for a few weeks. It wasn't convenient, that's for sure, but it was the option we had, so we took it.

A few days into our time there, Tom and Tony decided they would go out to the driveway and play some basketball. Now these two men are your classical American boys, which translates into being very competitive. Ashley and I were in the basement watching a movie with the kids, so we weren't present when the fight broke out. All we were left to do was piece together the two stories and come to our own conclusions. This is how I understood it: both of them had been drinking to start off the game, and as it continued, and the drinking increased, they started fighting. I feel quite confident they both started heckling each other as well whenever a point was scored. I think Tom was winning, so he started teasing his brother. Tony, as long as I have known him, has never been able to handle his liquor well, so he got mad and punched Tom. Then the two of them proceeded to fight it out in the front yard.

The next thing we heard was Tom standing at the top of the stairs yelling, "He's done it, Tony has lost his mind" or something to that effect. He told us he just started attacking him when they were playing basketball and I remember Ashley shaking her head and saying, "Oh no, here we go again." We both got up and rushed to our respective husbands to try and make sense of what had just happened. Trying to reason with two drunk men wasn't going to help anything, so Tom and I packed up the kids and our essentials and drove to my sister's house.

The next day we came over to the house to get the rest of our belongings when Tony was at work. We walked in the door, and Ashley had all of our stuff boxed up, and was very melancholic and very quiet while we were there. If we all had been a little bit more mature, we might have been able to hash it out right then and there, but none of us were that far along. In addition to that, we had had trouble with Tony's drinking before, and I think we were overly protective of our kids at that point because we weren't sure what he might do. I think we all had a sense this wasn't going to go away anytime soon and might be a problem for both of our families moving forward.

We were super upset about what had happened and definitely confused as to how it escalated to that degree. While all this was

CHAPTER TWELVE

happening I was continuing to get multiple phone calls for my lender requesting more documentation. Every time she asked for an additional piece of paper, it meant I had to drive down to Colorado Springs, get into the back of my storage unit, and sort through boxes to get her what she wanted. I had asked her multiple times to let me know exactly what she needed so I could get it all at once, but she did not seem capable of doing that. On about the fourth round of this, I finally told her that I wasn't going to go and get any more documentation. She got very upset with me and said, "You'll lose the house if you don't"don't."

To which I responded, "Oh well, that's a chance I'm willing to take because if you can't close on this with the amount of information I've given you, then it's not going to go through anyway." I don't think she appreciated my attitude, but at that point I didn't really care. I was right anyway because she ultimately had all she needed to close on the house.

So one day when Tom headed down to work in Colorado Springs, he decided to stop by his parents' house. Now I had explicitly asked him to keep the events of that night between us—his brother's family and ours. I was pretty certain his parents wouldn't be able to be neutral. This was one of many times I had warned Tom we shouldn't do something—the most recent was we shouldn't go live with his brother. As it turned out, he showed up to his parents' house and his mom was already crying. She begged Tom to tell her what happened, and he caved under the pressure. He explained his side of the events that night and told her Tony's version might differ. He told her she and John could talk to Tony and get his side of things. He also asked her not to get in the middle of things as that would make it worse. She told him she wouldn't, but that is not what she did.

We hadn't talked to his brother in a couple of weeks, and we were all waiting for things to simmer down. The other problem was we didn't see this just as a scrap between two brothers but an example of a much deeper issue—his drinking problem. When you add to that the temper that came coupled with the drinking, it became a very difficult situation. We loved his brother, but we didn't think it was good for him to be around the kids when he was drinking. We both thought he had some emotional issues going on impacting him deeply, and we wanted him to go get some help before we felt comfortable re-exposing them. Tony was resistant to getting help or seeing a therapist. Naturally he did not think he had a problem, so it became a battle of wills. Between both families, we made some poor choices in how to handle the situation—too many ultimatums, which created a rift later.

The situation with Tom's parents was even worse because they sided with his brother. They did not see his drinking as a problem and just thought the two boys were fighting as they always had. In all actuality, Tom's dad thought it came down to something as simple as Tony having beaten Tom up. John even said it to Tom directly. "You are just mad that your brother finally beat you up."

I think he was a little surprised when Tom didn't even argue with him about who won the fight but rather that his brother had a problem that made us uncomfortable around him. I will argue a lot of this goes back to the favoritism that developed out of that bicycle accident. Unfortunately for Tony, he always seemed to have impulse control issues, and I'm pretty confident it stemmed from the head trauma. I wish he had gotten the help he needed when he was young. Additionally, Tom's dad managed to knock back a few himself, so he didn't see it as a problem. It was a difficult position for us to be put in between keeping the family relationships going and not having our kids negatively impacted.

CHAPTER THIRTEEN

1999/2000

As the dust settled between Tom and Tony in came his mother to try and quote "fix the situation." She decided that she would seize the opportunity, when guests were visiting, to force the two of them in a room together. Apparently, Tony knew she was about to do this, but she never mentioned word one to us—so it was what you might call a giant ambush. Sue's brother and wife came out for a visit, and we were invited to their house to visit and have some food. Their oldest daughter had a close relationship with Tom and me, so we arranged for her to come and stay at our house during their visit.

When we arrived at the house and walked in the door, his brother was standing there. Tom and I grabbed the kids and started heading out the door. This could have been handled differently on our end—sure—but it could have been handled differently on her end as well. Tensions were already heightened, and she decided to pour gasoline on the fire, and the worst part about it is everyone was in on it except for us. That's right; we didn't even know it was happening, but apparently everyone else did. She followed us out to the driveway and begged us to stay.

Tom said, "Why is he here, and did you know?" To her credit she admitted she had set the whole thing up to get them to talk. Tom said she had no right to do that to us. Her response was she had talked to her father, and he said her house was neutral ground, and she was free to invite anyone she wanted to her house. Tom and I responded, "Of course you can, but you can't go and lie to us and not tell us that Tony is coming. You just made things worse."

What transpired next was a long period of fighting, separation, and total frustration. It took a couple of years before we ever really talked to his brother again, and I would say it was a good ten months before we could spend time with his parents. What happened between us was very ugly, but the ugliest thing of all for me was how they treated their own son. They called Sue's family as well as John's and told them everything that happened. I don't know what actually got translated to them, because Lord knows they wouldn't listen to our side of things, but the family members decided to get involved. We received angry, hateful letters from Tom's maternal grandmother and from his paternal granddad. These letters were pretty vicious and talked about how unfortunate our kids were to have us as parents. While I realize emotions were high, and people felt defensive, I also thought it was incredibly cruel. What family collectively turns their back on one of its members when they don't even know what happened? To this day none of them even know what we went through with Tom's parents and brother, but as the family saw it, everything was Tom's fault, and in turn mine because I was the worst wife ever—the out-law, not the in-law.

To add another layer to this difficult situation, I found myself pregnant again. I had taken a couple of pregnancy tests when I was staying with Tony and Ashley, and I told her about

CHAPTER THIRTEEN

it in secret. Surprisingly, all of the over-the-counter pregnancy tests came out negative, but I wasn't feeling right, and I knew something was up. So I eventually set up an appointment at my doctor's office and had them test my blood, and sure enough, there was another little midget growing inside my belly waiting to consume all my energy and food. Although I wouldn't necessarily say we were ecstatic about this, we really were open to having whatever children God gave us, so we started to prepare.

We were still not talking to his brother and very little to his dad, so it took a while for them to find out I was pregnant. We did not tell them and instead left them to find out through the grapevine. This seems like a cruel act, but a few things happened that didn't make us very excited to tell them. The first issue was that Tom's parents continued to defend Tony and wouldn't listen to what we had to say. The second had to do with his dad. One evening after I headed out to work, his dad came over to our house, stormed in the door, and started yelling at Tom. Tom got on the other side of the kitchen counter so his dad couldn't hit him if he lost control. John had been so angry through this whole ordeal and was never calm and rational, so we could never have a good or deep discussion. I was furious by his attempt to bully Tom in our own house and was ready to have the police called on him. I figured that might make him think twice before he lost his temper like that again. Tom said he didn't want to agitate the situation, which was probably wise. Either way, his mom and dad ended up not getting what they wanted because now we were even more unwilling to compromise.

When I was about seven months pregnant with our third child a mutual friend (Jane) of Sue, John, and ours reached out to us. She wanted to help us rectify the situation so we could start talking again. She was very unbiased in her approach to us, which made it easier for us to accept the olive branch. We decided to organize things through her and set up a meeting with Tom's parents and a third party—Jane did not want to facilitate this. So after a few ideas were tossed around, we decided on a Lutheran pastor they knew through his brother's swim team and who had been present at our wedding. We'll call the pastor Tim.

Tim wanted to meet with each family individually before bringing us together. We knew we were taking a big risk letting him go to Tom's parents' house first but decided that would be the best course of action. By the time he showed up for our appointment, it was very clear he had already formed an opinion. Once again, whatever the narrative that was being told by his parents was rather convincing. He seemed kind of judgmental at first and approached Tom and me as if to say you don't have a leg to stand on. Tom's parents of course didn't even know the real reason why we were still mad at his brother, so the information we had to share was quite shocking to the pastor.

We were trying to express to him how nervous we were to have him around the kids because of the drinking and his anger. The pastor started to dismiss this out of hand until a memory struck him of an event that happened at one of the swim meets. You see, his son and Tony swam together when they were kids, so he had known the family for quite a long time. Although he didn't go into much detail, he alluded to an incident where he had seen Tony's anger expressed in a public setting, and it was enough of an extreme reaction for him to remember it. The look he had on his face explained it all because it was very apparent he finally understood what we were saying—somebody finally understood what we were saying. Even if we hadn't handled the fight between the two brothers very well, there was at least some support for our position and understanding for what we were going through.

After we finished the rest of the meeting, we decided all four

CHAPTER THIRTEEN

of us (Sue, John, Tom, and I) would meet at another date. He got that scheduled, and we all arrived for the big meeting. The pastor thought it would be best to just try to rectify the situation with Tom's parents and worry about his brother in the future. I don't remember too many of the details of the meeting, other than to say it wasn't very comfortable, and it wasn't very easy. They were very angry to see me pregnant and not having told them. We argued over that a bit, as I tried to explain to them the four of us had not had a civil conversation since the incident occurred. It didn't seem like a very good opportunity to share good news, especially since we didn't really know how they would take it. I can see now it probably would have been wise for us to at least let them know, but we were angry and had decided not to.

Tom's parents were convinced they still had the pastor's support, but as the conversation continued, he let us bring up the drinking and the anger from his brother. They quickly started to dismiss this when the pastor shared his personal story at the swim meet from years ago. His parents were in shock, and that put a halt to their overconfidence. We finished the meeting after about an hour, and in the end, we were very grateful to Pastor Tim as he represented both sides fairly.

We slowly started to try and rebuild the relationship between his parents and us. One of the things I felt compassion for was they missed spending time with the two grandkids we already had and were basically separated from them for about six months. In that time, however, I never got the sense they were sorry for having taken sides or that they recognized they had taken sides or that they were wrong in any way, shape, or form. I imagine that they probably felt the same way about us. I think they saw the whole situation as Tom and I being the cause of everything, but they were never willing to talk about it in a civil way so as to resolve it. In other words, I felt like this situation, and the others to come, were always fixable, but only if both parties were willing to compromise—but both parties were stubborn.

Nonetheless it was important to us these kids have a relationship with their grandparents, so we moved forward cautiously. It took some time, but eventually things got a little bit better between us. The rift, however, between his brother and us still existed, and a happy ending seemed nowhere in sight. We were all doing okay, and our kids seemed none the wiser to what had happened, so they just resumed the usual grandparent/grandkid relationships.

As one can imagine, the stress of everything going on was wearing me down during the pregnancy and made it very difficult just to get through my days. I remember feeling so much sadness and stress during those times. It was a very dark period. As far as the relationship with Ashley was concerned, that pretty much ended the night of the fight. She talked to us when we came to pick up the stuff the next day. She also came over to my sister's house to visit with us a few days later. It was, however, shortly after that that she told me if she was going to make her marriage work, she would have to distance herself from us. A fact that even my husband and I could understand in the midst of the heightened emotions. I guess you could say we bid her farewell after that.

As for the purchase of the house we were trying to buy, not too surprisingly, it went through. Even though our lender made things so difficult and tried to make it sound like we wouldn't be able to purchase the house, the title company decided to send it through. We had closed on the house shortly after the incident with his brother and got moved in fairly quickly. In addition to all the struggles we were having in the familial sense, we were also

CHAPTER THIRTEEN

having monetary struggles. I decided to get a part-time job and deliver pizza. One more stress I could add to the pile of stressors we both were experiencing, or to be even more correct, my husband, unborn child, and I.

I finally made it through the pregnancy and was two weeks late. I was two weeks late with my son as well and used to joke all the time they were planning to go to college in my womb. This labor started out patterned the same way as my others. I would have contractions twenty minutes apart for a certain period of time and then fifteen minutes apart, ten, five, and then into hard labor for whatever time the good Lord wanted. In this case, I thought I would be a little bit quicker in the delivery because it was my third kid, but that was not the case. I got to the hospital and was not very dilated, so I walked the halls yet again. After a long time of laboring, I was just exhausted and demanded they go in and grab her out. I said she was swinging off of my liver, and they needed to extract her as quickly as possible. The nurses got a big laugh out of that. They finally suggested I have an epidural to which I caved and had one. I finally got a reprieve from the pain and was able to calm down and eventually deliver our new little rugrat, a beautiful baby girl, and we named her Agnes.

Agnes was, and is, an extremely vivacious and encouragable human being. She was very intelligent (even as a young thing) and loved to be the life of the party. Agnes had a way of throwing her little weight around to get what she wanted and as she got older was quick with a funny and sassy response to almost anything. She had beautiful blue eyes and won the attention of her daddy on most occasions. She is a strong person and a leader.

When I got home from the hospital my mom and dad both decided to come down and stay with me for a couple of weeks. Even though my dad and I fought a lot, it was good to have them both there to help. We were enjoying ourselves and adjusting to the new kiddo when my mom got an emergency phone call from Denver. My uncle, who was headed into eye surgery, had passed out in the waiting room, and my mom was his emergency contact. They had transported him over to the hospital. So my mom and dad discussed it and decided they should go and take care of him. I think they were with us for about a week, which was definitely helpful, as my husband never got more than two days off from his job to be home when the kids were born.

When they got back to Denver and evaluated the situation, they discovered my uncle was having a diabetic reaction. His blood sugar levels were very high, and they were trying to bring them down in the hospital. He wasn't feeling well at all, and it was not looking too promising. My mom and dad stayed by his bedside and kept us informed as they themselves were updated. He was having a lot of problems in other areas of the body as high sugar levels can cause a cascade of events in an elderly person. As I recall, he stayed in the hospital for about a week, and then they released him into a rehab facility. He remained there the rest of the time.

We slowly started getting more mobile as a family unit with the additional third child on board. I drove the kids up to Denver to go see my uncle in the facility. It was very difficult to visit my uncle as he had a huge temper and was angry at everything and everyone. Just like my mom, he had a difficult childhood—losing both parents and his aunt—so it had played a toll on him when he was young. When he got older, he met someone and fell rapidly and deeply in love as I understand it. She shared his love of the outdoors, fishing, hunting, and I do believe loved to play golf as well. He was completely smitten, and she was the love of his life as my mother told the story.

CHAPTER THIRTEEN

Unfortunately for my dear uncle, tragedy struck once again. His poor wife contracted cancer, and after a period of time, she ended up dying. This event, understandably so, rocked his entire world. My mom said that is when he started heavily drinking and spiraled into a depression. Since all of this happened prior to me coming into the situation, or being old enough to be aware of what was happening, I only have my mother's accounts to go by. I don't know how long he stayed in that state of depression, drinking, and despair, but he finally came out of it. When he did stop drinking, he joined an alcoholics anonymous group and stayed with them until the end of his life.

The uncle I knew—who was heavily scarred by all these events—was a very unhappy person. He loved my mom and our family and was there at every family event, birthdays, and holidays. My interactions with him, however, never went very well, and he seemed to have a big dislike for me and my personality. I found out years later other kids in the family felt the same way. He was always criticizing everything I did and would watch me like a hawk only to jump in and tell me when I was doing things wrong. It was just one more person for me to have disappointed. It was obvious though he really loved us because he kept showing up for all the important stuff. Like it or not, he was our uncle, and we knew he cared about us and tried to teach us about sports, lawn care, outdoor living, and nature. He respected and loved our parents.

The dreaded call finally came to us on Good Friday of that year. My uncle had passed away in his sleep, and we would have to prepare for a funeral. Since life likes to throw curveballs at everyone, I found this out at my post-delivery six-week checkup. I had my infant and three toddlers at the check up with me since I didn't have anyone to watch them. If you're counting, yes, it was

2000

an additional toddler, which was my friend's daughter, and her husband failed to come and pick her up when he was supposed to. I was a mess at that appointment and for quite a while afterward. I told my husband the horrible news when I got home.

2000

I wasn't very surprised when my mom called to tell me my uncle had passed because I knew it was coming. It wasn't just because he was so sick, but I could see it in his eyes the last time I went to visit him. I knew his soul was struggling to let go and be at peace. I remember going home that night and praying so hard for him to be in a state of grace (rectify his sins with God) before he died. I asked for God to let me know if he was going to be okay. My beautiful Lord allowed me a glimpse into his spiritual state. It was the Holy Spirit who came to me that night in a dream. I was in a large, completely white hospital room, with a lot of hospital beds all around me, when suddenly I saw my uncle jump off the bed located right in front of me. When he came out from under the covers, he looked so handsome and youthful, and he had a huge, brilliant smile on his face. He absolutely looked the epitome of someone at peace. He never said a word; he just smiled and walked away.

I knew at that moment my uncle was going to be okay, which brought me great joy. It was a day or two later my mom called to say he had died. I was so excited to share the dream with her and give her the reassurance I thought his soul was going to be okay. As I started telling the dream, however, my mom became very upset. She asked me to please stop talking because it was making her uncomfortable. It was one of those situations where the Holy Spirit provides information, but because it comes in such

CHAPTER THIRTEEN

an unorthodox way, it becomes almost impossible for anyone to hear. I, therefore, had to internalize it and keep it to myself. Luckily, however, to this day I know my uncle tried to settle things with God and will hopefully be in heaven with him and his loved ones. I am grateful to the Holy Spirit for sharing this message with me and giving me such comfort.

After my uncle died, my mom and dad started making plans for the funeral. They had to head over to his house to sort through his belongings, clean everything up, and get the house ready to be re-rented. We stayed at our mom and dad's house and started cleaning it to get it ready for all the company that would be coming. My parents were gone for a long time and were very worn out when they got home. My uncle had smoked for many years, and they said the walls were covered from it, and it would take a lot of work to deep clean it. They seemed very sad to have seen how he lived. We were never allowed to visit our uncle at his house, including my mom and dad, and he always came to see us. I don't think I ever even knew where he lived. I think my uncle was embarrassed by how he lived. I think it broke my mom's heart when she realized how bad it really was.

In addition to the task of cleaning his house, there was a funeral Mass to plan, and someone needed to write the eulogy. I don't remember if I volunteered to write it or if my mom asked me if I would, but either way I ended up doing it. It was a very difficult eulogy to write because my uncle was a mystery to me. He kept to himself most of his life and lived a very meager existence alone in his home. He never remarried after his wife died, and my mom said it was because she was the love of his life. He did, however, manage to make a lot of friends and play golf quite frequently with those same friends. He even played golf with some members of the Denver Broncos; although, he would never let us meet them. He would also "skunk" us pretty good whenever we challenged him to a tennis match. He would beat us badly without moving much on the court, while we ran around like crazy people.

I agonized over this eulogy trying to get it just right, which was an additional difficulty considering I still had an infant that needed my full-time care and two other toddlers. I eventually managed to get the eulogy written and sent it to my parents. They didn't like the first draft, so I had to rewrite it. Then when I sent the next draft, I got the impression my mom still wasn't very happy with the results, but we decided to just let it go and use what I had. I was very hurt by my mom's reaction to my eulogy because she seemed disappointed in it. Even with that I was confident the Holy Spirit had helped me write it, and in the end, it would read well because of that. When the time came to deliver the eulogy, it made people laugh, and it made people cry. My brother volunteered to read it and did a great job. After the funeral Mass, I had several people tell me it described my uncle perfectly and was a great tribute to him. I think we all know I have the Holy Spirit to thank for that.

Since I seemed to have no shortage of activities and events going on in my family at any given time, the weekend of my uncle's death was also the weekend my niece was coming into the Catholic Church. My oldest sister, who had always been a practicing Catholic, wanted to get her daughter baptized when she was born, but her husband wouldn't agree to it. There was a lot of fighting going on between the two of them just in general, and this added even more stress to the plate. Her husband was unhappy about a lot of things in his marriage and in his life, most of which was his own doing and well within his control to change, but he chose not to and instead liked to blame my sister for most of it. At least that's my take on things as an outside observer.

CHAPTER THIRTEEN

Sadly, over time, my sister and he ended up getting a divorce. I guess my sister realized that without him in the picture she could at least investigate Baptism and Confirmation for our niece. Her daughter went through all the classes and prepared for this very special event. It was a very long journey to get her there and such an important thing for her to receive her sacraments. Even though we were all hurting and mourning the loss of our uncle, we still wanted to be a part of her beautiful day coming into the Catholic faith.

The Mass and ceremony for her were extraordinarily beautiful and definitely an answer to our prayers—especially my mother and father's. You see, of all the things our parents have done for us in raising us, educating us, and making us good human beings and good citizens, the most important thing they shared with us was the Catholic faith. They were always saddened by the fact their granddaughter wasn't baptized, and it was a big concern for them. I remember them telling me how often they would pray for her to finally receive her sacraments. Which is why, while this was a day of great mourning, it was also a day of great joy and happiness. I remember how wonderful it felt to be there witnessing this beautiful event, and even though she may not be practicing her faith now, the Holy Spirit has his mark on her soul, and I pray daily that someday she'll return to the church.

After that very tumultuous time of burying my uncle and all that surrounded it, it was time for me to get back home and try to get settled in with my new life. At about three or four months after delivering Agnes, I started slipping into a depression. As you know already, I had suffered lots of depression throughout my life, so I was familiar with it. This, however, was a whole new thing, which would take years for me to understand and

2000

grasp. The depression this time around was pervasive, intense, and confusing. When I suffered from depression before, there were things I could do to help pull me out of it, but not this time around. It was a depression that seemed out of my control and made me into a rageaholic.

In the past when my depression would get bad I would start doing things differently, which is what I started doing this time around. I would leave my house fairly frequently to go interact with people. I would go to the park, let the kids play, and visit with other moms. I would go to McDonald's and let the kids run around the play area, go to swim lessons, and even go to the gym. I even started an intense food regime and got all sugar out of my diet (just in case it was causing some of my mood swings). Not one of these things seemed to help.

I felt incredibly sad for my husband as well during this time because I was nearly impossible to be around. I would get mad at the drop of a hat, and I'm sure he felt like he never knew which person he was going to get on any given day, his wife or the beast. I have tried to describe this over the years in an effort to make sense of it and help others make sense of it as well. When I would have an episode—as I later came to call them—it would be like this; I would start yelling at my husband or whoever was in the room, and I would have a surreal experience of floating out of my body and looking down on myself and wondering what the heck was the matter with me. I would tell myself to stop it but would quickly float back into my body and continue to rage. I could not stop it even though I could almost experience it from a third-person position, and not even that was enough to put an end to it. I could see the sadness in Tom's eyes as he didn't know what to do any more than I did. I didn't know what was happening to me, and thoughts of ending my life circled around in my mind.

CHAPTER THIRTEEN

I talked to friends of mine to see if they had ever gone through things like this, but none of them knew what I was talking about. I asked my family members as well, but there wasn't a connection for them either. It wasn't until one day, when I was struck by a vague memory of an Oprah Winfrey talk show, that things started to make sense. It was an interview with Marie Osmond, who at the time had six kids, and she described her depression. She explained that she got so sad one day and remembers looking at her kids—loving them—and thinking I can't do this anymore. She hopped in her car and drove away from the house leaving the kids behind. It wasn't long before she realized what she had done and turned around and came back. Luckily the kids were none the wiser, but what she described fit me to a tee. She said she loved her family and loved her children, but she hurt so deeply inside and didn't know how to make the pain stop. In the moment, she thought, If I just drive away from the house and my duties and responsibilities, the pain will end. That was my experience exactly. I loved my husband and kids, but my internal and emotional pain was so great I just wanted it to stop.

This is when I first heard the term postpartum depression. Prior to that, everybody just called it the baby blues, a phenomenon that happens when your hormones are adjusting after you've delivered a baby. Baby blues, however, only last a short while and at most about two months. When the condition goes on for a much longer period, the person is dealing with an actual postpartum depression, and that's much more intense and harder to treat. I have quite a few theories as to the catalyst behind severe postpartum depression, but again they are only theories, which I will be willing to share with you, but not until later.

This memory of an Oprah interview gave me a little bit of

insight into my emotional struggles and a sense I was not alone. At the time there were no good resources to help process a woman through this type of depression, so we were on our own to find the pathway through. Both of my sisters were trying to help us as well and could see I was struggling to get through and take care of my family. I would say they also started forming a bond with my husband because they could relate to how he felt. They were also trying to help me as well, but they had no familiarity with depression, let alone this form of it, so they weren't sure what to do with me. Everyone cared and everyone was trying to help, but there was no easy answer and no real "treatment." I would have to say my only saving grace was I had some awareness of my behavior and depression, so we could at least discuss it. In most cases, when an individual is struggling with severe depression, they don't know they are and are therefore in denial. I had seen multiple therapists over the years and learned everything I could from them. This created some level of self-awareness that may have helped me amid my depression.

It was during these episodes of depression and following therapy sessions that I learned the difference between situational depression and clinical depression. Situational depression is just that; it's brought about by a situation or an event and, over time, can improve when a person has gotten some distance from said event. Clinical depression is more difficult to treat as it tends to be more long-lasting and pervasive and can't be fixed just by changing your location, moving, or changing jobs etc. It requires more help, sometimes a longer period of therapy, and then, in even more difficult cases, medication. Postpartum depression was a category all by itself and not well known to the public. It took on the behavior of clinical depression but added a new level of mental suffering as it appeared to be strongly influenced by

CHAPTER THIRTEEN

hormones. The extent to which that was happening was unknown to us at that time.

So as I struggled with my mental health and three kids—four years old and younger—I could feel myself heading over the cliff. I was very proactive about trying to take care of myself; although, I was not sleeping well and could not make that situation any better. I worked on all aspects of my health. I was eating a very clean diet, stopped eating sugar, and removed all alcohol from my diet. I exercised five days a week or more, and I would leave the house daily and go on trips to the park or the store just to talk to other adults and get out in the fresh air (the same approach I took the last time I was depressed). While I realize these efforts probably made some difference, I didn't feel better.

When I would wake up in the morning, for a brief moment I would feel joy, and then in short order, I would feel an overwhelming heaviness and sadness which would stay with me throughout the day. I would look at my husband and kids and would wonder why I didn't feel happy. I was lucky in the fact I felt love for them (not everyone with postpartum depression can feel this), but I wasn't excited to see anyone, and I dragged myself through the day in what I perceived as a series of monotonous activities and events. Only to get to the end of the day and know the next day it would start all over again. I hated this drudgery.

For some unknown reason, I always seemed mad at my husband. It was like all of the disgust and self-hatred I had for myself got projected on to him. I would snap at him for no reason and lose my temper all the time. To say the situation was difficult is an understatement. I felt so helpless and sad I often thought about what it would be like to not be alive anymore (a feeling I was familiar with from before). I definitely didn't want to leave my husband or the kids behind, but I couldn't make the hurt or pain stop. Odd as it may sound, this was mixed with a strong desire to be a good mother, wife, and homemaker, which was an insane feeling to have. I felt so bad for my husband because I knew he wondered what the heck had happened to his wife and the woman he loved, and what could he possibly do to fix the situation?

I talked to God regularly during all this and begged for his help. I would not consider this any real form of good prayer but more a desperate attempt to have him either end my pain or take me off this planet. I knew I could not take my own life because of how much I loved my family and God and wanted to be with him in Heaven. I was definitely afraid that if I took my own life, I would be separated from God, and everyone I love, for all eternity. I am so glad to have had this strong connection with God because it is what kept me moving forward and kept me in the fight.

I remained in this depression for quite a few months, when finally I woke up one day and I could feel some of the weight had lifted off my shoulders. I slowly started to come out of the fog and feel happier and a little bit more myself. As the weeks rolled on, I got a little bit better every day and eventually felt "normal" again. I was engaging more with my family and enjoying my time with everyone. I was actually being kind to my husband again, and we were starting to feel affectionate. I was seeing light at the end of the tunnel, but it wasn't meant to last.

CHAPTER FOURTEEN

2001

It was a new year and a new period in our lives. The kids were doing well and enjoying our new home and our sweet puppy dog, who was now about a year and a half old. She was a beautiful golden retriever by the name of Madeline, and we all loved her very much, especially the kids. She was probably the smartest dog we ever had and incredibly easygoing and sweet. For some reason, much to our dismay, she started acting disobedient, and we were confused.

Mattie had started digging holes in the backyard, and she had never done that before. We read up on things we could do to break the behavior. One of the most recommended ideas was to put some of her dog poop in the hole and shove her nose in it. So we decided to try that. Tom did it multiple times, on multiple days, but unfortunately for us, this did not break the habit. I started thinking from a psychological standpoint, not that I think in dog thought, but I was processing through what could have disrupted her. Dogs are mostly instinct, and they don't do anything on purpose, but just in response to their environment, so I started trying to figure out what her trigger was.

2001

The more I thought about it, the more I realized it probably had to do with our new baby girl because that's when the behavior first started. I started wondering if our dog was feeling left out and started thinking of ways to make her feel more included. I also started researching dog training and came across a dog whisperer, if you will, that put out a number of videos on how to train your dog and keep them heeled when you're walking. To start the training, he suggested just walking square patterns in your front yard or at a nearby park fifteen minutes a day. So I loaded Agnes up in a front carrier and walked patterns in the front yard with my dog almost every day. That was just what she needed and she stopped digging. Everything returned to normal, and the bonus was we got an easy-to-walk dog out of the whole process.

About eight or nine months after Agnes's birth I got another surprise. I was pregnant once again. I wish I could say this brought a whole new level of excitement and joy, but it did not. If anyone has suffered from depression the way I have, you know how overwhelming it can be to think it's coming again. With each child, I seemed to be experiencing more depression for longer periods of time. Add to that the fact nobody seemed to understand what postpartum depression was or how to treat it, and you get a pretty good picture of how scared I was. I was so upset with the news I actually began to cry and proceeded to cry for quite a few days.

After Agnes was about seven months old, I had actually started to feel myself again and had lost some of the baby weight and just felt better about myself. The news of this next pregnancy led me to believe that would all be ending, and it wasn't that far from the truth. I had a relatively normal pregnancy this time around, and by normal I mean months of morning sickness,

CHAPTER FOURTEEN

severe ligament pain, and extreme fatigue. I know they say every pregnancy is different, but it appeared my pregnancies liked to mimic each other. I guess in a sense it made it easier to know what was coming, so that was helpful.

While I was functioning fine and able to get through my normal activities, I felt like I lived in a state of apprehension, which I'm sure did not make things any better. I had a lot of early labor pains with the fourth child. I had Braxton Hicks contractions two months before I delivered her, as well as actual labor pains. I was hoping to have an early delivery because my body was just worn out, and it was the summer. You see, in Colorado people don't really have air conditioning, so when it hits the high 90s to 100 and you're pregnant, it's pretty miserable. I must have forced Tom to go out for food or drinks every night when he got home from work.

At about thirty-six weeks, I was busy doing stuff around the house trying to get ready for our next addition to the family. One of the things we really needed to fix before baby number four was our back fence. We had shared fences on all three sides of us, and we shared the cost on the two side fences with our neighbors who hired a fence company to do it. When it came to the back fence, which was the longest of all, we knew we couldn't afford to pay for a company to come in and do it, so we decided to do it ourselves.

The day before we were to go and put in the fence, I headed to the lumber yard with all three of the kids to go load up the pickets and the posts we would need. If my memory serves me well, it was eight or nine posts and 125 pickets I needed to get. I went into the store and explained to them what I needed, and they pointed me out to the lumber yard. I proceeded to load every one of these by myself, and not one employee came to help me.

2001

Can you imagine seeing a woman eight months pregnant with three toddlers and not even attempting to help her put the wood in the back of her truck? I was pretty upset, but I needed to get it done, so I just drove home.

When I got back to the house, my husband was home from work, and his friend was there as well since he was going to help us put up the fence. They lost their minds when they found out I had loaded all of this wood entirely by myself. They took it upon themselves to drive over to the store and give the manager the verbal beating of his life. They didn't hold anything back, and I think the manager realized how incredibly foolish he looked. I don't even remember if they gave us a credit or discount, but it was really nice having these men protect and defend me because I had fought a lot of battles on my own throughout my life.

Nonetheless, once we finished that, we headed back to the house, had dinner, and went to bed. When we woke up the next morning, we got up early and started the project. Our friend had done fences before, so he was pretty proficient at it. We had cemented the post holes the day before, so the next day we were able to just line up the pickets and hammer them in. We had the project completed within two days and were so relieved.

The following day, however, it all caught up to me. We took the kids to the park to play and work out some of their pent-up energy, and I sat down on the bench unable to move. I started having contractions there at the park, which lasted for another eight hours. The contractions stopped as suddenly as they had started, and that was that. I knew it was early to have my baby, but truth be told I was ready to not be pregnant anymore.

I continued to have these intermittent labor episodes for the next four weeks. About two weeks before I delivered, I had a doctor appointment, and he assured me he wouldn't let me go

CHAPTER FOURTEEN

very far past my due date. Lies, all lies, haha! It needs to be said I had two different due dates, one at the end of August, and the one at the beginning of September. Naturally I was shooting for an August delivery. We had a family reunion at the end of August down in southern Colorado, and it was going to be very hot, but because I didn't go into labor, my family and I ended up having to go to the family reunion. It was a miserable experience for me because I felt so horrible. In addition, there was fighting amongst the nieces and nephews, and for whatever reason, my brother thought it would be a good idea to put me in the middle of it. Our kids were not even involved, so I still don't know why that happened, but I settled it the best I could, and then we headed home.

The last couple of months of my pregnancy were the absolute hardest of our marriage. My pregnancies were painful and difficult, and it made life equally so. I experienced sadness because we were still having trouble with his family and mine as well, and I was worn out. If I understood the purpose of suffering, especially redemptive suffering, at this time, it would have been much easier to endure. My mother tried for years to get me to offer up my suffering, but I was just too self-absorbed to inquire what she meant and figure out how to apply that in my life. In other words, if I had it to do over again, I would not complain every minute of every day but instead would pray for my spouse, my children, our extended families, and all of mankind. Unfortunately for my husband, all he got was the miserable, complaining, depressed, and unhappy version of me, and it kept him at arm's length. Tom added his own ingredients to the struggle that was our marriage. While I feel empathy and sadness for all he went through, I of course was not the only problem. There's also the part both of us played in our marriage.

2001

Tom, by nature, was a very introverted person and internalized his suffering, keeping everything "close to the chest," as you might say. For roughly a year he had been experiencing his own depression and questioning whether he should have married me and had so many kids so quickly. Don't get me wrong, there wasn't a day in his life he regretted having our children, but he never anticipated or expected how physically and mentally hard it would be on me and how hard it would be for him to navigate. He was probably thinking if only I had listened to her before we were married and ran in the opposite direction. To quote a line from a movie: "He has chosen poorly." In addition to the struggles everyone experiences in marriage, depression adds a whole new level to the process. To add insult to injury, we couldn't find anybody to confide in with an understanding of what we were going through, or at least if they did understand, they didn't want to share it with us. This made things even more difficult for both of us.

So, with Tom's makeup being what it was, he basically shut himself off emotionally from me and became an island unto himself. He never really let me in, and he kept himself emotionally at arm's length. To make matters worse, it appeared he was able to confide in both of my sisters, and they in turn confided in him. It felt as though whenever I walked into the room everyone made a wide berth around me and looked at me as if I was crazy. This was not an uncommon experience for me over the years, as depression seems to be the most difficult illness for people to comprehend and treat. The tendency is to avoid people with depression because it makes loved ones uncomfortable. This meant I lived alone in my marriage and very alone in my depression.

My husband and I were not talking very much, especially toward the end of my pregnancy. A couple days before my second

CHAPTER FOURTEEN

due date, I went into labor once again. This time I was up all night with my sister, who was visiting, and she timed contractions until the morning. She did not sleep, nor did I. When morning rolled around, the contractions came to a halt, and no matter what I did, I couldn't get them going again. In a state of despair and exhaustion, I called my doctor, and he suggested I go to the hospital to have them do an exam. He was confident that if they examined me, it would get my labor going again because it was my fourth child. I was so sick, tired, and frustrated that I just didn't have the desire to go and be disappointed.

The rest of that day was one of the darkest days in my memory. My husband wouldn't even talk to me or look at me, and I had no idea what to do. I could feel the anger coming from him and knew he didn't want to be around me. I took a bath and tried to get some sleep, but I didn't get much rest. When I awoke, I experienced what felt like true despair. I felt desperate to do something to fix the situation. I finally decided I might as well go to the hospital and have them do a quick exam to see if we could get labor going. My husband drove me, and when we arrived at the hospital I once again was not very far dilated and felt like I was going to scream. We drove back home and didn't speak a word to each other.

When we got home, we told my sister nothing was progressing. My husband decided it would be very good to go for a drive and clear his head. I told him that was fine. Once he left, in what seemed like instantly, I went into hard labor. I was having contractions two minutes apart, and they were coming hard. I don't remember what happened next, but Tom finally arrived back home, and we immediately headed to the hospital. It was a very long and painful ride. They got us into the room immediately, and the anesthesiologist came by to see if I wanted an epidural.

I passed on the epidural, but shortly after that one of the nurses checked on me, and I wasn't very dilated (surprise, surprise), and they said I had a very small window to get an epidural. I was desperate, exhausted, and just wanted to be done, so I said yes to the epidural.

I got the epidural and finally settled in but in short order realized I was very sick to my stomach. I told the nurse I thought I was going to vomit, so she brought the trash can over to my bedside and immediately proceeded to turn her back, and while doing so informed me she cannot handle people vomiting. Well, she wasn't alone, because my husband joined her in that corner of the room. I started throwing up within minutes of the trash can arriving and was hanging halfway off the bed with my head in it. Within a couple of cycles of vomiting, my sweet baby girl decided to make her appearance. This poor kiddo came right out and onto the hospital bed while her mommy was "hurling in the trash can." It seemed like an eternity before I could get my nurse and husband to turn around and come and help me, but eventually they both saw it and came racing over to the bed. What a glamorous way for this child to introduce herself to the world.

It was fairly late at night by this point, and despite the unorthodox way my sweet baby came into the world, she was just that . . . a sweet baby (we named her Alexis). We had yet another little girl (a fact that disappointed our poor son, who was hoping for a brother) and she was perfect and beautiful. My husband was as exhausted as I was, and after a few hours, we decided it was best for him to go home and take care of the other kids. He and I still weren't talking very much, but at least I wasn't pregnant anymore, which we were hoping would reduce the stress somewhat.

After a little while, they moved me up into the mother and

CHAPTER FOURTEEN

baby unit. Much to my dismay I was continuing to throw up, I assumed from the epidural, and did this for another twelve hours. To say that I was tired would be an understatement. I look back at pictures of myself from those two days in the hospital, and I looked like a heroin addict. My eyes were very puffy with dark shadows and pain covering every inch of my face. It's crazy how twenty-two years later I can still look at the picture and feel the emotions.

I was worried about going home because I was struggling with another issue. Our sweet Agnes had taken to screaming when she couldn't verbally express what she needed, get what she wanted, or get her way. This was no ordinary scream, mind you (because my kids never do anything halfway). It reminded me of a scene from the movie *Dumb and Dumber* when he says, "Want to hear the most annoying sound in the world?" and then delivers a high-pitched scream for the next minute or two. The concern I had was bringing this newborn home would bring about more of these soprano vocals from said two-year-old. This was a legitimate concern.

I decided to talk to the attending doctor, as well as my doctor, about these concerns. I received the usual amount of "she's just trying to learn to communicate, and we know it's hard, but just be patient with her." A little while later, I was in the nursery getting Alexis, I heard screaming down the hallway and heard the nurses in the nursery saying, "Oh my gosh, that kid has a set of lungs on her. I feel sorry for whoever has to take her home."

I walked around the corner and said, with a sound of defeat in my voice, "That would be me; she's my kid."

The nurses smiled and said, "We're sorry; that must be really tough."

I responded, "You have no idea."

Within a few minutes of this, the doctor also came over to me and asked, "Is that the screaming you were talking about?"
Me: "Why, yes, it is."
Doctor: "I had no idea that it was this bad," then she proceeded to apologize to me. None of which made anything easier because nobody had a solution to the problem.

I was also struggling with another problem and asked every nurse I could talk to, as well as every doctor, if they knew anything about postpartum depression and could recommend anyone who specialized in it. Nobody even knew what I was referring to, so they were unable to help, except for one nurse who overheard the conversation.

She came to me and said, "I went through something similar, and here's the person I visited." I desperately grabbed the sheet out of her hand, thanked her profusely, and then proceeded to put on my big-girl pants, get brave, and head into the room with our new baby Alexis and introduce her to her siblings.

Justin and Faye were both very motherly to her right off the bat. They held her in their laps, doted on her, and gave her a million kisses. Next it was Agnes's turn, and she did the same. She loved all over her and was very proud of her baby sister. I think at this point we really tried to build her up and help her realize what a great big sister she was going to be. She was still just eighteen months (about one and a half years) old, but this made her feel more like a big sister and less like a little kid. I would like to say she didn't start screaming, and Alexis was like a magic pill that kept her from getting upset, but that would be a lie. Something didn't go her way, yet again, the jaws opened wide, diaphragm expanded, and out came the minute-long shriek.

Eventually we got her to calm down, and after a little while, Tom decided to head home with the kids. He didn't stay very

CHAPTER FOURTEEN

long, and he was still very cold and distant from me, which made it even more emotionally difficult. While I realize I'm more sensitive to nonverbal cues, it did appear his anger for me bordered on hate. I can't say for sure that this is, or isn't, how he felt at that moment, but it seemed to rise off of him like a cloud of smoke. I don't even think he was able to hug me or give me a kiss. In this moment of having a newborn baby, which is supposed to be so joyous, it was anything but that. He gathered up the kids and headed out the door.

The next day they came to pick us up so we could go home. I was so ready to be out of that hospital and back in my own house, but there was also a bit of apprehension. It's a very strange sensation to know something is going on inside of you, that you have no control over, and that can manifest itself unexpectedly (postpartum depression). It's literally like having a ticking time bomb inside of you. That's what depression feels like for me, and unfortunately, changing locations doesn't stop it from coming.

Once we got home and settled, we started to talk and update each other on what had gone on the last few days. My sister (Lisa) was still there with us, helping take care of the kids and helping take care of Tom. The interaction going on between Lisa and Tom was kind of strange to me because they were interacting as if I wasn't there. They had formed a type of bond/relationship over those two days when I was at the hospital, I suspect out of being observers of my anger and depression. They shared a conversation that was like a constant "inside joke," which I was not a part of. It was like an insider's club, but you're not one of the insiders.

I realize someone reading this would consider me to be almost paranoid, but depression does feel like paranoia to some degree. If no one else in the room has ever gone through it or understands it, the tendency is to treat the depressed person like a fragile child and like there is something very wrong with them—like they are very broken and cannot be fixed. It warrants saying depression is one of the most fundamentally misunderstood mental health struggles. I heard a friend of mine once say that if someone came to you and said they had been diagnosed with cancer, your reaction would be to lean into it and immediately supply food, transportation, love, and support. Now that same person tells a friend they've been diagnosed with severe depression, and the reaction is just the opposite. It's as if they can't get out the door fast enough. Why do we do that, and what about mental health makes us so scared? Heck, there's even more compassion for alcoholism than there is for mental health issues because that is seen as a disease. The difference there, however, is even though it's difficult an alcoholic can choose not to drink, but someone with depression, or cancer, can't just choose something to make it go away.

As for my fourth wonderful child she was an easy baby just like her sister Faye. She slept a lot right from the beginning and she nursed beautifully. In addition, she hardly ever cried and was just pretty content most of the time. Alexis was held and taken care of by a lot of different people in her first year of life and was always easy going about it. She was and is intelligent, sharp, detail oriented, and very mechanical and good with her hands. She's confident and literally beautiful inside and out.

As if we didn't have enough bizarre stuff happening in our own home, there was an event that happened the day after I brought Alexis home from the hospital. The following morning, I was up nursing my daughter when my husband came out into the living room to inform me planes had crashed into the twin towers in New York City. We turned on the TV to watch the news in utter disbelief. We watched the news for several days after that.

CHAPTER FOURTEEN

My son recently said the school secretary called us the day of the attack and had us come and pick up our boy. I don't remember doing that, but I do remember the uncertainty we felt this may have been one of many terrorist attacks to come. Thousands of people died that day as the buildings caught on fire and collapsed. They also attacked the Pentagon, which was unheard of in the United States. It was a horrific scene with people running away from the buildings covered in black ash. I would say to this day it is still not completely clear what really happened. The official word was Osama Bin Laden was behind the attacks—a man living in Afghanistan no one had heard of before.

My sister had already gone back home by this time, but she and Tom had made plans to get together the following weekend. He was going to drive up to Denver, and they were going to go out for sushi, drink beer, and have fun. I was in a state of fatigue when this plan was made. If I heard it, I'm not sure I would have believed it anyway. The next few days were kind of weird from a big-world standpoint and still difficult between my husband and me. A couple of days before the weekend, my husband brought it up to me again he was going to go up to Denver. I was shaking my head and completely confused because what man would leave his newborn baby and three other kids and wife for a weekend to go and party?

The day he was going to leave turned into the biggest fight of our lives. For some reason, while I was downstairs vacuuming and trying to process what was going on between the two of us, it suddenly hit me. I was overwhelmed with the feeling Tom had completely fallen out of love with me, and he was thinking of separating. It was one of my sixth-sense moments, and I immediately began to cry and did so continuously until he got home. When he arrived, he didn't even greet me and headed directly into the bedroom to start packing his clothes. I walked up to him and said, "We really need to talk."

He said he didn't want to talk and that my sister was waiting for him, and he needed to get on the road. I said our marriage was more important than a weekend away, and we needed to work this out.

He was angrier than I had ever seen him, and he said, "I don't want to talk to you." For some reason at this time, I was very calm. I turned to him and said "I want to work on the marriage, and work on what's going on between the two of us, but if you go up to Denver right now, that tells me that you don't want to work it out." He exploded when I said this and started yelling, but it was the first time he had really talked to me in about a year.

I was crying, and very upset, but I knew we needed to hash it out. I started asking him what was wrong and why hated me so much. For a while he was just angry and spewing angry words at me, but eventually he said, "I don't love you anymore." I think that's when I collapsed in the chair and started to cry even more.

I said, "Yes, that's the conclusion I came to today."

I looked at him, and I said, "Can you tell me why?"

He looked over at me with tortured eyes and said, "You are not the person I married; you've changed and are always angry at me, criticizing me, and I feel like I can never do anything right." He proceeded to tell me everything he was angry about—which was a lot for me to take in. The cork had popped, and it was all coming out.

As I sat there listening to him, I felt more pain in my heart than I thought possible, and surprisingly a lot of it was for my husband and all he had been through. My Guardian Angel was there with me at that moment—and the Holy Spirit told me I needed to listen to my husband—and I gave him the chance he

CHAPTER FOURTEEN

needed to express all the pain from the last couple of years. When he finished, I looked at him and said, "Why didn't you tell me this when it was happening, and I could have tried to do something about it?" I said, "You waited so long, and now I'm afraid you've gotten yourself past the point of no return." For the first time in months, I saw his face and eyes soften as he realized I was compassionate to what he had gone through.

After a while, we both sat there defeated. I looked at him and said, "What are we supposed to do now?"

He said, "I honestly don't know." I asked him if he really wanted to get a divorce. He said he didn't know for sure; he just didn't want to live like this anymore. I told him I understood, and that I didn't know what I could do to heal myself, but that I would work on it. I also told him I still loved him and loved our children, and I wanted to make it work. I said our children didn't choose this, we chose each other, but they didn't have a choice, so I was willing to do what it took to make it work. I then said I would not force him to stay if he really wanted out. He stayed home that weekend, and we started trying to recover our relationship.

CHAPTER FIFTEEN

2002/2003

After a couple of months, we started getting a little bit better. I was still incredibly uncertain of the direction of our marriage, and I am sure he was as well. I admit I was in absolute shock when Tom told me he was thinking of divorce since that had never entered my mind. You see, I grew up in an environment where divorce was not allowed except under the most extreme conditions—physical abuse, drug addiction, etc.—so marriage was never optional for me. In my mind, once I had married him, I could not leave him and/or remarry, unless he had died. This, however, was not the environment he was raised in. He had grown up in a home where both parents stayed married, but on both sides of his extended family there were multiple divorces. Marriage wasn't regarded the same way for them. In other words, if things got bad, you could just leave, and it would be acceptable.

The problem is that even though you can talk a lot about your background and experiences in life, before you get married, there are always going to be things you don't even know need to be discussed. This was one of them. Over time, the more Tom and I talked about it, the more I realized he had somewhat of a fantasy about

CHAPTER FIFTEEN

marriage. I don't mean to undercut his commitment to me or the family, but his version of marriage was more like a fairytale in his mind, and when things got really difficult, he didn't have a way to cope with that. He saw divorce as a viable option, whereas I did not. It was so scary for me to think he and I might get a divorce, and here I would be a single mom with four small children and no job or career. I had given my life over to the family, and I wouldn't even know how to figure out a career path from here, not to mention the fact I did not want to put my kids in daycare and be separated from them.

As I had promised Tom, I started looking into therapy for myself. I contacted the psychologist the nurse had referred me to. Her name was Helen, and she was fabulous and just what I needed. This poor woman had gone through postpartum depression years before I had, when nobody knew anything about it. She could relate to so much of the pain and suffering I was going through. It was so nice to talk to somebody that understood. She wasn't a pushover by any means either. When I would get off topic, or start spinning out of control, she had a great way of reeling me back in. She would always ask me "What's the worst thing that could happen"; I'd tell her, and then she'd walk it backward for me. What she'd show me is the worst things you can imagine are very unlikely to happen. She would sometimes put percentages to it, which would give me a healthier perspective. This helped me make things more manageable.

As I continued to work on my mental state and my expectations, I was also working on my physical health. I would put my little kids in the stroller and go for long walks in the neighborhood, or a run, and head to the playground to do pull-ups, and rings, and monkey bars for my strength training. When Alexis got old enough, I was able to go back to the gym, which was also a very good outlet. I also returned to a reduced sugar diet and tried to eat healthier. Even with all of this, that wicked postpartum depression crept up on me again. Here we go for round three.

I was so blessed with my sweet Alexis as well as she was such an easy child and required such little maintenance. They say God always gives you the child you need at the moment you need it. It was true in this case. She never fussed, hardly ever cried, and slept a lot. Sleeping was so needed because I was not getting enough sleep of my own, and the combination would have been too much to handle. Alexis was cute and cuddly and wonderful. She still is; she's just a grown-up version of that now.

As time progressed, my husband and I started to get nervous about the possibility of getting pregnant again. We reached out to several people in our inner circle for some natural family planning (NFP) advice. It didn't appear anyone could help us, and in desperation I asked everyone I could think of at the church if they taught NFP or knew somebody who did. When I got a lead, I would immediately follow up on it, but for whatever reason, I was not able to connect with anybody that could help us and started to get desperate.

Tom finally decided he would need to do something more permanent, and since I was the one who had gone through the health struggles, pregnancies, and deliveries, he decided it should be him. I cannot begin to tell you how utterly opposed I was to do this, but I couldn't come up with any good answers. Looking back on it, we could have just tried to remain celibate until I could get a better mental handle on things, but we just weren't that mature or evolved in our faith. I knew making a permanent choice like this was wrong, but I think my fear took over. In addition, Tom was not Catholic and did not really understand the teachings of the faith on this subject matter, so for him, it just seemed a

CHAPTER FIFTEEN

pretty obvious solution. We went ahead and did it, and to this day it remains one of my biggest regrets and his as well.

To add a little splash of entertainment to the story, we had a bit of an adventure the day of his surgery, but to tell it correctly, we have to back up a bit. About four days before the appointment, we had some friends over to the house, and while they worked on my husband's car, I decided to take all of the kids to the playground. It was my four kids and a couple of others. So once we got to the playground, Faye asked me if she could do the rings. She loved to do the rings. So I hoisted her up there and watched her go across a few of them. She looked proficient, so I asked her if it was okay if I went and checked on some of the other kids, and she said that was fine. When I got over to the basketball court, I heard her cry out. I came running back over to her, and she had fallen off the rings onto her arm. She cried for a little while and then settled down as she always had, so we thought she was okay. We headed home shortly after that and got some ice on her arm, and although I thought she had broken her arm, she settled down so quickly I was hoping she would be okay.

From that day forward, she was fine unless she put any weight on the arm. Her forearm hurt only when it was weight bearing, which told me she had probably broken it. Tom of course was convinced it was fine and told me not to worry about it. It's a classic case of the mom over worrying and the dad under worrying. On the fourth day of her still having trouble, I decided it was time to take her in. I decided not to tell my husband because he had enough to worry about with his upcoming surgery and headed to the doctor. Sure enough, once he took the X-ray, he saw the break in her arm. After that he sent us to get a cast on her arm and then headed home. As soon as we got home and my husband saw her, he couldn't believe it. I told him the doctor had taken X-rays, and it was broken. What's that saying? Oh yeah, Mother knows best, haha! So we proceeded to load him up in the car and all headed over to his surgery appointment. It didn't take long, and then he was back home with us.

We kept rolling along, raising our kids and trying to rebuild our relationship. I was back in the throes of the postpartum, but at least I had my therapist to keep an eye on me. Another lovely gem that comes with this type of depression is a feeling of generalized anxiety. Now this is a term I was not familiar with but I got to know rather intimately over the course of the next six months or so. Generalized anxiety can bring about feelings of panic over things you don't necessarily have control over or may not even be a real problem. In some cases the anxiety can manifest itself over things that are not really happening—irrational fears. As an example, early on in Alexis's life I started panicking that I would run out of breast milk for my baby and wouldn't be able to feed her. It was an overwhelming feeling of panic that I wouldn't be able to nurse my child. It was irrational because I wasn't having any problems with my milk supply to begin with, but even if I did, I could still buy formula at the store if I needed to. My child would not go hungry.

As my anxiety increased, so did the concern from my therapist. She told Tom and I both to keep an eye on things, and if it got worse, to contact her. This is when she brought up the possibility of taking antidepressants. Now antidepressants had been suggested for me before with my postpartum depression after Agnes was born, as well as other episodes of depression in my past. I, however, did not want to take this medication because I saw what it did to people that took it. It may have helped them cope with their lives, but it made them disconnected and seemingly unemotional about most things. I had a real fear of using this medication—and this was not irrational.

CHAPTER FIFTEEN

Unfortunately for me, things did get worse in the anxiety department, and I was out of options. We had gone to church, and on our way home, I asked my husband to stop by one of the Christian bookstores so I could buy something. When he drove up to the store, it was closed, and we laughed to ourselves that of course it was closed because it was a Sunday, and it was a Christian bookstore. We got home about five minutes later, and I turned to him and asked him why he didn't stop by the bookstore. He turned around and looked at me with complete confusion on his face and said we did stop by the store, and it was closed because it was Sunday—remember?

I didn't remember having stopped by the store, and this sent me into a whirlwind of panic. I went into the closet and started crying. I asked Tom what I was going to do. I started worrying I might forget my own children in the car or in a store, and it was a real panic for me. I was so afraid I would leave them somewhere. Since my panic was so irrational at this point, my husband said I think it's time for me to call your therapist. He did, and she ordered me some antidepressants. I began to take them and started to feel moderately better, but it changed my personality.

After about two months of being on the antidepressant, my husband approached me and said, "I don't like what this medication is doing to you. You seem numb all the time." I agreed because I felt numb, but what else was I to do. I had no good options. Nonetheless we bravely decided I should stop taking them and see how I did. I don't know if it was because I was coming out of my postpartum depression, or I just felt much better when I was off of the antidepressant, but either way it was a turn for the positive. I stayed in therapy for quite a while, and it was very helpful.

Tom also started acting differently toward me, which was a

definite positive. He was acting like a new and improved husband who seemed to want to be a family. I'm not sure when it happened, but at some point we must have talked about whether or not he wanted to stay with me. He said he agreed we had made the choice to get married, and the kids had no choice in the matter, so he wanted to keep trying. I was thrilled to hear this but believe it or not still apprehensive. It's a crazy psychological thing that happens when you're on the verge of divorce, that your marriage feels more unstable and built on sand rather than rock. It was going to take some time for both of us to feel strong again.

As things were turning around, my husband came up to me one day and said he wanted to go through the RCIA (rite of Christian initiation for adults) program at church. He and I had talked about auditing these classes in the past as a way for me to learn more about my faith. I said I would love to audit the class with him to which he responded, "No, I don't want to audit the class; I want to take them. I'm thinking of becoming Catholic." I was absolutely in shock but decided to try and stay as calm as possible and proceeded to iron out the details.

We decided to go and ask his parents if they would be willing to babysit the kids once a week for the length of the course—which was thirty-six weeks long. We both wondered what they would say when they realized he was joining the church. So on one of our visits to their house, we asked them about babysitting, and they agreed to it. We made sure to tell them it was a class to learn about the Catholic Church, and then left it at that. They never asked another question about it for the entire length of time we were going. We thought this was rather odd considering they weren't exactly fans of the Catholic Church.

In addition to this, Tom and Tony had somewhat reconciled and were trying to rebuild their relationship. Tony also

CHAPTER FIFTEEN

announced he and Ashley were going to have a baby. It was a very exciting time for everyone, and we were glad things were going in a more positive direction. After all, it had been a very difficult few years, and we were all very worn out. I'm amazed by how much we were able to endure and stay married. I feel like none of this could have happened without the beautiful sacraments of our faith and the help of the Holy Spirit guiding and directing us, even when we didn't want to be guided and directed.

Tom finished the course, and the day arrived for him to come fully into the church. He had already been baptized when he was a baby, so he needed to do his first Reconciliation (Confession), first Communion, and Confirmation at the Easter Vigil. We had a good-sized gathering of people at this Easter Vigil, but unfortunately my parents couldn't make it because my mom was very sick—more to that story in a minute. We were all very proud of Tom and how far he had come. I was very moved that night because he received communion for the first time, and he had been longing for it. Truth be told, I was still a little bit in shock by the fact he had decided to become a Catholic. I assume that's what was happening with his parents as well, because right as he was walking up to receive his sacraments, his father handed him a folded up document talking about Martin Luther and how good the Lutheran faith was. John literally had thirty-six weeks to talk to Tom about any of this, and instead chose this night, the night when he receives the sacraments and joins the church, to give him an article on why the Lutheran faith is better than the Catholic faith. What he didn't know was that article confirmed even more the choice Tom had made.

As I had mentioned earlier, my mom was not doing well and could not attend the Vigil Mass for Tom. The story goes like this. My mom had been sick with a cold and a cough for a couple of months. Apparently the cough just kept getting worse and worse. On one particular night, after Mass, my mom got so bad with her coughing that she couldn't even walk. It was at that point in time my dad knew something more serious was going on, so he called an ambulance. They came and picked her up and took her to the hospital. I received a call from my dad the next day when I was at a friend's wedding shower telling me my mom was in the hospital. When I finished the shower I headed over to the hospital to see her, and things were definitely bad.

By the time I got there, quite a few of my family members were there and were talking with the doctors and nurses, and they were trying to get an evaluation. What we were eventually told is she had pulmonary embolism (multiple blood clots) throughout her lungs, and they were concerned one might break loose and go to her heart or her brain. A decision was made at that moment to put her on some blood thinners. In addition to that, they discovered she was very anemic, and she would also need to have a blood transfusion. My mom was very worried about this when she talked to my older sister because she was afraid of getting AIDS. My sister assured her everything was going to be okay, and my mom decided to take the blood transfusion.

After the blood thinners and blood transfusion, things went to the proverbial "hell in a hand basket." Unbeknownst to any of us, she had coughed so hard she had torn a hole in her abdominal wall, and with the additional blood, a lot of it went through the tear and into the abdominal cavity itself, causing severe abdominal swelling. In addition, the staff told us she was also struggling with her blood pressure because it was very low. We were told at that time they couldn't give her any pain medication because her blood pressure was too low, so she was suffering immensely and could not get any relief—it was horrible to watch her go through

CHAPTER FIFTEEN

so much pain. One of the nights in the ICU it was believed she suffered another heart attack. My older sister and I stayed in the hospital and slept on the couches in the ICU waiting room for most of that first week. We were afraid she was going to die, and we wanted to make sure somebody was with her. Our dad asked us to make sure she didn't die alone.

As time went on, and more fluid began to build up, it started to become clear she was going into renal failure. This went on for a couple of days, and while they were doing the best they could to take care of her, it looked like her organs were starting to shut down. When I would walk into the room to see her and pray with her, I could hear her talking to people. I was told later this is what they call ICU hallucinations, but I know it was different than that. I could tell she was actually talking to some of her loved ones because her voice was so sweet, and she would say things like, "I miss you; I haven't seen you in so long." I was 100 percent sure this was going to be the end, and I was preparing to say goodbye and let her out of her suffering.

God, however, had other plans, and as things got worse for my mom, the doctors came in with their prognosis and evaluation. Basically they said her kidneys were shut down and the only thing left to do, to keep her alive, would be to start her on dialysis. The doctor said she would most likely not make it through dialysis because of her low blood pressure, but he left it up to all of us to decide what we wanted to do. The whole family was there, except for one person, so we decided to discuss what we should do. I was of the mindset we needed to ease her pain as much as possible, and then let her go; others were not in that same mindset. When it was clear the conversation wasn't going in the direction my dad thought it should, he finally stood up and said, "I am making the decision, and we are putting her on dialysis, and God will decide the rest from there." I was upset with this because I thought it was an unnecessary attempt to try and keep her alive, but that was not the case as I found out later.

The moment came to start dialysis, and they began their first treatment, and much to their amazement, she lived through it. Getting the fluid off of her body was of immense help. From this point forward, we just kept the process going, and she slowly started to get better. She was in ICU for a couple of weeks, but once she started getting better, they moved her over to the rehabilitation area of the hospital. It was very clear to all of us she was going to make it and be able to go home again. One of the nurses from the ICU unit told us she has seen this happen a lot where the doctors are convinced a patient is going to die, but he or she ends up recovering. She said it happens when they have a lot of loved ones around them, and that always gives them the will to fight. Let me tell you, when it came to fighting, my mom was a champion at it. She was the toughest old broad I think I ever knew.

CHAPTER SIXTEEN

2004/2005

Well slowly but surely my mom started to improve and looked forward to the day she could get home. It was a kind of interesting process for my younger sister and I, watching my mom go through what she had. As I had mentioned earlier, she had been in ICU for about two weeks and was not able to eat anything. Once they moved her to the rehab unit, her appetite was still tanked, and she didn't eat hardly anything for another two weeks. It finally occurred to my sister that after all of that time, you would think my mother would have lost a lot of weight, but she did not. She approached the doctor about this, and his only comment was that they had much bigger things to worry about than our mom losing weight. My sister clarified, however, that was not the point she was trying to make; she was trying to explain to him how unusual it would be for anyone to go for that long without any real amount of food and not lose weight. She told him our mother complained for years while we were growing up she could never lose weight no matter how hard she dieted, and here we were seeing proof of that before our very eyes. I think this finally got the attention of the doctor. I do not remember how much investigating they did in this subject matter, but I did hear they had determined my mom had a metabolic imbalance that caused her to not be able to shed the pounds. I've often wondered if I suffer from the same thing.

Aside from that, it was a welcome relief to know our mom was going to return home. When she made it back home, I decided to be brave one day and have a deep conversation with my mom regarding her near death experience. If you remember me telling you, this was always a very difficult subject matter for my mom, so it was hard for me to approach the discussion. I asked her what it was like for her when she was in the deepest throws of her unconscious state. When she began sharing with me her experience, it was with much fear and trepidation. She told me it was nothing like she had read or heard from others. She said she never saw a bright light or heard kind voices or felt warmth and love. Instead she experienced the opposite, and for her it was cold and dark and overwhelmingly scary. It scared her so much that all she wanted to do was get out of there. That is when she told me she had expressed this desperation to my dad in a private moment between the two of them. She begged him to help her live. In that moment, I saw my dad in a completely different light and realized how much he had done for my mom to save her from the abyss. He was her hero.

Even though my mom had returned home, we were definitely not out of the woods yet. She still needed a lot of care and had to be transported to dialysis three times a week. My dad took her when he could, and in the meantime, my sister and I balanced the rest of the visits to the dialysis center. As mentioned before, I lived in Colorado Springs, so I had to drive up to Denver with all four of my kids a couple of times a week. I did it, without thinking, because that is what you do for your family. The stress on

CHAPTER SIXTEEN

my husband and I, and the kids for that matter, was immense. I was trying to balance taking my kids to school, taking care of toddlers, and going up to Denver to help my parents. Talking to my husband recently, he reminded me of how difficult getting up to Denver was because our cars kept breaking down, and we had to borrow his parents' extra vehicles periodically just to get up there.

As if that wasn't enough of a stressor, I think God believed we could handle even more (however, he didn't ask me directly or I gladly would have informed him I thought he was wrong). My dad managed to injure his knee, and it appeared to have probably done some soft tissue damage. As the story goes, my dad told me he went to the doctor, they took X-rays, and there was nothing broken. I tried to explain to my dad that soft tissue injuries do not show up on an X-ray, and it might do him some good to go back and have an MRI done. Once again, when the fifth child speaks, it's as if we are talking in a foreign language. Either nobody understands what we're saying, or they just stop listening; either way, the results are the same.

The following accounts of these events came from my sister as I was not present during the event. One evening as my dad was heading downstairs, he put his weight on his non-injured leg and it immediately gave out, causing him to tumble down the stairs. For whatever reason, my mom decided to call my older sister Anne first to let her know what had happened. My sister told them to call an ambulance, and she would drive over and help. When she got there, he was lying at the bottom of the stairs and was in a lot of pain when the ambulance showed up. They somehow managed to get four men and a gurney down the stairs, which was a very tight space. My dad was a big man, and it took all four of these gentlemen to lift him up and put him on the gurney (wish I had video of that). My sister followed the ambulance over to the hospital, and someone else came and stayed with my mom.

They checked my dad into the emergency room, and after a while of being there the doctors came out and told my sister they were going to release him. My sister became very emphatic, which is unusual for her, and said, "He can't go home; he can't even walk." The doctor then proceeded to examine him only to find out he had a complete tendon tear and would have to have surgery. Suddenly they realized they would need to check him into the hospital, and he would be staying there for a while—a fact my sister knew from the minute she saw him at the bottom of the stairs in my parents' house. What can you say; common sense is not so common anymore.

I of course came back up to Denver when I found out what had happened to my dad, and we took turns at the hospital with my dad before, during, and after his surgery. We also still had to take care of our mom as she needed to be transported to the dialysis center during the week. She of course wanted to see her husband, so we had to transport her over there to visit with our dad. The only real blessing in all of this was the dialysis center was part of the same hospital where my dad was undergoing surgery and would be recovering. I cannot tell you what a difference this seemingly small fact made in mine and my sister's hectic lives.

Luckily my dad went through surgery very quickly and started recovering nicely. When he was at the hospital, and my sister and I were performing our juggling act, it became clear to us that something needed to change in the at-home care of our parents. We talked to my dad together one of the times we were in the hospital visiting him. We explained to him we thought they would need a lot more additional care than she and I

CHAPTER SIXTEEN

could provide. Surprisingly our dad agreed (at that moment), and we started talking about assisted living facilities. I had already offered for them to come down and live with me and my family in Colorado Springs, but they did not want to do that, for reasons of their own. So the minute my dad showed any kind of interest in the idea of assisted living, I got to work.

I called about eight to ten assisted living facilities around the hospital and the area where my parents lived. I talked to the managers of the residences at all these facilities, got pricing, and set up walkthroughs. I put so many hours into making these phone calls and arrangements. I had to talk to my dad about some of his finances, which he was not too surprisingly very guarded about, but I needed to know where he was financially. Just when I thought I had a couple of good options for facilities around the area, my dad pulled the plug. A few days after our initial conversation, when I started going over some of the details with my dad, he got very angry and said we can't afford assisted living, and that's not going to work. As quickly as the search started, it ended.

When my dad was released from the hospital, he could not be transported in a regular car, so my sister-in-law pulled the back seat out of her van and drove him home. She transported him around to all his doctor's appointments because we had no other way of getting him there unless we called one of the handicap transportation vans. I will always be grateful to her for all the help she gave my dad. When my dad was home and situated, my sister and I set up a meeting between the four of us.

The two of us talked about the meeting long before we had it to make sure we were aligned in our approach with my dad. You must understand our dad was—what shall we say—one of the most stubborn men we have ever met in our lives. He was also very headstrong and opinionated, which did not make for a good overall balance. We needed to talk to him about hiring help to come into the home, and we were very sure it wouldn't go over very well. As usual we were not wrong in our calculations.

We sat down with Mom and Dad and said they needed more help than we could provide on our own, and if they were no longer open to the idea of an assisted living facility, then we needed to talk about hiring a company to come into the house and help. I had already contacted a few of these in-home care companies and narrowed down what I thought was a good match. We continued to discuss the in-home care options; which consisted of anything from cooking, cleaning, and running errands, all the way to doing laundry, driving them to doctor's appointments, and if need be, bathing and dressing. We figured we could start out small and build into more assistance as they needed it.

Once I suggested they needed this additional care, my dad immediately stopped me and told me they didn't need any help. He basically tried to shake me off abruptly and inform me they were self-sufficient. Since my sister and I both knew what was coming, we were prepared. I looked at my dad and said if that's the case, then you are no longer going to call us when you need someone to take you to a doctor appointment or run mom over to dialysis or pick up your prescriptions, etc. . . . I told him from now on he would have to do this stuff on his own. I also told him the next time he fell down the stairs not to call me because I'm not going to come. At that moment, I looked over at my sister and said "don't call her because neither one of us is going to be coming." I knew this was the only way to handle my dad and get him the help he needed. Believe it or not, he started to argue again when my mom told him to shut up, sit down, and listen to us.

When we left that night, I handed him a contract for one of

CHAPTER SIXTEEN

the agencies I had contacted, and all he needed to do was sign the contract, and we could make a phone call and get someone over to their house right away. The next morning, my dad called me on the phone, and like a defeated child he said he signed my stupid form and that I should be happy because I got what I wanted. To which I responded, "I'm very glad, and it is what I wanted because now I know you'll be taken care of." (Not the response he expected.) Within the next couple of days, they brought over a care worker, and my parents immediately bonded with her and started to relax. It was one of the best things we had ever done.

While things were getting a little bit better for my parents, I still had my life to attend to and all the issues and problems we were struggling with as a family. Things seemed to be better with Tom's parents as well as his brother, and we were slowly reconnecting. We were doing our best to balance our time with his parents and brother's family as well as my family. During this time, Justin and Faye were both doing school and starting sports. We were a busy family, that's for sure, and we loved being involved in our kids' activities and schooling.

Justin attended a private school just a couple of blocks from our house in a very quiet neighborhood. We really loved the school, but I had found out about a highly recommended charter school from some friends of ours, so we were interested. We decided to go to the open house and see what it was all about. This charter school was remarkable as they had students excelling in academics and followed a different model of teaching than we had ever seen before. They gave us material on studies showing the different types of learning and the number of repetitions it took for various students to learn. There were kids considered low repetition learners, medium repetition learners, and high repetition learners, and all these students could and would be able to learn the material, it just would take longer for some than others. I found this fascinating as I was an individual that needed a lot more repetition than most of the students around me. I felt like this type of school would have helped me a lot.

We were sold on the idea of going to the school, and luckily, because our daughter was entering kindergarten, this bumped our son up on the waitlist so he could attend as well. It was a very rigorous school and was located all the way across town, which required a lot of driving. I was willing to put in the time and the effort if it meant that things would be better for my kids. So we got them enrolled and started school.

My kids did well; although, Justin had to play catch up because he had not been at the school for the last couple of years and therefore had a lot to learn. He was a very smart boy, however, so it didn't take him long. Faye loved her teacher and the class, and she was doing very well and was one of the top students. I couldn't believe it, but they were teaching these kids how to do cursive in kindergarten, and she learned it very well. They even gave me a book at the beginning of the summer to teach Faye how to read so that by the time she entered the school she would already be reading. The summer reading program with Faye was a battle though. This was one of the few times I ever saw that sweet-tempered child get defiant, and defiant she was. I fought with her every day that summer to get through her training, but alas she completed the book. That child loved Dr. Seuss more than any kid I have ever seen, and for years those were the only books she wanted to read on her own.

Justin was doing quite well in school, even though he had a much tougher teacher. She was very abrasive and difficult to get along with, and I was a bit worried right from the start. This woman was a rule follower and time oriented, and I am not either

CHAPTER SIXTEEN

one of those things, so I was worried I would mess things up for my son. There were a couple of times I did mess things up for him, and he ended up getting punished for it. I made him late for school a couple of times, and on one occasion, I forgot to sign his homework, even though he asked me to do it. When I found out he had gotten punished for that, I marched right into the classroom and challenged the teacher. She tried to explain the purpose for the rules and why they couldn't make exceptions. I responded by saying life is not black and white and rigid but instead is always moving, changing and adapting, and that it wasn't fair to punish the child for the parents' mistakes. She removed the mark against my son that time but told me she wouldn't do it again. It was actually a good experience for both of us, the teacher and I, and for some reason brought us closer.

As time went on and we adjusted to the new rules, and the superstructure of the school, I started to see some problems. To begin with, my son is naturally a perfectionist and overachiever, being the oldest child and all. He was so hard on himself that he kept getting sick, and one of the illnesses had culminated in him rupturing his eardrum. I was starting to see a pattern related to his health and the intensity of the school, and I didn't think it was a very good thing. In addition, there wasn't much time for socializing, playing, or kids getting to know each other. The PTA tried to do more social activities outside of school, but very few people would attend, so there was no good way to get these kids social time together.

I went in to talk to the interim principal at the time to explain my concerns regarding the lack of socializing. She was less than interested in hearing my opinions on things and more interested in telling me how things were. She immediately attacked my children and said they must be troublemakers, which she thought would be the only reason I would be in there talking to her. She got my blood boiling, but I took a deep breath, got very calm, and said if you think that's the case, go and talk to their teachers. I challenged her to investigate it and to see how my children really were doing in their classes. To the best of my knowledge, I don't think she ever did this. I think she didn't enjoy what she did for a living, and it appeared the position had been thrust upon her, and she wasn't really taking to it very naturally. Either way, the combination of my son's illnesses and the lack of social activities for the kids made us decide we should probably pull them out at the end of the year and maybe go back to our old school, and that is what we did.

Unfortunately, when we got back to the old school, the principal had left, and a new principal had taken his place. She didn't run to school the way the prior principal had and had managed to chase off a lot of families. You see, this was a private school run and supported by a church community, and when this principle took over, it literally split the church in half. We came in on the tail end of that, so it wasn't great timing. In addition, there were a limited number of teachers at the school, so my son and daughter were in a combo class of first, second, and third graders and only one teacher.

Their teacher was a very kind person and very good at teaching science to the kids, as that was her major interest. The problem, however, was she had no idea how to manage a classroom, let alone one with kids of mixed ages. To put it bluntly, it was absolute chaos when I walked into the classroom, and it was stressing my kids to be in the classroom all day. They would come home from school and tell me how noisy it was and how the disruptive students were never disciplined, and my kids couldn't get their schoolwork done.

CHAPTER SIXTEEN

I visited the classroom on a number of occasions to talk to the teacher, and she was actively working at trying to implement new ideas to make the classroom function better, but to no avail. On one occasion I got called into the principal's office only to find out one of the students got triggered by something another student had said, and he picked up a chair and threw it across the classroom. This child was only in first grade. You can see things were not under control. I decided it wasn't fair for me to judge the teacher without spending an entire day in the classroom so that is what I did. I arranged a day to come in and stay the full day—seven hours. It was loud, unruly, disruptive, and very frustrating to watch. I witnessed the teacher asking my son to sit in the back with a couple of the students and teach them math. Yes, that's right; she was asking him to tutor the other kids.

I had talked to the principal on several occasions about what was going on in the classroom, but she always reacted defensively. It got bad enough they even had the superintendent show up for a couple of unannounced visits, and they didn't get a good report card from the superintendent. Even with all of this, it wasn't enough to get the principal to do anything. So after about six months, I decided to take them out to homeschool them. My response to the principal was that I was paying tuition, and my kids were having to teach the other students or getting ignored in the classroom, and I can ignore them for free at home.

As you can tell, I was dang frustrated with the whole situation. So we pulled them out of school, brought them home, and I started to teach. I never had a desire to homeschool my kids, and when it got thrust upon me, I did not handle it very well. I cried so much over the course of the next year because I did not know how to homeschool my kids. Now I am so grateful God closed every door to me and forced me through another—the homeschooling door. It was the best thing we ever did for our kids because it brought us all closer as a family, presented us with the opportunity for unlimited learning, and most of all deepened our faith and absolute love of God. It made my children whole.

While all this drama was going on in our lives, Tony and Ashley found out they were having another baby. She ended up delivering a beautiful baby girl she named Taylor, and she and Tony appeared to be doing much better. Ashley and I didn't have an extraordinarily close relationship anymore, but I got along well with her family, and we got to see them regularly at family functions. Tony seemed to be very close with Ashley's family as well and especially close with her father. He would come out a lot and help them work on things in the house, building projects etc.... We were glad just to be able to talk to them again and get to know the kids.

Not surprisingly, my health was still an issue, so my chiropractor started me on a natural thyroid medication. This was a game changer. Even though it was a small dose, it was enough to make me start seeing the world differently. For years I had a hard time experiencing joy (even with my wonderful family), but this small hormonal support gave me a taste of what life could really be like. You know, it's a strange thing when you spend most of your life in a certain psychological state. It doesn't always occur to you other people aren't living the same way. I was in absolute shock most of the people I knew lived like this most of the time. You might find this a little surprising yourselves, but it made me somewhat sad—almost feeling a little bit jipped—that I hadn't gotten to experience this throughout my life. Ultimately, God was working behind the scenes in all of this, but I didn't know it, so I couldn't give him credit yet.

CHAPTER SEVENTEEN

2006/2007

We were living day to day and trying to hold ourselves together. Somewhere along the way, we decided we wanted to redo our kitchen / living room area. We decided we wanted to repaint both rooms, lay new hardwood flooring—laminate as it was finally decided—and put in nicer baseboards to make it look more updated. We were novices at this, so naturally there was a learning curve, and it took longer than anticipated (although I don't know many projects that get done in the time calculated anyway). We were able to buy a table saw cheaply, which made the cutting of the boards a lot easier. It became a family project, and I still have memories of all of us kneeling in the living room holding floorboards and trying to slide them in and connect them. The little kids didn't always have the strength to do it, so it was quite entertaining. It brings a smile to my face even thinking about it now.

The smile quickly got wiped off my face as the next catastrophe hit. The crawlspace flooded, and when we went to clean it, we realized my husband's stamp collection from his granddad was soaked and destroyed, along with my beautiful wedding dress. I remember pulling the boxes out of the crawlspace—filled with emotion—taking them out to the corner—and tossing them in a heap of trash. Everything we had to throw away that day was covered in mold, so there was no way to recover it. A day later, the wicked witch of house projects decided to provide us with another hurdle. She made sure our refrigerator and oven conked out on us. Oh, what joy this brought.

We would not be deterred, however, and replaced the appliances, fixed the leak, and continued to replace the floor and finish painting. We eventually finished that project, minus some final trim work, and fell in love with the results. For the last couple of summers, I had also been working outside in our yard trying to do a beginner's version of landscaping. I decided I wanted to have a garden and proceeded to dig out a large section of the backyard to put in a nice vegetable garden. It just so happened our house was built on a hill, so the only way to get the chunks of grass and debris out of the backyard was with a wheelbarrow, and I can't even remember how many trips up the steep embankment I made. I laugh now because I always liked to have the opportunity to get my cardio and strength training workouts in and thought it was very special the family allowed me this opportunity to fulfill that dream.

The summer before, I had decided to re-sod the entire front yard, which was a comedy all on its own. You see during that time there was a drought in Colorado, so we had severe watering restrictions. I, being the person that I am—more action-oriented than pre-planning—just decided I was going to dig up the yard and then lay the sod. I knew I would have to get a rototiller, which is a device I was not familiar with and still to this day have not become an expert in, to start this project. This entire landscaping vision I had was, shall we say, an open wound in

CHAPTER SEVENTEEN

our marriage. I have no idea why married couples fight over the stupidest things, but landscaping was our "coup de gras." We had bickered and fought for months, maybe even a couple of years, over what we were going to do with the yard. The yard was quickly declining and being overtaken by weeds, and I did not have the time to take care of it, and my husband did not have the interest. I thought it was time to redo the whole front yard, and he did not think it was a worthwhile expense. Lines were drawn.

After a couple of conversations with friends, and others who had redone their yards, along with a bit of investigation, I decided it needed to be done. I let my husband know for a couple of weeks beforehand what day I was planning on doing the rototilling and that I was going to go and rent a rototiller. He never said anything, and when the day finally came—as I was heading out to get it—he picked a huge fight with me. Fueled with anger, and too much coffee, I went over to scoop up my dirt-chewing machine. The men helping me went through a brief tutorial, attached the trailer to transport the rototiller to the back of my car, and waved goodbye. When I got to the house, I had no clue how to get the damn thing off the trailer, let alone what I was going to do next. So after screaming in the front yard for a couple of minutes my husband finally yanked the machinery down off the trailer, put it on the yard, and walked away. After what seemed like hours, I finally started getting the hang of the machine and felt pretty confident. Confident that is until I hit a buried telephone line between my neighbors and us. Now I was panicking. The next call I made was to a friend of my husband's who was a landscaper.

Josh raced over to the house immediately, dug into the dirt to find the telephone line, and like a seasoned professional, or someone who had made this mistake a few times himself, quickly reconnected the line and buried it back in the ground. I know what you all are thinking, that I didn't call utility services to have it all marked beforehand, but that would be incorrect as I did call them, and they did not mark the area where the telephone line was. It didn't matter at this point because the problem was fixed, and I was back up and running. I finished the rototilling, reloaded the machine onto the trailer, and returned it to its original location.

I had scheduled to have sod delivered to my house a few days later and felt so good and confident I had done this project mostly on my own. As I started talking myself up to friends and family members, I discovered yet another interesting fact. Apparently, if I was going to get permission from the city to water more frequently with the new sod, I had to add a mixture of compost like material into the ground before I could lay the sod. This created two more problems: 1) I had to order the soil to be dropped off, and 2) I would have to re-rent the rototiller to mix it all into the yard. And guess what was next on the agenda? That's right, a fight with the husband, and this time his parents decided to jump on board. They all thought it was a waste of time and money to lay new sod, and they were not nice about it; they were downright mean. It really upset me they all ganged up on me, and it added even more fun to the situation.

I didn't care anymore if he liked it or not because I was halfway through the job and because I wanted to finish this task and make my yard look beautiful. I pushed through my anger, sadness, and frustration and moved forward. I rescheduled the sod delivery, scheduled a delivery for the compost, and re-rented the rototiller. Once I got all the compost mixed back in, we had a sod-laying party. I couldn't believe it, but my husband came out to participate—as did our children—which came as no surprise

CHAPTER SEVENTEEN

since they loved doing projects—and finally our neighbors even came and assisted. It really didn't take long, as the front yard wasn't that big, and I was relieved. Once a couple of weeks had passed with regular watering, the yard started to look beautiful, and I couldn't have been prouder of the results.

I proceeded to continue the project in the backyard as well, finished digging up the garden, and dug out a play area for the kids. I got a bunch of sand delivered and hauled it down into the designated area in the backyard—once again by wheelbarrow—and the kids were loving this giant sandbox to play in. I got all the soil ready in the garden, contacted Josh once again, and hired him to put in a drip system for the garden. After he finished, I planted all the vegetables. I was quite excited about the drip system because we were going out of town for two weeks, and I knew, with the system in place, the garden would get watered while we were away.

We left on our trip with everything in place and a bit of peace in my heart not having to worry about my freshly planted vegetables. When we arrived back home and I went out to see the garden, it was very clear the vegetables had indeed gotten watered. The problem, however, was it was overwatered, and there were pools of water all over the garden. I called Josh immediately to come and look at it, and he discovered one of the valves had gotten stuck open, so it watered the entire time we were gone. By then it was too late, and at least half of the vegetables were ruined. This is one of those moments where you throw your arms up in the air and say, "Come on, now you have got to be kidding me." Of course it was no joke, just my usual brand of reality. If you are quietly laughing at this part of the story, you are not alone. At some point, things become so ridiculous you must laugh, and laugh we did.

2006/2007

Yard work wasn't the only difficult thing happening; my husband was also struggling with his job. He had been working at the utility company in town since our oldest son was born and had really enjoyed the job. He had a wonderful boss, great coworkers, and was growing his skill set by working on numerous projects and taking classes on networking to add numerous certifications to his bag of technical tools. He was growing his resume as well with all the experience he was getting. Eventually, however, as life always keeps moving, his boss decided to move into another position, and his replacement was, what shall we say . . . lacking in skills and aptitude for managing people.

The next year, under her tutelage, several people quit, and unfortunately a coworker of Tom's took his life. Now I would never place the blame for this suicide in the hands of his manager, but she certainly did not make it easier for him, or anyone else, to work under her. It was becoming more and more clear to us Tom was probably not going to last much longer in this job. So we decided it would be best for him to cut loose. He interviewed and got a job offer for a company up in Denver. He worked that job for almost two years, driving to Denver in the crazy traffic and sometimes horrendous weather, to make money for his family. I will forever appreciate how hard he has always worked for us.

As our home repair project and landscaping soiree was happening, my husband had been actively job searching because his company in Denver was laying people off and downsizing. Tom was also very worn out from the commute, and it was time to give him a break and find a job closer to home (little did we know that home would be changing). I was in the backyard, literally laying down the last few paving stones in the yard, when Tom announced the news. He had been interviewing for a couple of

CHAPTER SEVENTEEN

positions and had just gotten a job offer for a bank in western Colorado. He was very excited about the job, and it looked like the pay and location were going to be a good fit. No sooner had we finished renovating the house to our liking than we were going to be putting it on the market and selling it and then moving.

It looked like a great opportunity for Tom, and we were quite excited about the change. It was very clear to us we would not be able to move up there with him initially as I would have to stay behind with the kids to try and sell the house. The market was starting to take a downturn, so we were trying to get it sold as quickly as we could—this was during 2006 and 2007. Luckily the only thing we really had left to do was put in a new carpet upstairs, and it would be ready to sell. We had a friend that just happened to be a "stager" (a home decorator of sorts) and helped us make our house look like a model home.

While all of this was going on, my husband headed up to the mountains to start his new job. He found a room to rent from one of his coworkers, and we helped him move his stuff up into the house before he started his new job. After we got him situated and spent some time meeting his boss and some coworkers and checking out the area, we drove back home. The place we were moving was a four-hour drive from Colorado Springs, so it was a good long haul and would prove to be difficult for trips back and forth in the future. We left, and he started his new job, and we began the process of listing our house and preparing for showings.

We went with a realtor that lived two doors down from us and was a good friend of ours, and sometimes that's not the best choice. As coincidence would have it, or more importantly timing on the behalf of a realtor, we were both selling our houses at the same time. The interesting part of this scenario was her floor plan was exactly like ours. The difference, however, was we had upgraded our home, and she had not, and it made our home show better in the long run. I'm assuming that's what frustrated her. Either way, we had never bought and sold a home until this experience, so we trusted her, until we couldn't trust her anymore.

The market was already getting difficult for people to sell homes, and for some reason she decided to list our houses $5,000 higher than the comps in the area. After one week of no showings, I had her show me the price comparisons, and when we realized we were sticking out there like a sore thumb, we told her to drop the price of our house by $5,000. This became an argument between our realtor and us until finally I asserted myself. I told her to do what we were asking her to do. It wasn't but the next day when we had three showings and received our first offer.

While the market was difficult for sellers, the first offer we received was for a double contingency, which Tom and I both thought wasn't very smart. Somehow our realtor convinced us it would be a smart move because the market wasn't good. We sat out there for a month, with no ability to do any showings and all kinds of complications on the buyer's end. When the double contingency did not go through, we asked our realtor to go ahead and return their money to them and allow us to return to the market. This precipitated a two-week battle between us, our realtor, and the buyer's realtor. Our realtor argued and fought with us at every turn.

To add insult to injury, and to make this story more entertaining for the reader (which I can only assume was the purpose for all of this, sarcasm emphasized), I ended up with another stress fracture in my foot that required me to be on crutches and a root canal from hell that landed me in an oral surgeon's office. I really do hope at this point you are not shocked by what you read,

CHAPTER SEVENTEEN

but are either nodding emphatically like you know what that's like or you're laughing your head off at the image this description has conjured up. Either way you interpret this, the truth is I was in mind-numbing pain and at the end of my rope. So I did what I do best, and I cracked the proverbial whip.

Apparently I did a no-no and emailed the buyer's realtor directly, explaining exactly what I wanted done. I told her I did not think our realtor was representing us and our desires, so I wanted to make it perfectly clear. Unless our buyers were willing to forgo their earnest money while asking us to wait for even longer than the contract, I said we do not have a deal. She tried to explain to me how foolish I was, and I quickly responded by saying we will return the earnest money to your clients tomorrow, and this contract will be null and void. I think both realtors, and potential buyers, were pretty ticked off by my taking matters into my own hands, but I didn't give a darn. I waited for the angry phone call from my realtor the next day, to which I responded you work for us, do as you're told, or you will not be working for us anymore.

Shortly after this event happened, I figured out the truth of what was going on behind the scenes. Our realtor was making a side deal with our buyers to sell her house to them. When I got wind of that, I immediately contacted her broker, told him what I had found out, and said unless he wanted me to take his brokerage license as well, he had better contact her and end our contract within the day. Our realtor, being the coward she was, sent one of her family members over with the dissolved contract. I was very kind to her daughter but very angry at our realtor. If I had had any strength left in me, I definitely would have gone after her real estate license, but she lucked out because I was busy taking care of four small children and a root canal and fractured

2006/2007 CONT. . . .

foot. If you are visualizing me walking around on crutches, with a swollen face, and looking like death was knocking at my door, your visualization is correct. What a clown show!

    We quickly dissolved the contract with our realtor, hired a new one, and got the house back on the market. Needless to say, we had an offer within the week, from out of state, sight unseen. They flew out after signing the contract to do a walk-through and luckily fell in love with the house. The kids and I continued to pack up the rest of the belongings and prepare for our move to the mountains. At this point, you might ask if there were any adventures going into the move, and I will not disappoint you. Yes, there were many.

2006/2007 CONT. . . .

A few days before our move date, I had purchased a part for my husband's car to keep it from overheating, as this was the vehicle we were going to be driving in. I had someone help me put the part in and left the junkyard thinking everything was okay. The next evening, the night before the move, it started to snow of course, and our lovely little vehicle—with its beaming new part—started overheating. I had driven it over to a parts store to deposit roughly five gallons of old oil that we had in the garage. The car, with its wonderful handling and overheating engine, had managed to hit a bump and tipped something over in the back as well. I wouldn't find this out until a few minutes later. I drove up to the auto parts store and went in and asked if they had a receptacle for old oil. They said yes, I proceeded to go out to get the oil, only to discover it had tipped over in the back of the car and was slowly pouring out everywhere. So in the freezing cold and with an overheating car, I proceeded to take a

CHAPTER SEVENTEEN

plastic cup and scoop the oil straight into a trash can. I imagine I broke ten EPA rules, but I didn't give a dang. I had had enough.

As I had mentioned before, my husband was up in the town we were moving to and waiting for us at our new location. He was not able to come back down to help with the move and was arranging a new rental house for us to move into. The next morning, the day of the move, our moving truck arrived and began the process of emptying our house and all of our belongings. We had a neighbor right next door we were very close to, so she was taking care of my kids.

All of a sudden she came racing through my front door yelling that something had happened to my youngest daughter, Alexis, and she was injured. I ran next door to see what was going on. When I went into the house, they told me she had been swiveling around on a chair, it fell backward, and she hit the back of her head on the hearth. She had a good-sized gash on the back of her head and was bleeding quite a bit. We looked around for steri-strips, but there were none, so I asked if they had any superglue. Everyone looked at me in astonishment except grandma, who simply turned to me and said, "I will go get some." As soon as she got back from the store, we cleaned out the wound and superglued it closed. I had learned this trick from a friend of mine, and apparently it is the method used quite frequently in hospitals now as well. What can I say; I was a trendsetter.

While all this was going on, we were watching the news to see if Vail pass was closed. They did indeed close it, and we continued to pack the moving truck up in the meantime. We were hoping for a break in the storm, to thread the needle so to speak, and luck was in our favor. We had to get an additional car dolly to tow behind the truck because of my favorite overheating vehicle. We were left to ride in the front of the moving truck. We had a good—if not very long—ride up through the mountains to get to our new home. We scheduled the unpacking for the next day and proceeded to get ourselves ready for nighttime. As is always the case with moving, or traveling, a couple of the kids got sick, so we had to battle that little demon as well. So I scrubbed out the bathtub, got them all warmed up and cleaned up, and we headed to bed. The next day, we got everything unloaded from the truck and started the unpacking process.

We didn't know anybody up in the area except for Tom's coworker, so he kind of helped integrate us. The neighbors weren't exactly what you call friendly, so it took some time to form some friendships. There were a lot of kids in the neighborhood, who appeared to be unattended most of the time, and they managed to find their way to our house pretty quickly. This worked well for me as I loved taking care of kids and just being there for them, but it became a difficult process for my kids. Some of the boys and girls from the neighborhood were mean, sometimes kind of cruel—especially to my daughters. After a while it became clear their parents helped form their behavior. There was a young gentleman living the block over who was Justin's age, but they seemed to fight quite a bit. They ended up on the same baseball team, and the competitiveness came out. The two of them didn't actually form a friendship until shortly before we moved, which was quite the bummer.

This was a very small town we were living in and was barely even on the map. Normally I'm a city girl, and I like activity and options, so this was a big stretch for me. I can't say I loved it right off the bat, but I sure felt a lot of peace living up there. For the first time in my life, I was able to sleep. I had experienced so much insomnia for so many years I didn't think I would ever be able to sleep again. I actually struggled to get out of bed

CHAPTER SEVENTEEN

sometimes because I enjoyed sleeping so much. It wasn't until a few years later that we figured out a lot of our peace stemmed from not being close to our families and the stress that came along with that. It was especially difficult with my husband's family as they liked to put us in the middle of things. God, you knew what I needed, and provided it for me and for my family.

Shortly after we moved up to Rifle, it was my daughter's birthday, so my brother came up with his family to celebrate. This was a nice blessing because she had no friends yet and would not have had much of a party without them. We were so excited to have everybody there and decided to go ice skating in a nearby town nestled in the mountains. It was a great birthday, but some difficulties ensued with my family back home. It is not for the pages of this book to share any of the details of what happened, but my poor sister and niece had a huge crisis in their life. I think most of us remember how difficult teenage years are, and this was no exception. My sister, who at this point was divorced, definitely did not have a good co-parent to help with her daughter's struggles. So she was in crisis, called me, and we began to execute a plan for her daughter's welfare. This plan would change forms and continue for many years to come. She's such a beautiful and accomplished young lady now, proving that we can all recover our lives with God's help, and our hard work. I hope my niece realizes how very hard we have prayed for her healing.

As time went on, we got the kids involved in sports and activities, and that made a difference. We used to drive up to Glenwood Springs fairly regularly to participate in gymnastics, baseball, and enjoy our favorite pizza joint. Glenwood Springs is such a beautiful place and if you ever get the chance, you should definitely stop by and visit it. Things were going fairly well on the homeschooling front, as well as my husband's job. I benefited

2006/2007 CONT. . . .

from this new work location as they had a gym in the building, and I could go work out in the mornings. Add to that the access to free coffee, and you have my perfect day.

We drove down to Denver and Colorado Springs quite a bit to make sure to visit the family. My mom's health was still pretty bad but was in a holding pattern. I didn't leave Denver until I knew she would be okay as well as my dad. It was good timing as my younger sister, Lisa, also moved back to Colorado and could be there if Anne needed it. So when we came down to visit, I would pick up prescriptions, go and buy groceries, and make meals for my parents. My kids were very close with my mom and dad because they had a different relationship with them than some of their cousins. Because of my ranking in the family—being number five and all—my parents were too infirm to do much in the grandparent arena. In other words, where their older cousins got opportunities to be taken care of by the grandparents, taken out to eat or to kids' play areas, or the kids' sporting events, my kids got something else. My kids learned to be caretakers and spend time interacting with their grandparents. They didn't get to experience much of the typical grandparent relationships—which is a bit of sadness for me—but they got a lot of quality time with their grandparents and got to know them well.

We spent a lot of time going to visit Tom's family as well, and things were continuing to go okay. We were glad for the opportunity to reconnect, but logic told us it probably wouldn't last long, and it didn't. His family, parents, as well as his brother and family, decided to come up to visit us. It was naturally going to be fairly tight quarters because we didn't have a lot of bedrooms to host them in, but we made it work. On the day of their arrival, as we were sitting in the kitchen visiting, my son came to me and said his rabbit had died. We had two pet rabbits they

CHAPTER SEVENTEEN

loved very dearly, and his rabbit had passed. I went out to the backyard to help them get him in a container to figure out where to bury him. This rabbit experience was the oddest thing of all because none of the adults seemed interested in helping me take care of this sweet pet my son loved so much. I remember being told by one of the visitors we should just throw it in the trash. I spun around on that person very quickly and said, "Is that what we should have done with your pet dog when she died?" I said, "How insensitive can you be?" That gives you an idea of how the rest of the weekend was going to go.

I decided to load the kids and the rabbit up in the car, shovels in hand, and drive them to one of our favorite hiking trails. We dug a deep hole and buried the rabbit. We put stones on top of it to make sure the animals wouldn't get to it and said some prayers. We cried for a while and then loaded back up in the car and headed home. We ate dinner, visited for a little while, and went to bed. We woke up the next morning, had a nice breakfast, and visited again. Everything seemed to be going along reasonably well, minus the dead rabbit incident from the night before, but what a silly thing to be keeping track of, right?

Nonetheless, that evening after dinner we decided to play some card games. Now I tried to avoid playing any kind of card games, board games, or games in general because it seems to bring out the worst in my husband's family. If you add to that the consumption of alcohol—which there was a lot of—you have a problem in the making (this is probably why my husband rarely drank alcohol). Needless to say, no one wanted to listen to me when I recommended we just sit and visit or do something else. There have been quite a few times in mine and Tom's marriage where I have warned him something bad was going to happen and not to push forward. This was one of those times, and it didn't end well

2006/2007 CONT. . . .

    For some reason, Granddad decided he wanted to give Justin a hard time about girls. It is important to understand my son was a very private person, especially when it came to matters of the heart, and in addition he was still incredibly young. It was misplaced—and in my opinion inappropriate—prodding. He asked Justin if he liked any girls, and this made him blush. The more he blushed, the more granddad pestered him. As if that wasn't bad enough, Tony had to jump on the girl harassment train, and the two of them would not back off. They were both warned by their spouses to knock it off, to which they ignored the warnings and pushed forward. I finally got up, looked at both of them, and said, "If you keep doing what you're doing, I will not have my son held accountable for what happens." I then proceeded to leave the room so that I wouldn't get mad.

    Within a minute or two of me exiting the room, my son stood up and got up in his granddad's face and started yelling at him to leave him alone and back off. I imagine Granddad was in shock because he didn't say much after that. Justin stormed out of the kitchen and into the living room where I was. I just comforted him because I definitely wasn't going to discipline him after he had been provoked. My husband proceeded to have an argument in the kitchen with his dad and his brother. His brother actually had the nerve to tell my husband our son was rude and had no business talking to his granddad like that. My husband responded to both of them and said "you started it and wouldn't leave him alone, so my son has every right to defend himself."

    After a few minutes, everyone calmed down and Granddad came out into the living room where Justin and I were sitting. Believe it or not, my son stood up, walked over to his Grandad, and apologized. He told him he had no right to talk to him that way, and he was sorry he had done it. Granddad immediately

CHAPTER SEVENTEEN

apologized to him and said that it wasn't his fault. He actually took responsibility for having provoked the whole fight. It wasn't often, or almost never from my memory, he apologized for things he had done, but it was nice to see him respond in this manner.

Everyone kind of settled down, and we all decided to get ready for bed. I could tell Ashley was very upset with Tony as well as Grandma with Granddad. The funny thing is the two of them could never see the similarities in their relationships. They both lived with husbands that had the same temperament and personality and had a tendency to lose their temper. Both women reacted in the same manner toward their husbands. They would try to communicate with their spouses, and when that didn't work, they would just shut down. It's like they knew the ship was about to hit an iceberg, but they had been in that position so many times they knew how to navigate away from the iceberg, but that just meant the rest of us were going to get sunk either way.

We got up the next morning and they all ate breakfast, gathered their belongings, and headed out of town. It was all rather civil the next day. As soon as they left, my husband and I got to talking, and I told him I felt like something was really wrong between Tony and Ashley. I said, "I can't tell you exactly what it is, but I think something very bad is coming down the pike." Little did I know how accurate that statement was. And little did I know how once again we would get dragged into the middle of the drama. We thought the distance would preclude us from being involved. How wrong we were.

CHAPTER EIGHTEEN

2008/2009

I had a hint something was awry in Tony and Ashley's marriage because of an incident my son and I experienced a few months prior. When we were down in Denver visiting family we got a call from Sue and John that her brother Steve had suffered a heart attack and was not doing well. He had been transported to a hospital in a small town in Oklahoma, and they didn't know how he was going to do. At the moment we found this out we were visiting my aunt and uncle on my dad's side of the family, who were struggling with their own health problems, and we were trying to make sure we spent time with them as often as possible.

I believe I have mentioned before how close I was to Tom's Uncle Steve. He had a heart of gold and would literally give the shirt off of his back for anyone that needed help. He was a craftsman, handyman, and a mechanic all wrapped up in one. He and I spent a lot of time together in the early years of my marriage with Tom and became quite close. He was the one member of the family I always felt like I wasn't judged by and was always accepted just as I was. Tom was always very close to him as well since he lived in Colorado Springs when Tom and Tony were

CHAPTER EIGHTEEN

growing up. Steve was my friend. So you can imagine how upset I was, as well as the rest of the family, when I heard he had suffered multiple heart attacks.

So my husband and I came up with a game plan for who would go out to Oklahoma to see him. It was decided Justin and I would drive with Tony down to Oklahoma and spend a few days there. I felt like this was a good opportunity for us to get some one-on-one time and try to get to know each other again. We actually had a very good trip and enjoyed some good and funny conversations. Tony was actively swimming at this point in time and was able to tell me about all the swim training he was doing. I of course could share my addiction to exercise as well, and it created a good common ground. He enjoyed time with Justin as well and enjoyed a lot of playful banter.

When we arrived at the hospital in Oklahoma, we got in touch with Sue and John, who naturally had also driven down to spend time with Steve. We met at the hospital and proceeded to find his room and invade his quiet little space with a bunch of worried, loving, and needy family members. Steve was awake when we came in, and although he looked very pale and very sick, he still gave us one of his beautiful smiles and seemed quite happy to have us all there. When it was getting close to the end of visiting time a decision was made about who should stay in the room with him and spend the night.

This was one of my most fond memories that night in the hospital room with Steve because it was a bonding moment for Sue and me. You see, the hospital had allowed for two of us to stay in the room, but they only had two chairs—neither one of which was very comfortable—so we sat across from each other, put our feet up on each other's chairs, and proceeded to get some sleep. In that moment, someone observing that setting would never have known all the misery in the background of our lives together. After a couple of days, when it looked like Steve was going to be okay, we decided to head home.

The weirdness came when we returned back to Denver to spend the night at Tony's house. Ashley was having a party with her sister and some friends of theirs—they were all very drunk—and nobody even greeted us when we came in the door or acknowledged we were there. Tony and Ashley hardly talked to each other at all, and he proceeded to take us downstairs and set us up in the guest bedroom, which was the den. Justin and I only slept for a couple of hours, and then Tony took us to the train station so we could ride back to our small town in the mountains where loved ones would be waiting for us. Ashley never even said goodnight to us or greeted us in the morning, so I knew something was up.

As I told you, my life was always full of adventure whether I wanted it or not, and this train ride was no different, so I might as well add this story to the mix just for your entertainment. You've heard the saying "fiction imitates life," but I assure you there was nothing fictional about our life—this stuff really did happen. Justin and I hopped on the train, which was supposed to take four hours for us to get to the station in Glenwood Springs where our family was going to pick us up. That did not end up being the case, and we were rolling into the seven- or eight-hour category by the time we finally arrived at the station in Glenwood. We were exhausted, and I was emotionally drained from all of the travel and the stress of what happened to Steve, and all I wanted to do was get home, but the conductor couldn't manage to make that happen.

After the third stop and delay on the tracks, I finally talked to one of the ushers and asked him if they could please let me off of

CHAPTER EIGHTEEN

the train with my son and our luggage as my husband could come and meet me at that location, and I wouldn't have to wait anymore. I begged him to please let us do this as I was emotionally spent and the train was stopped anyway, not going anywhere, and they wouldn't tell us why. Shortly after this request I was met with an angry, hostile, six-foot, 230-lb. man they called the conductor. He cornered me in front of my son and started yelling at me that I had no right to ask to get off the train.

I was crying at this point in time, and he was bullying me in front of everyone, but no one did anything about it. I tried to get some level of compassion out of him by explaining the situation we had just come from—visiting a very sick loved one in the hospital—and he said if you want me to call an ambulance to come pick you up because you're a basket case, then I'll do that. He was a hostile, angry, and very cruel man. I told them to leave me alone, and he finally left the area. When the train finally made it to the station, I was met by some paramedics who said that they had received a call that I was in medical distress. I turned to them and said, "No, that was a bogus call made by the conductor," and pointed him out and said, "You can go thank that man for wasting your time."

I was so angry about the situation and what had happened, and I tried to file reports with Amtrak because that is the company he worked for. It became very clear to me in a hurry he was allowed to do this and the company would back him no matter what. It didn't matter what he had done to me on that train because he obviously had all the power, and Amtrak gave it to him. I could have taken him to court and sued him, but we thought it wiser just to let it go as my husband has had firsthand experience on the power and control these government bodies have over "we the people in this Free Nation."

2008/2009

Now we fast-forward to the visit from Tom and Ashley and Sue and John. So a few weeks after we parted ways with Tom's family more bad news came crashing down—the news we were expecting. Tony and Ashley had not been getting along very well, and the result of that was a decision to separate. I knew that even though we lived four hours away somehow we would be dragged right into the middle of it. We talked to Tony about it at length, and he gave the breakdown on what was going to happen next. We also talked to Ashley, as we were still friends with her, to find out what the plan moving forward was. Their "plan" as it were was to live in the same house with the kids but to share time. So in other words, he would live there half of the week, and then she would live there the other half. Does anyone see anything wrong with this?

We didn't know for sure all the details as to why they were separating, but we knew personally—having been close to the situation—that they were fighting quite a lot. Ashley also had some additional stressors in her life that added to the task of raising two small children and had pushed her over the edge. We kept in contact with both of them, and of course we conversed regularly with Sue and John. We were trying to be helpful and supportive, but we had our eyes focused mostly on the children— which we found out later was not appreciated by the family. In other words, they wanted us to focus more on Tony's suffering. While we knew he was going through a lot, we also knew through experience that the kids can sometimes be put on the back burner when two people are fighting.

This led to the next big fight and separation with his family. We had a trip planned to Atlanta, a business trip for my husband and a leisure trip for me, and we asked his parents if they wanted to watch the grandkids while we were gone. They had agreed to

CHAPTER EIGHTEEN

do it a few months prior, but because of the separation / pending divorce between Tony and Ashley, emotions were heightened. When we arrived at the house to drop off the kids before our flight, we had a short conversation with his parents about Troy's (Tony's oldest child) upcoming birthday party. They explained to us they were going to have a party for him there at their house, which seemed like a good idea, and they were trying to do it as soon as we got home. They didn't, however, share the rest of the information with us. For the brief time we were there, Sue appeared to have been crying and was making a lot of derogatory remarks about Ashley. We foolishly thought she would be okay when she was in front of the grandkids.

We left on the trip, and after the first day of the visit, we got a panicked phone call from Tom's parents when we were out to dinner. So we called them when we got back to the hotel, and they told us they were going to have this birthday party for Troy, but that Ashley was also going to send out birthday party invites, and they didn't want us to tell her they were doing a birthday party for him. My husband said, "That doesn't make any sense; why can't we have a combined party between both families?" This made his parents very angry, and they said, "Tony doesn't want to do a co-party with her." They said she had destroyed the marriage, and they didn't want to be around her and didn't want us to tell her they were doing this birthday party. Tom said we were not going to lie to her and proceeded to tell his brother he needed to talk directly to her and not ask any of us to be in the middle of it.

It's important right now to envision those scenes in the movies when somebody has been seeking justifiable vengeance finally tracks down and locates the perpetrator, and after dumping gasoline all over the perpetrator's house, the vigilante strikes a match and then tosses it over his shoulder onto the trail of gasoline, and the house blows up in the background. That is the best image I can give for what happened next after Tom told his parents and brother we would not lie to Ashley about her son's birthday. We ended up in an hour-long fight and screaming match on the phone because of it. His parents were so mad at us because they were convinced we had taken Ashley's side. No matter how many times Tom said we were not taking her side, we were taking the side of the children, they still couldn't understand it. We came to no resolution, but exhausted and tired of fighting, we ended the call.

    I was so freaked out at this point in time. I knew that I needed to fly home and go take care of my family. I was so worried about leaving the kids with the grandparents because their anger spilled over into everything. I just knew they couldn't separate their anger from the grandchildren and that my kids would be swept up in the middle of all that. But we decided to stay put and finish the trip and that they wouldn't hurt our children. We stayed, and I suffered through the rest of the trip. When we arrived back at their house to pick up the kids, they were so ready for us to be there. We had a curt encounter with his parents and then proceeded to load children up and drive back to Rifle.

    Our hearts were torn in two hearing about all of the stuff that happened in those few days they were at Grandma and Grandad's house and we were away. I more than kicked myself for not having stuck with my original instinct to go back home immediately and pick up the kids. When they finished telling us what had happened, the kids asked us not to leave them alone with the grandparents again because they said they were angry at them the whole time, and it made them cry. They told us their grandma hated Ashley and that she kept saying really mean things about her.

CHAPTER EIGHTEEN

They didn't understand what was going on in any great detail because they were still young, and they didn't need to know all the details. In addition, one of our daughters (Agnes) had a very difficult time falling asleep one of the nights and came to Grandma begging for comfort. She told Agnes it was her fault for watching a scary movie before she came to Grandma's house (the decision to watch the movie was mine and Tom's), and she would just have to go to sleep. Agnes went upstairs and proceeded to crawl into bed with Faye, who tried to comfort her. Apparently Grandma stayed outside with Grandpa and never came in to check on her. I looked at my husband, and I told him "I will not let them be subjected to that again—EVER" (I was very angry at that point). That was no problem for Tom because he was just as angry. What grandparent doesn't know how to separate the mistakes adults make from the children?

So as one can imagine, things went downhill after that. When we received the invitation from Ashley, my husband reached out to his brother, told him he'd received the invitation, and asked his parents when they were doing the party for Troy because he had just received the invitation from Ashley for Troy's birthday party. His parents responded super edgy and said they had already had the party for him, and we could just do whatever we wanted. Tom texted Ashley to let her know we probably wouldn't be able to get down to Denver for her party but thanked her for sending the invitation.

2008/2009 CONT. . . .

We were having our own fun as we had decided to make a move to a small town on the other side of the Mesa. Once again we rented a moving truck, roped a few friends into helping us, and headed to the town of Montrose two hours away. We really loved it over there and had wanted to move that direction for about a year. We moved into a small cul-de-sac and made some good friends in the neighborhood. The location was perfect as we had a grocery store within two blocks of our house, a Starbucks right behind our neighborhood, and much to our demise, a Sonic next to that. Let's just say our time spent in that location cost us a pretty penny in so many ways.

I immediately enrolled the kids in various sports so that they could get to know other children in the town. There were some really great families we met from the local Catholic parish, but after a while, we realized we just couldn't stay at that church anymore. Something beautiful was happening with my husband, and his relationship with Jesus and his church, and it was making some serious changes in his heart. Tom announced to the kids and me that from that point forward he had decided he would receive communion on the tongue and kneeling. He said we did not have to do that; it was just a direction he was going to go. We didn't really know at that time what all of it was about, but something just immediately felt right to all of us, and we told him we would do it as well, and do it we did.

The priest, however, was not quite as thrilled with this change as we were. Much later we would find out all the background and negative connotations that came with that gesture of receiving communion; for the time being we were what you might say ignorantly delighted to receive communion on our tongues. It was very awkward at first because they had no portable kneelers, so we were quite a distance below Father's hand, and he made quite a fuss about this. For respect of his priesthood, I will give him the benefit of the doubt and say he was trying to be respectful of the sacred host. The problem was he made

CHAPTER EIGHTEEN

a public spectacle of it. One day after we had received communion, he announced from the pulpit that if someone was going to receive on their knees, then they would need to crawl forward and come closer to him so he wouldn't have to bend down. It needs to be stated here we were the only ones receiving communion in this manner, so it wasn't hard to figure out who he was pointing a finger at. This was enough motivation to find another parish, and luckily we found one thirty minutes west of where we lived. The priest was very conservative and very solid in his knowledge and understanding of the faith. It was a very good fit.

While we were adjusting to our new location, and new church, things got bad down on the front range. Naturally my mom was still on dialysis, but she was struggling with severe nausea and dizziness, which had gone on for about six months. She told her doctors multiple times how sick she was, as well as the staff at the dialysis center, but it appears they didn't investigate. She got very sick and had to be transported back to the hospital only to find out she might die again. She was in the hospital for about a week in critical condition. They ended up doing dialysis on her for four days in a row because she had so much fluid on her kidneys.

When they completed the dialysis, they discovered she had twenty additional pounds of fluid they had taken off during the dialysis. What had happened was she wasn't eating very much because she was so nauseous; she had therefore lost weight, which her body replaced with fluid. The employees at the facility didn't know this because she continued to weigh about the same before and after each of her dialysis appointments. It was a perfect storm of things going wrong, and she almost didn't make it. What they found out later was at the root of her nausea and dizziness was the drug Statins, which used to lower her cholesterol.

2008/2009 CONT. . . .

My mom told her doctor the drug made her sick, but he insisted she keep taking it.

During my mom's recovery I received even more horrifying news. My husband greeted me at the door late one night after I returned from Justin's baseball game. He told me my cousin Dave had suffered a heart attack and been driven down from the mountains to a hospital in Denver. I was so upset, confused, and angry that I didn't even believe my husband. I argued with him for a few minutes because it all seemed so unreal, but it was not. He definitely suffered a heart attack and was going to have to have bypass surgery. This meant I would have to get the kids packed up and ready again to go back down to Denver and spend some time with the family.

A day or two later, I drove down to Denver and headed over to my cousin's house. This was Dave's sister (Carrie), and she needed someone to watch her son while she went to the hospital for her brother's bypass surgery. I came down to stay with him and later to go visit with my parents. When I got there, she was in need of some groceries, so I headed over to the store to get her and me a few things. She headed to the hospital the next day, and everything went according to plan. Dave, who was only six years older than me—placing him at about forty-eight years of age—required five bypass surgery. It was a long and involved surgery, and it was a success. After he came through recovery and got settled in his room, my cousin Carrie came home. We visited for a while, and I headed over to Grandma and Grandpa's house.

When I got to their house, my dad informed me my mom was ready to be released from the hospital, so with much excitement we headed there to scoop her up. She looked weak and tired, but she was very eager to get home. Once we got home, I sorted through all of her medication, read through her release

CHAPTER EIGHTEEN

forms and instructions, and organized all of her medications. It was getting late, and the kids were hungry, so I had to head to the store, yet again, and get groceries for my parents' house as they had none.

I was in the parking lot at Costco unloading my groceries and one of the employees came to help me load the back of my car. When I turned around to grab my purse out of the cart, it was gone. There were only three cars in the parking lot—mine and two others—and I discovered the employee was the one who took the cart before I could retrieve my purse. When I asked him where it was, he said with a blank look on his face that he didn't know and he hadn't seen it. This began a frantic search to no avail. I asked if we could see in the employee's car, but he wouldn't let us, and there was nothing we could do about it. So in about a thirty-second span of time I lost all of my credit cards, id, and wallet. I was so angry and upset someone would do this, but I had to get home and feed everyone, so I left.

I headed back home with all of my groceries and proceeded to make dinner for everyone. My parents felt bad for me, but there was nothing we could do about it. The following day I was preparing to go home when another medical emergency occurred. This time around it was my dad. The whole family was over visiting when he quietly whispered to me in the living room he was having some heart palpitations.

I asked him a few more questions about what was going on and details regarding his heart issue. He said his heart was fluctuating significantly and that he was worried that he might be having an arrhythmia. So I told him to go and take his blood pressure while I called my cousin (she was a nurse) to ask her for suggestions. She said take his blood pressure three times and get the average of those. So I told my dad what she had suggested, and when he finished getting the readings it became very clear to us that he probably needed to go to the hospital. I called his doctor's office, and they told me to take him there immediately. I explained to my sister what was happening, and she started to get a little panicked, so I asked her if she could go get the car ready. As it turned out, she had to run to the gas station and fill it up, which gave her some time to pull herself together. When she got home, I loaded Dad in the car, we calmly explained to our mom what was going on with Dad, and then I drove him to the hospital.

He was indeed having problems with a heart arrhythmia, and it took a few days to run all the needed tests and to sort it all out. In the meantime, I was back and forth between the hospital and my parents' house working with my sisters to try and make sure our dad was going to be okay. They finally got on top of what was happening with my dad's heart and started him on some medication, which helped him turn the corner. I think my poor dad was so worried about my mom, which was probably what caused the heart problems. After a day or two of the medications being in his system they released him to return home. We finally got our mom and dad back at home and on the road to recovery.

I finally made the long drive over the mountains and back to my home. The kids and I were quite happy to be back in our hometown. Tom was down in Denver with me for a small period of that time, and then he headed back up to Montrose for work. The morning after I arrived home, I called my cousin Carrie to check in on Dave. They had released him from the hospital, and his sister decided to take care of him at her house so that they could keep an eye on him. It was ten days post-surgery when I called her, and she sounded horrible. She had just found her brother on the floor, and he was having a stroke. She had

CHAPTER EIGHTEEN

already called the ambulance and was taking care of him until they got there. She was a wreck and asked me if I could call all the extended family and let them know what was happening. I collected myself, picked up the phone, and proceeded to make the difficult phone calls to all of our loved ones. The news was hard for everyone to take, and there was quite a bit of crying and confusion. I finally finished the phone calls and collapsed on the floor and cried myself. The road ahead for Dave was going to be a very long one, and none of us knew what the outcome would be.

All the above events were just more ingredients added to the pot of soup that was our lives. As for Tom's family, as time progressed in this complicated, chaotic relationship, I found myself receiving phone calls more frequently from Ashley. Tom's parents and Tony were very angry with us, as well as his grandparents, aunts and uncles, and probably a good majority of Sue and John's friends—although I can't prove that. I just know that on the couple of occasions we came down to Colorado Springs, some of Sue and John's friends would make some slight or remark about Tom and me. It was pretty apparent we were being talked about behind our backs, and not in a positive light, that is for sure. The details of what was being said, however, is still unclear to this day. Yet somehow we knew God was taking care of us.

When the grandparents got involved, they really got involved. Not one of them ever called us directly to ask our version of the story but took it upon themselves to make decisions—with one side of the story—and added Tom and me to their "Most Wanted List." His maternal grandmother again took Tony's side in the fight and decided to write us off. We never really got an opportunity to talk about it again. It is a very lucky thing for her we could find our way to forgiveness. Tom's grandmother has since passed, but shortly before she died, we called her on the phone to check in on her, and she told us that she loved us and that she had talked with her pastor and was ready to go. That was as close to an apology as we could get, but I was able to accept it. My husband and two daughters drove through a snowstorm out to Oklahoma to see his grandmother and say goodbye. God in his infinite mercy toward us continues to try and teach us mercy toward others.

Even to this day we do not regret having taken the side of Tony's children in this whole miserable ordeal. I feel like it cost my husband his whole family, and he also had to watch his wife get mistreated as well. It could not have been an easy thing for him to deal with. My husband made me proud because he was principled and stood up to his family for the sake of the children put in the middle of this divorce. Of all the ugliness that went down during this time, the thing that hurts me the most is how Tom's own family turned on him. I can't say for sure, but it appears no one stood up for him with the possible exception of Steve, who never showed any favoritism and never treated us differently.

Tony, as well as Sue and John, were not including us in any activities with Troy and Taylor because they were mad at us. They didn't reach out to us or let us talk to the kids or be involved in any way. Surprisingly, Ashley was still including us and inviting us to the kid's activities and events and gave us opportunities to talk to them. She included us in their birthdays, holidays etc., so we continued to have a relationship with her. This was honestly quite an innocent pairing for the sake of the kids, but Tom's family seemed convinced we took her side in the divorce. Looking back on my behavior and the way I handled these situations, I could understand why his brother would have felt that way. I definitely should have handled things better than I did, and I allowed myself to get too close to Ashley and too close to the situation. I was worried about Troy and Taylor because they

CHAPTER EIGHTEEN

seemed very unhappy and hurt, and their dad always seemed angry. I thought I was helping the situation by being there for the kids and Ashley, but I probably made things worse. The one thing Tom and I couldn't understand is why his parents seemed more concerned with how Tony was doing than they were with the grandkids. Tony and Ashley were adults and made their own choices, but the kids had nothing to do with it. Sue and John should have known that.

Things started getting really ugly, and Tom and I ended up in a fight with his dad and his brother. There were a lot of ugly emails going back and forth, and the whole thing was quite a mess. We sent an email to his dad and brother trying to explain what we were doing and why we were doing it. It was at that point in time his dad told me it was none of my business, this wasn't my family, and I had no right to be involved in it at all. I had been married to Tom for about thirteen years at that point and to be told I wasn't a part of the family was very hurtful. It was, however, a kind of freeing moment because I realized I didn't need to keep trying anymore. I had been trying to help communicate with the family and get to a resolution so we could all live in peace. What finally dawned on me was I was actually trying to fix the problems Tom, Tony, Sue, and John had been experiencing for years. In other words, like so many of us, this was part of their family dysfunction, and I had no place in it. It was for them to fix or not fix; it wasn't up to me. So for one of the first times of my life, I gave myself permission to just gracefully step out of it and let the chips fall where they may.

As if this heap of dung sitting atop all of us over this period from 2008 to 2009 wasn't enough, I guess we need one more pile of poop to add to the heap. My husband lost his job in 2009 due to the housing market crisis and his position at the bank. The process before he was let go from his job was six months of hell, and he suffered a lot during this time. They attacked his work production, his commitment to the job, and ultimately his work ethic. We ended up hiring a lawyer during the process because we knew something was going to happen with his job and that they might try to sabotage him. That is indeed what they did. Luckily, since we kept track of all the documentation, they had nothing to support their claims. So when it came time to collect unemployment, they ended up having to pay out. Tom will always have my respect and admiration for working so hard and waking up every day to go to that miserable job, all for the sake of his family.

Tom's grandmother died during this timeframe as well. He had been searching for a job for a couple of months and managed to land himself a good position. The job, however, was in Washington State, so we were in the process of packing our house and preparing to move yet again. We were not able to go out to Oklahoma for the funeral because of it. We tried to explain the situation to his parents, but once again they got very angry with us. They thought we were being selfish, and Tom did not value his relationship with his grandmother. They had no idea the six months of agony he had gone through with his job nor the two months of full-time job searching he had done after being let go. To be honest, they didn't seem to want to know. It's still a very strange subject that comes up every now and then, and they always seem surprised when we talk about him losing his job. It is like they still don't understand he was let go from his job, the one he was using to support six people. We even had to draw money out of our retirement fund to float us during that time because we had no savings.

Shortly before we moved we had First Communion for Alexis. We had invited Tom's whole family to come to the communion,

CHAPTER EIGHTEEN

even though we were all still fighting, because we thought this was the proper thing to do. There was no RSVP from either his parents or brother, and we only heard from his parents the day before the First Communion. They informed us they would be staying at a motel nearby and would meet us at the church, never once mentioning his brother was coming as well. When the day came, they showed up late to the ceremony, and his brother showed up with another woman and a ring on his finger. It appeared he had gotten married, and of course we were never told. This did not sit well with our kids, and they were very confused. We finished the ceremony and headed into the reception hall where things got really ugly.

Tom's dad insisted Justin go out to the car with him so he could give him some stuff. Justin did not want to go because the reception had already started, and he thought it was improper to leave, but in obedience to his granddad, he went out to the car. When he got out there, his granddad started unloading the gifts he brought them and then proceeded to get really angry and tell our son how mad he was at Tom. Justin did not know what to do, so he decided to head back into the reception. Tom's dad came in as well, and he and Sue proceeded to start a fight with us in front of everyone. It was a horrible situation, but the benefit was my sister was there and witnessed the whole thing. In the meantime, his brother stood behind a wall watching the whole thing happen. They never said a word to us and never engaged in any conversations. They didn't even bother to congratulate Alexis on receiving her first communion.

They left very quickly after that in a fit of rage, and we returned to the reception and tried to make the best of it. I think one of the greatest gifts the Holy Spirit did for Alexis in that moment was to provide her with holy forgetfulness because she doesn't remember any of what happened. She just remembers how much fun she had and how happy she was to receive Communion. After everything had finished, we wrapped up the party and headed home. Our sister came back to the house with us, and we sat up and talked for quite a while about the whole disgusting affair. This just made us all the more glad to be moving away; although, it made us sad to be leaving my family behind as well. It was definitely what needed to happen for the sake of our family, and that is why God took us away. Luckily we moved to a very beautiful place, so there was no shortage of visits from my family down the road.

The day arrived for us to move to Washington State, and the night before our big move we got a call from U-Haul saying our two trucks were no longer reserved. This reservation had been in the system for two months, but they just weren't going to honor it. They left a message on a Sunday night, so I couldn't call them until the next morning, which was our move date. When I contacted U-Haul the next morning, they said somebody else requested it, and our trucks got diverted to a different location. I hope you are laughing at this point in the story as the old adage seems to be the story with us: "If it weren't for bad luck, we'd have no luck at all." This was yet another opportunity for me to learn to handle adversity prayerfully and peacefully, but I did not.

After yelling and pitching an adult-sized fit, I set about problem solving. I contacted Budget truck rentals and proceeded to try and track down a truck. They had one for us in a nearby town, so Tom drove over there, picked it up, and then dropped it off at our house so the movers could pack it up. I then found another truck. This time we had to drive an hour one way to pick up the second truck. My husband raced over there, got the truck, and brought that one back for the movers to finish packing. We

CHAPTER EIGHTEEN

could not fit everything in the trucks because they were a bit smaller than the ones we originally had reserved, so by the end of it, I was just giving away whatever was left in the garage that we couldn't take with us. When all was finished, we hopped in the trucks and my car and headed out to the Great Northwest.

After three days of driving and an epic road trip vomiting adventure, we arrived at our destination. My husband's new boss waited for us at our new house, along with a group of men to help us unload the trucks. In addition, she ordered pizza for us. I cannot tell you how wonderful this experience was. We immediately felt welcomed and supported. His boss was always this supportive and loving. She is a really great woman and has raised an amazing family. After visiting with our new friends for a while, we started getting ourselves situated for bed. The next morning, we talked about getting unpacked, and by that evening experienced our first exposure to "twilight." When the sun goes down in the summer in Washington it hovers just at the horizon for a couple of hours before it sinks down and disappears. This makes for a beautiful and long-lasting sunset. It also makes for a disruption in one's internal clock. In other words, when it's 10:00 at night, it still looks like it's 7:30 p.m. That certainly took a while to get adjusted to.

The rest of the year was pretty wonderful. Our family came to visit shortly after we moved there and fell in love with the area. It was very nice having the family around and made us a little bit lonesome when they left. The town itself where we lived was famous for having events all summer long. So we got to be in the Fourth of July parade, experience the Arts Festival, and eat and enjoy every version of raw and cooked oysters at the "Oyster Run." That fall we signed the kids up for soccer, dance, and baseball. We also immediately got connected with the Catholic Church in town. We met families we immediately bonded with and also

2008/2009 CONT. . . .

enjoyed a lot of activities there as well. We really enjoyed that parish and for about six years were involved in most of the events that the church hosted.

All right I realize the story is now sounding almost too good to be true—or in our case pretty impossible to believe—so I'll throw in a nice end of the summer surprise for all of us so you realize you're still reading about the same family. In August, our sweet daughter Faye had an accident that landed her smack dab in the emergency room. She and Alexis were playing on some mattresses in the bedroom, and she fell off the bed and tried to catch herself with one arm, at which time Alexis fell on top of her and broke her arm. This was no little break, mind you; she broke both bones in her forearm completely. I wrapped her arm with ice and an ace bandage and raced her over to the ER. When we walked in the front door, I told them she had broken her arm, and they requested to see it. I told them that it was definitely broken, but they insisted on unwrapping her arm and looking at it. They took one quick look, and they understood what I already knew.

By the time we got back into the exam room, she was in excruciating pain. Luckily the doctor that night happened to be very good with little kids, and he said they would not take an X-ray until he made sure that she was out of pain. They gave her a dose of pain medication, and once her pain subsided, we took X-rays. When he came out to talk to us, he informed us she would be needing surgery, an obvious fact that for some reason I hadn't even realized. The next morning they did surgery, but she was still in enormous amounts of pain. We eventually realized the medication they had given to her—which would be the medication they would send her home with—wasn't working. They finally tried a different medication, and once that started to work, we were able to go home. This was all a very nice wrap up to 2009.

CHAPTER NINETEEN

2010/2011

Tom had started his job a few months before we moved, so he was already pretty well situated and connected. We were of the understanding that with this new job he would be traveling 25-50 percent of the time. This was a choice we were ready to make at this time in our lives but avoided doing that when the kids were little. In the beginning he took a couple of trips, and we started to prepare for that adjustment.

As luck would have it, however, his boss decided it was time for a change. They had a software product that hadn't really been marketed yet because they didn't have anyone who could take charge of the process and manage all the potential onsite implementations that would come their way. Tom's boss, Marcy, thought he would be a perfect fit as project manager for this product. After explaining what the job would entail, she asked Tom if he would step into the role. He and I talked about it at length and decided it would probably be a good career move. So he stepped into the new role and got it off the ground. As is always the case with my husband, it never takes very long for him to learn any new job and to streamline the operation. This

2010/2011

position was no different, and in just a couple of years, it became a pretty competitive product out in the marketplace.

We were definitely adjusting to our new environment and new location. We lived in a very beautiful place on an island north of Seattle. It was the location of the ferries that serviced some of the San Juan Islands. We were obviously surrounded by water (being an island and all) and had these beautiful and heavily forested hiking trails throughout the island. Walking through these forests was quite heavenly, and the scent given off by all the trees and plants was wonderful but almost impossible to describe. I wish I could bottle it up and put it in a candle. Maybe somebody already has.

We were also starting to develop deeper friendships with some of the families we met at our church—St Martha. There was one family in particular (the Smiths) that we grew very close to, and to this day our sons are best friends. The funny thing is it took them almost a year of knowing each other before they really started to bond. At this point in time, all four of us (the parents and Tom and I) were already friends. I guess in a sense the boys had no choice but to become friends or be very bored when both families were together. The Smiths had a friendship with another family whom they had known since they both started having kids. The two families brought us into their inner-circle and showed us a lot of love and kindness.

There was no shortage of really good families at St M's, and we spent time with most of them. For a number of years it was an almost "perfect" parish. Our faith and knowledge of the teachings of the church we're continuing to grow. It was in this growth we found ourselves wanting a more traditional Mass. The Mass at St M's was a very traditional Novus Ordo (New Mass), and we were all very drawn to that. This was due to the efforts

CHAPTER NINETEEN

of the previous priest, and our new priest kept the liturgy (Mass) virtually the same for a number of years. It was a very reverent, beautiful, and sacred Liturgy, and it definitely fed our souls. I even ended up joining the choir, and the girls eventually took violin lessons from some of the older girls in the parish. All in all, it was a great experience for our whole family, but as the saying goes, good things never last, but I'm getting ahead of myself.

We were continuing to do school from home, and I was trying to make sure the kids had a well-rounded education. By this stage in the game, we had participated in private school, charter school, virtual online school, and were now in the "design your own curriculum phase." As no surprise our kids all learned at different rates and different repetition levels. Some of our kids learned very quickly and never seemed to struggle very much, while others, similar to me, took a while longer and needed more repetition. None of it really mattered to me because the beauty of homeschooling allowed us to set our own pace and spend more time with each child as he or she needed it.

One of our favorite things to do was read together. We would choose a book we all wanted to read, and after the kids finished their school work for the day, we would sit down and read out of the book. Every one of us took turns reading a chapter. It was something I had chosen to do just for the fun of it, and it was a great way to help the kids read out loud and learn how to pronounce words. I had no higher aspiration for reading than that, but it ended up being one of our greatest memories. The kids and I still talk about it and how much we loved reading *The Chronicles of Narnia* and the other books we had chosen. I guess it was something that brought us closer to each other. It puts a smile on my face even now. If you get a chance, I highly recommend trying it yourselves.

2010/2011

Once a year we participated in testing for the kids. I wasn't concerned with the results as much as I wanted them to get an idea of what it would be like taking tests in a school setting. I had no idea what our kids would do in the future, but I wanted to make sure that if they decided to go to college, they would understand the testing structure and how to operate in the classroom. Naturally they did not enjoy this formal, timed structure of testing, but I think it served its purpose. As it turned out, they did fairly well on the standardized tests, which was helpful for me to know.

As the year went on our sweet lovable golden retriever started to get sick. She was about twelve years old at this point in time, and she quickly started to decline. I remember vividly the first time I knew she was going downhill. I put her on a leash to take her for a walk, and she sat down and refused to walk with me. I think I knew then it was only a matter of time. Sometime later she got much sicker and could hardly hold herself up when she walked. She wasn't eating very much food and would sometimes aspirate into her water bowl. It got to the point where I had to change her water out every time she drank because it was so dirty. I would also have to carry her out to the yard for her to go to the bathroom. One day, when my husband was out of town, I noticed she didn't manage to urinate in the yard for about eight hours. I knew she was probably in kidney failure.

So when my husband got home from his trip, we prepared for the inevitable. We knew it was time to take her to the vet and say goodbye. Before we headed to the vet, we took her over to the beach, put her in the water, and let her sit for a little while to say goodbye. She was a water dog through and through and loved to swim in the ocean. It was definitely her happy place. When she was finished, we dried her off, loaded her back into the car,

CHAPTER NINETEEN

turned on the heat to warm her, and headed to the vet. When we got there, I told them I thought she was in kidney failure, which they did not necessarily believe. They did a physical exam, ran some blood tests, and determined she most likely had cancer throughout her body. We as a family gave her all our last-minute hugs, and said our goodbyes, after which Tom and Justin headed back into the procedure room. A short while later, they both came out with tears in their eyes. We all started to cry because she was the best dog anyone could ever ask for.

We went home and loved on our dog Sadie. It was so hard not having Maddie around, but it was such a comfort to have our sweet Sadie to hug and love on. This is why we continue to have two dogs in our home. They serve as good companions for each other, and they fill that empty void after you lose one of your dogs. Even though we were all hurting, and we knew nobody could replace that dog we loved so much, we also knew it wouldn't take long before we'd get ourselves a new dog.

In December of 2010, disaster struck again for my daughter Faye. It was the week before Christmas, and I had a lot of shopping to do. The kids really wanted to go roller skating, and I wanted to make sure they got to enjoy themselves a bit. So we made a plan to go up to the nearby town to go roller skating. The girls brought a friend this time too. The plan was to leave them off at the facility while I ran my errands, and then come back and pick them up after about two hours. The kids were older now, so I didn't worry about leaving them there to skate. I don't remember why Justin didn't go with them and stayed with me instead, but either way, it was a good thing he did. I was in line at the photo department at Costco when Justin came running in the door. He said Faye had fallen and broke her arm again. I was in disbelief because she had two pieces of titanium in her arm from the previous injury, and I didn't understand how she could break that.

Justin finally snapped me out of it and said, "Mom, we have to go now." So we headed out to the parking lot, jumped in the car, and raced over to the roller-skating rink. By the time I got there the ambulance had already been called, and Faye was already in a great deal of pain. I knew the ambulance was going to cost a lot of money. We didn't have very good insurance, and the previous surgery had put us in debt, so I asked if they could give her medication, and I could drive her to the hospital. The paramedics said they would not be able to administer the medication unless she was in the ambulance. I was not going to put my daughter through needless suffering so into the ambulance she went, and we followed behind in our car.

I needed to contact my husband, and I knew the phone call wasn't going to go well. He was very angry, and very upset, and in as much disbelief as I was. Nonetheless he told his boss that he needed to go to the hospital. When he showed up, she was in the exam room waiting to get splinted. There was nothing they could do for her at this point, and we would have to go home and schedule her surgery. Right before they came to put a splint on her arm and set it, I asked Faye if I could take a picture to send to my family. She was so mad at me because she was in so much pain and didn't want to remember it. I took a quick picture anyway, and I will say it got her a lot of sympathy packages in the mail. Our daughter's friend that had come roller skating with them was absolutely amazing through the whole process, completely calm, and seemingly unphased by what had happened. We had to call her parents to come and get her and proceeded to tell them what a great kid she was.

Once we got back to the house it was time to start the endless

CHAPTER NINETEEN

string of phone calls to orthopedic surgeons to see if someone could operate on her. The problem we had was the surgeon she had before, while he had done an excellent job operating on her arm, had a horrible bedside manner, and my daughter did not want to go to him again. As it turned out, however, with it being Christmas week, the list of orthopedic surgeons referred to us were all either busy or on vacation. No matter what we did we couldn't get another surgeon, and if I wanted my daughter to have this operation before Christmas, which she and I both did, I would have to arrange it with him. So I set the date for surgery.

The surgery went extremely well; although, it took longer than expected. Interestingly enough, I had mentioned to the surgeon I was worried she might have low bone density because she kept breaking her arm. After it was finished, the surgeon told me there were no problems with her bone density, as it took him longer to do the surgery than expected because so much bone had already grown over the previously installed plates in her arm, and he had to remove it to get the old plates out and put in new ones. We laughed pretty hard at that, and my husband and son both said, "See, we told you; she just doesn't know how to fall." That was the running joke for quite a while in our house, that Faye needed to learn how to fall correctly. This time around our surgeon had developed a good bedside manner. He was very sweet to her and made sure she was comfortable. We found out later the surgeon ended up having a baby of his own, so I think that softened him a bit.

Pain management was much more effective this time around, and we were able to get her back to the house sooner than the last time. Faye was so sad and so defeated, and she just cried when we got home. She knew how long it took her to recover the first time around and knew it would be a long road again. In addition, she was on a competitive swim team, and she knew it would set her back quite a bit. This really bothered her because she was such a competitive athlete and was trying to advance to the next level. Add to that the fact it was now Christmas Eve—and she was supposed to play music at Christmas Eve Mass—and you can see how an almost thirteen-year-old girl would feel as though her life had ended. She decided she wanted to at least go to church and watch her sisters play their music for Christmas Eve Mass. It was, however, too much pain for her to endure with the drive over to church and all the commotion. She looked at me and said, "Mama, I hurt too much. I need to go home," and home we went. I lay on the couch next to her, held her good hand, and we both had a good cry. It was a difficult Christmas for sure.

Over time Faye's arm started to heal, and she was getting some of her strength back for swimming. She was not, however, able to put any weight on it, and unfortunately to this day she still can't do any push-ups or weight-bearing exercises. That's okay, though; who really wants to do push-ups anyway? Faye was really taking to the swimming, and we were enjoying the heck out of watching her compete. As we rolled into next year, each of the kids was getting better in their sports and really making visible improvements. Alexis was in gymnastics and would have done even better if she had had some decent coaching. As it turned out, we should have switched gyms a lot sooner than we did, and she might have been able to stay in gymnastics for a longer period of time. It drove me crazy going to our practices and watching her coach from the viewing area. This lady did not know what she was doing at all, but every time I talked to the owner, she made excuses for her.

Somewhere around this time, I'm not exactly sure when it happened because I can't distinctly remember the dates, my

CHAPTER NINETEEN

niece came to live with us. She had been in college in Kansas and was really enjoying it immensely, but her parents didn't have enough money to continue to send her to that school. She tried to negotiate a way to stay in school, but the school seemed very reluctant to assist her with her financial needs. I don't know all of the details, but it appeared to me that if she couldn't pay, then they kind of booted her out.

Needless to say my niece (Tricia) was very distraught over this and immediately called me. We were very close, especially when she was young, and she had leaned on me and my family for quite a few things. She had experienced a lot of difficulties in the home, and her mother was struggling with some depression issues, and they didn't always get along. I really wanted to help the family, but I'm not sure the methods I used were very constructive. At this point in time, however, she had been living away from home and was appreciating that. So she asked my husband and me if she could come and live with us out in Washington. I told her she would need to think about it, pray on it, and talk to her parents. It wasn't very long after that conversation she called me up and said she was going to move out with us. I was pretty confident because of the short duration of time she really didn't do any of those things I had recommended. Nonetheless we gave her the green light, and her parents moved her out to live with us.

The year Tricia spent with us was very productive for developing her independence, but I don't think it was necessarily a good thing for her spiritual development. She lived with us for a while and struggled to get work. She was definitely in a depression, so her motivation levels were very low. In addition, she was not very helpful around the house or helping me take care of the kids. It would have helped me immensely if she was in a good frame of mind to assist me, but unfortunately that didn't happen. I felt badly for her because I knew she was hurting, and I wanted to help her, but I had to take care of my family, and my family was feeling the strain. The kids were sharing a room with her and felt pretty put out that she wouldn't clean, help them do chores, etc. So I tried to motivate her, but when I realized it wasn't working, I had to set a deadline for her to get a job and move out.

The rest of what happened over the course of the next six to eight months still hurts me a little bit when I reflect upon it. Ultimately, Tricia hadn't been working much before she moved out, so she had no extra money at all after she did first and last month's rent. It was a real struggle for her financially for quite a while. I really wanted to jump in and fix things for her, but I knew I had to let her figure things out on her own. I was very upset with my brother and sister-in-law at this time because they were not helping her financially and weren't offering much emotional support. Part of the frustration I was experiencing had to do with the fact we knew the college she went to was too expensive, and we tried to warn my brother not to send her there because he wouldn't be able to afford it. He can be a stubborn old goat and wouldn't listen. So when everything went downhill for her and the school, I felt like he almost washed his hands of it. I eventually called him and talked to him. I explained to him his daughter was really struggling. After that call he started to engage with her more frequently.

When we helped Tricia find her new apartment, we also went about tracking down some furniture for her. We purchased an old couch from the church rummage sale, and somebody donated a bed for her, and we got a kitchen table as well. We helped her move everything in, and then the girls and I went and purchased a broom, a mop, cleaning supplies, scrub brushes,

CHAPTER NINETEEN

laundry detergent, dishwashing soap, etc. We did our best to get her established. The poor kid didn't have any money to buy a car, so she had to walk to her jobs, which caused her to be late on more than one occasion. This tended to get her in trouble. She finally decided to go and buy herself a bicycle, which we thought would be a great idea. The only problem is she got in a bike accident shortly after that and the bike was broken and she was a bit banged up. The poor kid just could not seem to catch a break.

While all of this was going on, my poor mom started to get sick again. She ended up going into a nursing home for a little while because of an open sore infection on her toe. My dad had been watching over her and trying to take care of her, but the sore on her toe went from bad to worse in almost twenty-four hours. One of the ladies they had hired to come in and do chores at their house was trying to help my dad change out some of the bandages on my mom's toe. Apparently the sore looked small the first day they bandaged it, and when they went to re-bandage the next day, it had significantly grown in size. My dad said it looked very bad, so they took her over to the hospital.

When they got to the hospital, she was checked in, and they started to evaluate the infection. Naturally they got a lot of antibiotics on board and started doing some diabetic wound care. The cleanup of the wound and antibiotics did not seem to be doing the trick. Eventually it was determined she had MRSA poisoning, and it had damaged the tissue around her toe, so she was in need of an operation to remove the toe. They did surgery to remove the toe, and once she started to recover, they sent her to a rehabilitation facility. She was there for a little while, and everyone was assuming she was going to get better, but that was not happening.

During this period in my life, everything seemed like a

continuous cycle of ups and downs. Everyone handles life struggles differently, and I have been likened to Scarlett O'Hara and her famous saying "I can't think about that now; I'll think about that tomorrow." That is pretty much how I function. I don't spend a lot of time dwelling on the past but keep plowing forward. This design in my processing is actually a gift as it keeps me functioning, but it also never allows me to slow down and evaluate things when that approach is needed. No matter how I look at it, God provided me with the right gifts to handle all my situations—which he does for all of us—even if we can't see it.

We were still living in Washington and my dad continued to update us on my mom's health situation. I had asked my dad if I needed to come home for the surgery or her recovery. He told me not to come for the surgery, but that they would keep me posted on her condition. It was a long drive from Washington to Colorado, and he didn't want me to drive home unnecessarily. So after she went to the rehabilitation facility for recovery, we were about to embark on an adventure of our own. Tricia's sister Hazel was going to be in a dance competition in Seaside Oregon. We had been to the area a couple of times ourselves and really loved it, so we thought it would be a great idea to go down and watch her competition.

Tricia, Justin, the girls, and I all made plans to go camping out there. We figured it would be a cheap way to go, and it was summer, so it would be nice weather—we thought—and then we would get to spend some time with my niece / the kids' cousins. We were all very excited, and I was so excited that I thought it would be a wise idea for me to injure my back. I think you'll agree I don't like straightforward things. Apparently I like to add additional obstacles to make life a little bit harder for myself. It was a fluke accident: I was lifting a box of some fruits and vegetables

CHAPTER NINETEEN

(those will kill you every time). I twisted wrong and bulged a disc. It took a good two hours for me to be able to move enough to get in my car and drive home. I actually headed straight for the chiropractor, and after the adjustment, I started feeling better. I went to him for the next three days.

I was still in a good deal of pain, but it was time for us to pack up the car and head out for the camping trip. Tom could not come with us, so he asked the kids to make sure they took care of me. And of course he proceeded to set me straight on the things I could and could not do with my back injury. This approach is definitely fair enough considering how stubborn I am and how hard I push myself sometimes. Luckily for me the pain was severe enough I couldn't push through it.

We had a great drive down to the Oregon coast and headed to our campsite to get set up. After we were situated and got some food, we headed into town to go see the first competition. Over the course of the proceeding days, we had an absolute blast watching all of the dance competitions and getting to see Hazel perform. I had never been to anything like that before, and it was very enjoyable. The only one I think that wasn't entertained was Justin, and you can't really blame him for that. He wasn't much into the Arts and greatly preferred doing sports. He was a good sport (play on words) and went along for the ride.

The first night of camping was decent, but from then on, things didn't go so well. It proceeded to rain on us, and some of the time it rained so hard we couldn't even get the fire made. In addition, we didn't have a very large tent, so it was hard to sit inside and do anything. The camping part was not working out so well, so I asked the kids if they wanted to try and find a motel. My question was met with shouts of cheering and woohooing. We went into town, scrambled around for a little while, and found one of the last rooms available. It was very nice staying in a warm bed and not in the rain.

When the trip was almost finished, I called my father to check on mom. He gave me the bad news, and it didn't look like it was going to improve anytime soon. This is the point in time when they realized the infection had continued to spread even with the toe amputation, so they would have to do something different. They had moved her from the rehabilitation facility back to the hospital and were trying to evaluate what to do. So we packed up all of our belongings, said a heartfelt goodbye to Hazel and her dancing troop, and drove back to Washington.

When we got home we had only twenty-four hours to wash everything up, repack, and hit the road to drive out to Colorado. My dad called me the morning we were about to leave, and he said he thought we might need to drive straight through because he wasn't sure if mom was going to make it. My dad seldom made statements like this, so I knew he was concerned and very worried. The problem was we only had two drivers Tricia and I. Justin only had his learner's permit, but that would require me to be awake for his portion of the drive. Not to mention the fact that while I was appreciative Tricia was willing to drive, she could be a kind of crazy driver, so that was a little nerve-racking. So we packed up everything, and everyone, and hit the road. Tom said he would come later if we needed him to.

It was a long, exhausting drive, and we were worried about my mom's condition. We were also exhausted from the previous travels and my back injury. I drove the first part of the trip, and when it came time for Tricia to drive I asked her if she was ready. She said she didn't think she could do it because she was too tired. I told her to go into the convenience store, get a large coffee with lots of caffeine, roll down her window, and let the wind

CHAPTER NINETEEN

blow in her face if she had to, but she was going to have to drive. I knew I couldn't do the whole drive by myself, and I needed to close my eyes and try to get some sleep, and that is what I did.

When I awoke the car was moving about 85 mph and the rest of the kids were asleep. I told my niece I was awake and ready to switch with her whenever she wanted to. She pulled over at the next location so we could switch spots. By this point in time, Justin had awakened as well and was ready to take his shift. We had been driving through the night, and it was fairly early in the morning, so I figured it would be a safe time to let him drive, since he was only fifteen years old.

We finally arrived in Denver, exhausted and worn out but glad to be with the family. We got to my parents' house and quickly unloaded our luggage and then proceeded to head to the hospital. We got over there and connected with my dad and sister. They took us over to the room immediately, had us put on protective gear because of her MRSA poisoning, and let us come into the room. My mom was very happy to see us, but she looked very bad. We could tell she had been suffering a lot, and it definitely broke my heart. I gave her a big hug, as did the kids, and I hung out and visited for a while. After a couple of hours had passed, we decided to take the kids home to get them fed and to bed, or just to relax if nothing else.

The next week of our lives was a lot of emotional ups and downs. Since my mom's amputation didn't manage to remove all of the infection, she was looking at a lower leg amputation to correct the situation. We talked to doctors, nurses, and of course all of the family to determine what to do. My mom was not eating at all, and the nurses asked us to encourage her to at least drink her protein shakes. She didn't want anything to do with it and could only manage to take a couple of sips out of a straw. This was devastating for us to watch because we knew she would have to have surgery to stop the spread of the infection, but she was so weak that she most likely wouldn't make it through, and her not being able to eat was a sign of her weakening health.

One afternoon my brother and I went outside to stretch our legs and get some fresh air. While we were there, one of our mom's nurses was also out there and started talking to us about her situation. He basically said that if she did not feel like eating, she shouldn't have to, especially at this stage in her life. There was something subtle in what he was trying to communicate, so we continued to ask him questions. He told us then that when his grandfather was dying, he didn't want to eat either, and they decided just leave it be. This is when I started to realize she was getting ready to die. We quickly fell into more relaxed conversation about different types of jobs and how he had come to be a nurse. He was a very interesting person, and it served to be a very good distraction. Shortly after the conversation, my aunt pulled up to the entrance of the hospital where we were standing and waiting for her.

She wanted to see my mom and drove up from Canyon City with my uncle to do just that. We were all very eager for her to get there as my mom and she were as close as any two sisters could be. We took her up to the room, and she went in by herself. They were in there for a number of hours, and although we do not know all the details of what was said, we do know that our aunt recommended that if our mom wasn't going to receive a great benefit from having her leg amputated (a.k.a., living significantly longer) it wasn't worth the immense suffering and struggle on the back end. I do think this was sound advice from my aunt because she, after all, was a double leg amputee herself. She had suffered from diabetes as well. I definitely think my mom took her words to heart.

CHAPTER NINETEEN

So at the end of the week, one early morning, when none of the family members were in the room with my mom, she told the nurses and doctors she did not want any more dialysis or lifesaving measures. She had finally made up her mind she was going to let go and let nature take its course. I had for the first time in a week had an opportunity to take my kids and some nieces and nephews to a water park to decompress. No sooner did we get into the park, get situated, and get into the water that I got a phone call from my brother. He told me it was going to be the end for mom, and I should try to get there as soon as I could.

Luckily a friend of mine was with me, and she offered to take care of the kids so I could go to the hospital. My husband had also decided to fly out, so I had to make a drive out to the airport to pick him up. I was a little bit worried because I didn't know how long we would have, so I scooped him up and drove him right over to the hospital. When we arrived, we went right into my mom's room. I stood next to my mom and told her that Tom was there. She was incoherent at this point in time, but she looked down at the end of the bed—winked at him—and slipped away again. That was enough to satisfy my husband and me. She got her chance to say goodbye.

Throughout the day, all of my siblings and nieces and nephews came into my mom's room to say their goodbyes. As the day progressed and night time rolled in upon us, my mom's condition deteriorated. Most of my brothers, nieces, and nephews went home, but my two sisters and sister-in-law stayed by my mom's bedside until the end. We sat next to her for the last few hours talking to her and praying with her. She never regained consciousness, but we were very blessed to be with her. Then all of a sudden something in her behavior changed, and I could see on her face that something was happening. My sisters looked at the monitors, and they noticed her blood pressure and heart rate were dropping. I turned to the girls and said I think it's time. My dad was in the waiting room and asked us to come and get him when it was time, so my oldest sister ran out of the room to get him. By the time they both got back, put on their protective clothing, and entered the room, she had already passed. I have regrets I didn't go and get my dad in place of my sister so that she could be with my mom in her final moments. It just happened so fast, and I was awestruck. We could literally see my mom tracking someone with her eyes across the ceiling. She smiled, sighed, and then took her last breath. It was the saddest and most beautiful thing I'd ever seen.

My mom died on July 23rd, which would later have some major significance in our lives as well. We stayed for the next week helping to plan my mom's funeral. The day we buried my mom, we drove back to my parents' house, immediately packed up our belongings, and started the long drive back to Washington. It was a two-day drive, and shortly after returning, we closed on a new rental house we had been in the process of trying to lock down when we were in Colorado. The house was located on one of the most popular beaches in the town we were living in. We were very excited for this opportunity, but it came with a mixed bag of emotions.

As soon as we finished the paperwork and signed the rental agreement, we started to pack our house. As the timing in these things always conflicts with something else, my husband and son were also preparing for a trip overseas to Madrid, Spain. It was a Catholic event called World Youth Day, which brought together youth and young adults from all over the world. The talks, Masses, and seminars all occurred over a week's time. We had been fundraising and planning this trip for two years, so we

CHAPTER NINETEEN

couldn't very well have them stay home and lose out on all that money; besides, my mom wouldn't have wanted that.

I went through an amazing period of spiritual growth during this time and also suffered immense pain and mourning. I was at home with my three daughters and a house to pack up, along with a new home to paint. The house we were moving into hadn't been taken care of in a while, and a lot of the rooms needed painting. Our landlord was kind enough to let us choose our own colors and do with them what we would. All of my support system, not just my husband but my friends as well, was overseas in Spain. I had to navigate this entire process by myself—with the help of my kids of course. In addition we solicited the help of some of their friends—also children their same age—and I was very grateful for their help. The only problem was they were all a little too young to be painting without a lot of supervision, so I had a lot of spilled paint to clean up every day.

I was struggling to get any quiet time to pray, cry, and just be with our Lord. I remember during that time going to our local parish and just sitting in the sanctuary to get some quiet prayer time. This was the first time I realized how important sacred silence was as I had never longed for it in the past the way I was longing for it now. The parishioners didn't seem to have a good understanding of the importance of that sacred silence whenever they were in the main church. So people would come in and talk to each other, make noise, shuffle around, and in general rob me of my only peaceful time—at least that's how it felt.

Thanks to Our lady (Mother Mary) looking out for me, and knowing how much I missed my own mom, she must have gone to her son in my stead. They provided a huge gift for me on this particular weekend. There was a guest priest visiting us who was part of the Divine Mercy apostolate. He was scheduling times for spiritual direction. When I got a chance to meet with him and share with him my struggle, he looked at me and said he could help. He told me that every time I was hurting, sad, or missing my mom, to just turn to Christ and say, "Jesus, I trust in you." This literally became my mantra for months to follow. I probably uttered it a hundred times a day in the beginning because that is how much I hurt. He gave me great solace, and it helped me survive what seemed like the impossible.

Once Tom and Justin returned home, we began the process of moving. We planned out a day when all of our friends could help and in short order got moved into our new home. If you're counting, this was our fourth move in five years and was taking its toll on me. I had certain expectations in my heart that when my friends returned home, they would rally around me as I processed through the death of my mother. I had buried a lot of family members at this point in my life, but burying a mom is a much different experience. I just assumed they would want to know what I was going through and be there to talk to me. The problem, however, was that most of my friends hadn't lost anybody close to them, and I guess it freaked them out a little bit. Their reaction was pretty much the opposite of what I thought. At least from my perspective it felt like they pulled away entirely. It seemed as if the subject matter was so uncomfortable, and they were so unsure what to do, that they just avoided the topic altogether. I was so lonely, and even though my husband and kids were there for me, I knew I needed more. I just wanted my friends to check in on me and see if I was doing okay. It turns out I only had God to lean on, and lean on him I did, and it brought us so much closer.

CHAPTER TWENTY

2012/2013

Moving into the following year, it became apparent to me, and more importantly to my family, that I should start setting some boundaries for myself. I needed to make some changes in my schedule, and those changes were going to be very difficult. As it stood, I was working a part-time job a couple of mornings/afternoons of the week; as mentioned before, I also had all four of my kids in separate activities. I had a couple of my kids working part-time jobs, and all of this required me to transport everyone... everywhere. My husband and I tried to divide up the driving the best we could, but he had a full-time job, and it required his full-time attention. So the majority of it was left for me to work out.

When I was raising my kids, there definitely seemed to be a lot of pressure for us as stay-at-home moms in society. Stay-at-home moms felt as if it wasn't good enough for us to just raise and educate our children but that we needed to make ourselves "useful" in society. Whether this is a real or a perceived interpretation of the times, I cannot be sure, but I felt the pressure nonetheless.

2012/2013

So in an effort to be the best version of a stay-at-home mom, I guess, I threw myself into every volunteer opportunity I could. I was busy donating my "free" time to my local church parish at almost every function, volunteering for all of my kids' sporting events and activities, assisting at a local nursing home with my daughter, and most importantly volunteering at a place called "Gleaners." "Gleaners" was a sort of food co-op, which received food donations from local grocery stores that had outlived their shelf life, to be consumed by the members of Gleaners. We were free to shop up to three times a week with whatever produce and additional food they had acquired. The requirement, however, was making sure to volunteer a certain amount of hours every week. It was a great benefit, but one more thing I had to do two to three times a week. I was homeschooling my kids, working a part-time job, transporting four kids to six different events, running a home, and volunteering everywhere. In January I actually had a nervous breakdown, full-fledged meltdown, shaking, crying, and crumbling on the ground.

So, after a while, I started looking through my long list of activities and volunteer functions with my husband to decide what I could cut back on. One would think this task would be easy, but it was far from that. If I suggested cutting back on any church activity, I would get immediate pushback from those in charge of the event. In trying to reduce or eliminate my "Gleaners" shopping and volunteer hours, my friend, tried to convince me not to give up (as did my husband because it saved us money). If I tried to lean out my volunteer time with sporting events for my kids, the coaches would try to negotiate with me in an effort to keep me volunteering. I was met with obstacles and roadblocks everywhere I turned, which made mitigation next to impossible. It was an exhausting process, and it was because of this that I literally

CHAPTER TWENTY

reached "the end of my rope," hit "the final nail in the coffin," went off the "proverbial cliff"; in other words, I had a nervous breakdown from trying to eliminate things that might cause me to have a nervous breakdown.

Since I was not in a psychologically sound or emotionally strong place, this back and forth stuff was too difficult for me to navigate. So I got angry and very reactive, and I decided I was done doing any of it. I basically removed myself from EVERYTHING I was doing. I quit volunteering for Gleaners, all church events, my kids' sports and activities, and anything else anyone asked me to do. It was a very painful process for me and brought me to tears, but it had to be done. I had no idea what I was going to do with my free time, but what I knew is I needed free time, free time to think, free time to pray, and free time to realize what my duty in life actually was. I hadn't had free time in my life since I was a child, which really isn't an exaggeration, and without it, I wouldn't be able to get a handle on my health or the direction my family was going.

Not too surprisingly my mass exodus from my volunteer services was met with much opposition. It came from every direction, Church, sports and activities, family, and even from friends. I could have used someone playing mediator for me, but that was not in the cards, so I had to stay strong and decisive. As I pushed back, I discovered the negative impact society had had on me (as I had mentioned before) and my role as a mother. Society during this time, and even more so today, had minimized and reduced a mother's role to nothing more than daycare and babysitting. In a sense, we weren't considered real women until we had gotten ourselves a career. So it forced us to focus our attention more on our needs, and those of the outside world, then the needs of the family. All of that was about to change.

2012/2013

    I couldn't believe how different things felt for me to not be as harried as I had been and be able to sit and relax and enjoy. I had so much guilt over not being there for my kids at times they needed me. One of the stories that still haunts me to this day is my son being so sick and me not being there to tend to his needs. He was a teenager at this time (sixteen years old,), and the poor kid ended up getting mononucleosis. He was a hardworking kid and had been burning the candle at both ends, so I wasn't surprised. He had a bad sore throat and extreme fatigue, but he wouldn't call in sick to his job. I had a motherly instinct he actually had "mono," so I took him to the doctor. She didn't believe me either, even though the glands on his neck were so swollen it stuck out. Nonetheless, I convinced her she may as well test him and rule it out. She ran the test, and it was positive.

    Not that it was any shock to me, but this meant he would be able to stay home and get some rest. The doctor wrote a note for Justin to take to work requesting a minimum of a week off. So we left the doctor's office, picked up some snacks for him, and headed home. The issue I had was I had a Fourth of July party I was throwing in the neighborhood, my Gleaners volunteer hours and shopping to do, and a million other things. That poor kid sat downstairs in his basement bedroom for days on end, sleeping and watching hours of endless TV—*When Sharks Attack* was the show of the week. I should have been there that whole week taking care of him, cooking whatever food he needed or wanted, and comforting him. Instead I would run all of my errands, race home, and quickly throw together some food and some drinks to bring downstairs to him, and then race off again. I felt like a horrible mother and will never get those moments back. Luckily for him, he doesn't seem to remember any of that.

    Time went on, and I surprisingly started appreciating the

CHAPTER TWENTY

slowness of my life and the time I got to spend with my kids and husband. I finally had an opportunity to experience "peace," and it really made me protective over my time. I developed a close relationship with my kids and husband, and we grew closer as a family. It was because of this relationship with each other, and spending concentrated time together, which allowed us to pray more. Naturally in turn this caused our faith in God, Jesus Christ, and his church to grow exponentially.

We had started attending Mass in the Traditional Latin Rite more frequently along that time too and shared our time between a parish on the island connected to us and going down to Seattle to the fraternity parish there. My husband was so interested in the TLM (traditional Latin Mass) that he decided he should learn how to serve alongside the priest at the Mass. I may have mentioned this before, but it begs repeating that Tom is an incredibly intelligent man, so he was able to access some training videos on YouTube and learn to serve the Mass that way. I would have needed on-the-job training multiple times to have mastered it, but he seemed to get it down in just a few tries.

While all of this was going on, we were also learning prayers in Latin. This all started when our daughter Faye approached us about learning the rosary in Latin. She came home from one of her confirmation classes with a sheet of paper that had the "Our Father" and "Hail Mary" printed in Latin. So my husband took the ball and ran with it. He looked up articles and videos on pronunciation, and we started practicing it. Not only did we learn the rosary, but he had us start learning the Divine office— Liturgy of hours—as well. It was amazing how much we learned about the parts of the mass through this process. My husband was very wise.

One of the great things that happened during that time had

to do with a very special and kind priest we met on Whidbey Island. Apparently some of his parishioners were interested in having the Latin Mass at their Church, so they approached him about it. He had learned to say the Mass by training with one of the fraternity priests, so he was already in a position to start doing it. In addition, he was a good shepherd to his flock and was trying to provide what they had requested. When we got wind of this, we immediately connected with him, and my husband started serving Mass at his parish along with our son Justin. He offered the TLM every other weekend, which gave us a break from driving down to Seattle every week. It was a wonderful period of time and a great relationship we formed with Father. This lasted for about two years, which was just enough for us to prepare to drive down to Seattle weekly.

It goes without saying, although I am going to say it, there always has to be some suffering thrown into the mix, so God reached out his very loving arms and gave us a "gift," which we would not see as one until much later. Our son was getting ready to do his Confirmation and our daughter Faye decided she wanted to go through the class at the same time, but she was a year younger than she needed to be. Our kids were doing confirmation at our local parish because we hadn't integrated with the parish down in Seattle yet and because they had a lot of good friends at the local church. The problem with that was it was a diocesan parish, and there appeared to be very strict rules around what age a kid could receive their confirmation—mind you that age had changed over the years a number of times. So she needed to go to the priest and request permission to join the class.

The parish priest/pastor serving at our local church was what you might call a little green. He hadn't been a priest for very long, and they put him in the position of pastor, which we

CHAPTER TWENTY

realized later was probably too much for him to handle. Needless to say, we didn't think a request from a fifteen-year-old girl to receive her confirmation would turn into such a big deal, but it did. Once she met with the pastor and requested permission to join the class asking what she needed to do to, it became a confusing process. He told her she would have to talk directly to the Archbishop (a priest who is placed in a leadership position of a large area which consists of multiple churches and priests) to get permission, so she wrote a letter to the Archbishop. We planned it out on one of his visits, to give him the letter and tell him what she was asking permission to do. The response from the Archbishop, not too surprisingly, was the permission had to come from her pastor since he is personally familiar with her and the Archbishop was not. In other words, he was our local priest and knew his parishioners better than the Archbishop, and he'd be better able to decipher if she was ready or not.

After that, two other girls stepped forward requesting the same thing, and both of them received completely different responses from the pastor. So there were now three girls wanting to get confirmed at fifteen, and each one being told they had to do something different to "prove" their worthiness. The classes were getting close to starting, and none of the three girls had received a definitive answer from the pastor. To make matters worse, there were very strict requirements regarding attendance for these classes to qualify to receive the sacrament of Confirmation. It was turning into a giant mess.

The pastor was very young and introverted to boot, so he had a hard time dealing with confrontation. What he then did was to push off the decision to a lay person (a parishioner in the parish) who was volunteering to teach the class. This put him in a difficult predicament and did nothing to settle the confusion and anxiety the parents were experiencing. This frustration started to build and came to a climax on one fateful Sunday, which divided the parish and caused a huge fight to erupt. At the end of the day, feelings may have been hurt, but if the pastor had just been consistent and made a decision, we all could have lived with that. The fight was so big it caused some irreparable damage to some of the staff and parishioners. Once again while the fight was happening, our pastor wasn't even there to mediate or even try to control the situation.

After this explosion happened, and we were trying to move forward with confirmation classes and the necessary requirements to get confirmed, our daughter started to experience some very real doubts about the faith. You see, she witnessed one of her good friends getting treated extremely cruelly by the confirmation instructor and the priest. The instructor, on the day of the incident, told this fifteen-year-old girl that she would not be allowed to attend the class. From the information we had, there was no reason for this decision to have been made as she had done nothing wrong and did not warrant this kind of a reaction. From what we could surmise, the instructor was responding to comments the pastor had made about this young girl and her family—in other words, gossip. Faye also started to wonder about the role our pastor played in all of this and was having an extremely tough time reconciling it all. When you're fifteen years old it is not easy to separate the priest from the man. In other words, a priest is still human and can make mistakes, but his role as a priest is still valid. In this case, the man outside of the priesthood had acted immaturely and caused harm. This caused a great struggle for my daughter for the next two years.

As the months passed by we, the parents of the three fifteen-year-old girls, tried desperately to set up a meeting with the

CHAPTER TWENTY

pastor. It finally happened, and we were able to meet face-to-face with him. We walked through all of our grievances and explained to him what we were upset about. While we were there in the office visiting with him, it appeared he was trying to make amends. We accepted that and agreed to move forward. It didn't take long, however, and he returned to his usual behavior. By this point in time, the kids were pretty well over it all and were looking for a change. Justin and Faye were still in confirmation class, and we needed to finish that up and get them confirmed before we did anything else.

When the time finally came for the confirmation, it turned out to be quite a beautiful ceremony. We had some relatives travel from out of state to be there for it, which was really quite nice. Faye's cousin (Tina) also came out for the confirmation, which was her closest cousin. We were limited on space in our house and maximized on visitors, so we decided to rent a hotel room for Faye, Aunt Mary, and Tina. The boys shacked up in Justin's room, and the rest of us managed the best we could. We all managed to get ready at our prospective places and made it to the church on time. They got confirmed, and we had a big celebration afterward. It was pretty wonderful.

Toward the end of the week, when my brother and his family were about ready to head back home, my daughter and niece took me aside privately to talk. It's necessary to fill in a little detail here. As I had mentioned before, there were some struggles with my brother, sister-in-law, and their children. My sister-in-law was having some health problems, which seemed to be impacting her ability to take care of her children. The problem was she didn't realize it, and it was having a major impact on her kids. So a few of the kids had talked to me looking for some help and guidance over the years. I had spoken to my brother on numerous occasions regarding this issue and asked him to get his wife some help. He was not successful in doing so, and it was now heavily affecting their daughter, Tina. Tina asked if she could stay with us for a while longer. So my husband and I spoke to my brother and arranged to keep her for another week.

At the end of that week, when it was time to take her back to the airport, something significantly shifted in her. I have this memory, frozen in my mind like a snapshot, of Tina on our way to the airport. I was driving the car, and I remember looking back in my rearview mirror, and when I saw her face, and our eyes locked, I saw what looked like despair. Every fiber of my being told me not to put her on that plane and send her back home, but I didn't have any other option. After all she was not my child, and I had no authority over her.

Things got very bad for her after she returned home. To begin with, she ended up getting very sick and it lasted for quite a while. Eventually they took her to a doctor and finally discovered she would need to have her tonsils removed. She went to a hospital in Denver to have this done, and her mom went with her. She had been losing weight, and definitely not thriving, so we were hoping this would help. While the surgery fixed her health problems, it seemed to have exacerbated the emotional problems she was struggling with.

One night I got a call from my brother and he said Tina had been taken to the hospital and was on suicide watch. She was then placed in a facility and was not released for a month. What I found out later, from Tina's therapist in the facility, led me to the conclusion Tina was not telling her the truth about how she felt or what was going on with her. I discovered this when I talked to the therapist. I was concerned we couldn't get Tina stabilized and out of the facility and frustrated it was taking so long, and I

CHAPTER TWENTY

needed to understand why. Tina gave permission for me to talk openly with the therapist about her situation, and here's what I discovered.

The therapist lost her opportunity to build a bond with Tina early on because her actions gave the appearance she had sided with Tina's parent. This was like a red flag for me, and I immediately told her she lost her chance to help Tina. I said Tina needed to feel as though you were on her side 100 percent, and that is not what she experienced. The therapist said she was on her side and was trying to help her, and I told her I knew she was, but Tina did not know that. I explained she had been feeling as though she had been screaming for help for many years, and her parents were not listening. I then told the therapist that when she spoke up for Tina's parents, it appeared she had taken their side in things, and Tina couldn't trust her. I then told her I thought it was too late for her to get that trust back. She agreed, and so we went about problem solving the rest of it. The reason they couldn't release her was she could not guarantee she would tell her parents if she was actually suicidal. So we had to come up with a solution.

That is when we decided she should go and live with her Aunt Mary in Denver. When Tina got out of the facility, she stayed temporarily with her parents as my sister was making arrangements for her to live at her house. Eventually she got everything arranged, and we were able to move my niece up to Denver. My sisters and I had to talk at great length about what was needed for Tina moving forward. We decided she needed to get a job, and she would need to get into school. My sister-in-law had been homeschooling her, but because of her health issues, she wasn't able to give Tina what she needed education-wise. She was behind in school, but we just didn't know how far behind.

2012/2013

It was fairly easy for my sister to get Tina applying for jobs, and in short order she was working. This was something she had told us she had wanted to do for a while. She had wanted to get a job so she could make some money and get out of the house once in a while. When it came to school, however, that was a whole other difficulty. My sister worked painstakingly at trying to find the right school and the right fit for my niece. She talked to many of the principles at the various schools in their area and eventually found a place for her to settle into. She was definitely getting on her feet thanks to my sister's help. As a side note, all the stress of this had caused me to develop Shingles. I was in a lot of pain for about six weeks suffering greatly. It took about 2 weeks to even discover I had it, but once I did we started treating it. What can I say no good deed goes unpunished.

The problem with all of this was the impact it had on our daughter. Little did we know how much of this darkness, sadness, and suffering our niece was going through had impacted Faye. It wasn't until years later we put together a majority of the pieces to that puzzle. Our daughter was exposed to things we didn't even know about, and had been the target of comments and criticisms that had really scarred her. I think this may have negatively impacted her emotional development as well. That will be a story for another day, or another chapter.

In regards to the matter at hand, it's suffice to say that once Justin and Faye got confirmed, the interactions with our pastor at our local parish continued not to be very good, so we decided it was time to make a change for our family. My husband and our four kids were all on board with the idea of traveling down to Seattle to attend the fraternity parish. This was an hour and a half drive one way, with a lot of heavy traffic, and I was not feeling very certain about it. I didn't realize it was such a positive

CHAPTER TWENTY

thing for the rest of my family until I started complaining about the drive. That's when I found out what was really going on.

I personally was having a hard time letting go of the parish we belonged to. We had made a lot of friends there and had a lot of good years and meaningful experiences. My son served at a lot of the Masses at that parish with two of his best friends and had just started the process of discerning the priesthood. In addition, my girls had multiple opportunities to play various musical instruments, sing in choir, and participate in all of the church functions. I also sang in choir, volunteered for various functions, and overall enjoyed my time with the families I met there. I guess I naturally assumed my husband and kids would have a hard time tearing away from this environment. What they told me one day, on our way back from a TLM Mass in Seattle, was they were tired of the drama at our local church, and they didn't like the way our pastor was handling the situation. In addition, very much to my surprise, my husband and kids told me they enjoyed the drive to and from our church in Seattle because it gave us all a chance to talk to one another about church-related topics, as well as anything else going on in our lives. They said the drive was time well spent, and it made them all so close to us and to each other. That pretty much put things in perspective for me, and I realized we would be making a permanent change.

CHAPTER TWENTY-ONE

2014/2015

What can I tell you about 2014 other than to say discernment, discernment, discernment. We were in the throes of helping Justin decide what he wanted to do with his life. At this point in time, he had been thinking about the priesthood for a while and had visited a couple of religious orders. He had specifically visited a religious order in California about three times and was wondering what he should do. I had never been exposed to any discernment process when I was growing up. My family didn't really talk about that kind of thing. Since my husband had converted to Catholicism, he didn't know much about the process either.

We were hoping to receive a lot of guidance from our priests and pastor, but that didn't exactly happen. We had been pretty much going it alone for a number of years with our kids. We talked openly about vocations to the priesthood and religious sisters, and whenever possible visited with religious sisters, seminarians, and priests alike. In addition we were blessed with a beautiful retreat held once a year which included priests, and religious from across the country that came to one location to help the youth learn about what they do. The priests and

CHAPTER TWENTY-ONE

religious' would eat meals with the teens, play sports, and do talks over the course of those long weekends. It gave the kids a chance to ask questions and learn about priestly and religious life. It was a beautiful experience and helped our son and daughters know what it was like to live as a religious sister or as a priest.

As Justin got further along in his discernment, we were blessed with a little angel to help him along his course. We had met a gentleman from the monastery my son had been visiting. He actually was the real reason we even knew about the monastery to begin with. He was the brother to one of Justin's closest friends (Jacob), and he had formed an attachment to our family, and even more so we had formed an attachment to him. He was a religious brother (Brother J) and was still going through his formation at the monastery, so we were only able to visit with him when he was home on his breaks. In the meantime we just emailed him. He was a great help to our son, and of course to us, as he helped explain the process. He had a very special and unique gift for putting people at ease, sharing the truth of the teachings of the Catholic faith, and making people feel appreciated. He was also a fabulous leader for young boys and men. He naturally knew how to listen and interact with them.

As our son's discernment got more serious, we started to realize there was a good chance he might join a seminary or monastery somewhere. As he prayed for direction from God, he asked a couple of priests for some help. They both, independent of each other, told him he would need to break up with his girlfriend to properly discern. This was going to be a big event as he had been dating this young lady for about three years. She was the daughter of one of our closest friends and was a very sweet young lady. They were both very young when they started dating each other, so I was surprised they had lasted so long. Nonetheless, poor Justin could see the writing on the wall.

After tormenting himself for quite a while, he realized it was time to pull off the Band-Aid. The night he broke up with his girlfriend, Katrina, was a painful night for all of us. My girls were close friends with her and two of her sisters, so it was like breaking up with both families. Katrina was absolutely devastated, as was our poor son, and they both wore their pain vividly. The night they broke up, and she got home, there was no opportunity for her to just cry herself to sleep and mourn her breakup. That's when we found out she had too many responsibilities to take care of at the house. When we found that out, I asked the girls to go down to her house and be with her to give her some support. I was home with our son trying to give him some support, but he seemed much more concerned about her well-being. I assure you this is a trademark of Justin's—to always be more concerned with somebody else's pain and sadness than with his own.

So the next night my daughters drove down to Katrina's house to help her with some of her chores and give her some companionship. On their way back home that night, the car broke down, and they called us to let us know what happened. We immediately called triple A and arranged for a tow truck to come. Since the driver claimed he would not be able to transport the girls in his tow truck, Katrina offered to come and get them and then drive them up to our house. I didn't want her to come that far, but she did it anyway, and I was very grateful.

When she got to our town, I asked her if we could go for a drive so I could talk to her. I wanted to check in on her to make sure she was doing okay. She was upset Justin had broken up with her, but not surprised. She said she always knew he felt a tug in that direction, and she blamed herself for letting herself get

CHAPTER TWENTY-ONE

so close to him. I told her there was nothing either one of them could do, that this was just life. She was clearly trying to accept what had seemed inevitable to her for quite some time, but her heart was broken, and there was no fast way to heal that.

We talked for quite a while that night, and she opened up quite a bit with me. I learned a lot about her life, hopes, dreams, and struggles. She had some very personal, extraordinarily painful, and emotionally devastating experiences throughout her life, and she was trusting enough to share them with me. One of the events in her life was very serious, and she had some serious scars from it—the wounds weren't even closed yet. I thought she needed to get some help. I told her what I thought and she agreed but was concerned her family might not be so supportive in that regard. We finished the heavy-duty talk and decided to separate for the night. When I went home I had all of the stories she had shared with me swirling around in my head, and I was not able to sleep. I doubt she got any sleep either after all she had been through.

I shared with my husband some of the stuff we had talked about, and he agreed we should help her get connected with somebody for therapy and to work through the problems. Our first thought was a priest we both knew and who we thought would have a good approach on how to help her. I called Katrina up the next day and talked to her at length about the idea I had. She was definitely in support of the idea and knew she needed to talk it out. I called and set up an appointment with the priest, and the two of us drove down together to meet with him.

He was very compassionate, kind, and caring. He comforted her and told her he could help. He seemed grateful she had reached out to him and told her he would help her in any way he could. He said he would also like to talk to her parents so they could be aware of her needs. While we understood that this needed to happen, Katrina and I were both very concerned they would not take it well. We tried to tell the priest our assessment of the situation, but he thought it was best to handle it that way. So we went forward with the plan.

When her parents found out Father was coming over to talk to them about some emotional struggles she was going through, they exploded. I'm assuming it was an embarrassment they didn't know their daughter was struggling, but either way, they did not handle it well. They both got very angry at me for inserting myself into the situation. They basically told Father they didn't want me coming over to their house when he went to sit down with them. It was the beginning of the end for our friendship. This process with Katrina ended up lasting quite a while, and my husband, girls, and I were still very involved—if only from a distance. She called me on a regular basis when she needed help or comfort.

While I was in the process of helping Justin's ex-girlfriend, another blow came our way. It was an incredibly unsettling blow, that is for sure. An individual my family knew very well had served time in jail. This was a person that we not only knew but whose house my kids had been to on a number of occasions, and not only my kids, but my brother's kids as well. We didn't know anything about this and would have liked to have been informed if my brother had any knowledge of the crime. After all, maybe we don't want that kind of negative influence. When my sisters and I found out about this friend's record, we decided to tell my brother and sister-in-law about the subject matter. The worst part of this was that our brother knew about it the whole time and never told us. It's one thing to let your own kids be influenced by that person, but it's quite another to expose someone else's kids without telling them.

CHAPTER TWENTY-ONE

As it turned out, my brother and sister-in-law not only knew about his criminal record but they hadn't even told their own children. There had been a good deal of rebellion going on in the family at this point, with some of the older siblings, and this news just added to the frustration. It's important for me to make clear my brother and sister-in-law are very good, kind, and religious people, who didn't intend to cause harm to their children or other family members. To be honest, they almost seemed emotionally numb when we brought up the subject in the first place. Their children were hurt when they found out this friend of the family, whom they had known so long, had some serious skeletons in the closet. The whole situation upset my husband and I and both of my sisters. The news also severely impacted my niece Tina, and that ultimately hurt my family in the end. So my husband, kids, and I all got hit with a double whammy, if you will.

Meanwhile, as this was going on, I feel as though I neglected my poor son yet again. He was grieving too after the breakup and in the meantime still processing his priestly call. He had so much weight on his shoulders; it was pretty painful to watch. Toward the end of 2014, he went back to the monastery for another visit and to decide if that's where he was going to enter. When he returned home, he filled out his application, wrote up his essay, and turned it all into the monastery. He wasn't very convinced that he would get a call back. He did, however, receive a call back, and they told him he had been accepted to the Monastery and would be entering in August of 2015.

Then we spent the next few months preparing for his entry into the monastery in California. There were a lot of steps he had to go through to be ready to enter that fall. We were all trying to wrap our minds around the idea he would be leaving us in just a few months. I know he was excited, and I know he was also scared, but he felt as though God was calling him to it, and he was going to be obedient to that call. We wanted to make sure we did as much stuff with him as possible before he left, which ended up being a long list of activities. One day when I was walking with his friend Ben, and talking about Justin leaving, Ben turned to me and said he's really leaving isn't he?, "He's really going, isn't he?"

I looked at him confused, as Justin had been talking about this for a couple of years, and said, "Yes, he is." Ben started talking about what he was going to do with his own life because he didn't have a plan.

I smiled sweetly at him and said, "Justin tried to get you to go with him on some of these visits, but you were reluctant."

Ben said, "I know; I just don't think I was ready at that time." I agreed with him, and suggested that maybe he could start visiting some seminaries himself. He did and later entered a seminary.

As the date for Justin's exit from the home started getting nearer, everyone was trying to make last-minute plans with him. I feel like we had a million going away parties for him. In addition, Justin wanted to do one last road trip with his friends before he entered, so they planned a two-week excursion out to Clear Creek monastery from Washington State. The road trip was to take place one month before we left to take him to California. Prior to his leaving, however, I had to make an unexpected road trip out to Colorado for my uncle's funeral.

My uncle had died unexpectedly, and I wanted to make it home to be there with the family. The memorial service was lovely, and it was very good to see all the family. We spent some time with my dad, cousins, and siblings after the funeral, getting

CHAPTER TWENTY-ONE

caught up and just loving one another. I got the privilege of traveling with my youngest daughter Alexis on this road trip, which gave us a great opportunity to spend some quality time together. It was a really sad, but really great, road trip, until we made the drive back home.

She and I stopped at a hotel halfway home so I didn't have to drive through the night. We got a hotel room with a pool and a hot tub—our usual requirements. The two of us were playing around and enjoying ourselves when all of a sudden I jumped in the pool, feet first, and when I hit the bottom, I felt some serious pain in my right heel. I proceeded to hobble over to the hot tub and try to relax a little bit, but the darn thing was still hurting. I was talking to a couple also taking a soak in the hot tub and they asked what had happened to my foot. I repeated the story. The wife looked at me and said "You may have broken your heel." I just laughed this off as it seemed ridiculous I could have hurt myself that badly just jumping in a pool.

Needless to say, when I woke up the next morning I couldn't put any weight on my heel. I had a twelve-hour drive ahead of me, so I took some ibuprofen and proceeded to drive us all the way home. A few days after I got home, I went to the orthopedist, and when she took an X-ray she discovered I had broken my heel. She seemed a little amazed I managed to drive another twelve hours in that condition. We all just kind of laughed because that's pretty normal for me to do the impossible when I think I have no option. If I don't know I shouldn't be able to do something, then I just do it. She had me buy some hiking boots and wear them all the time as a way to repair the broken heel. It looked silly at times, but it did the trick. Truth be told I'm pretty sure my Guardian Angel did most of that drive since he's very gifted and can do almost anything.

2014/2015

2 weeks after I arrived home Justin and his friends took off for Clear Creek monastery in Oklahoma. They took my van, as that was the biggest vehicle any of us had to transport four big men and their luggage. That two-week trip was quite the adventure for all of them. They fought with each other, laughed with each other, slept in a tent by the side of the road, slept in the van, and broke down one mile outside of Clear Creek monastery. They walked about a mile to get to the monastery in 100-degree weather. They left the van until a couple days later when they finished their visit. They took it to a shop in the nearby town and waited for the repair to be done. Once finished, they went back on the road again. We were beginning to think they may never make it home, but they returned nonetheless. They were haggard, road worn, and glad to be back. To this day, however, it remains one of their favorite memories. It was definitely a dude's road trip.

Before the engine really had a chance to cool, we packed up the van again and headed for California. We had multiple stops planned along the way, which made for an exciting family trip. Justin wanted to see a place called Crater Lake in Oregon. It was absolutely beautiful. The lake was the deepest blue color I've ever seen, and the hiking trail we took to the top of one of the lookout points was fairly brutal. It was worth every minute. We got to the top and took a bunch of family pictures and then hurried ourselves back down the trail so we could get on the road and get to our hotel.

We got to see the Redwood Forest and made our way into Sacramento. One of the days we headed into San Francisco to do some of the touristy stuff. Shortly before we left, however, I decided I should throw my back out—which appeared to be a common theme. I was basically crippled up for the rest of the trip. It didn't hold me back though, and I went into San Francisco

CHAPTER TWENTY-ONE

with the rest of the family. We took a water taxi across the bay, and when we got to "San Fran" we ate some lunch and went to investigate some of the Catholic churches, Sts Peter and Paul, which was beautiful. We finished the day with a baseball game at AT&T stadium. The crazy thing was one of my brothers flew into San Francisco that very night for a business trip. So we managed to connect with him, meet him at the stadium, and visit for about two hours. It gave him a chance to say goodbye to Justin.

The next day we drove down to Orange County and to our hotel. It was now getting very close to having to say goodbye, and none of us wanted to face that reality. The day finally came, and we drove him to the monastery. We met a couple of the priests there, and our good friend Brother J as well, and got a tour of the grounds. These were very small grounds, mind you. This will probably surprise you to know that neither the girls nor I had ever stepped foot in this location, and other than Brother J, had never met anyone else from the monastery. That was the craziest thing of all to not even know where he would be living and who he'd be living with.

Well we had put it off as long as we possibly could and the time had come to say goodbye. We had no idea when we would be able to see him again. It was probably about the most painful thing I'd ever done, and I think the rest of the family would agree. We all hugged him, told him how much he meant to us, and told him we were proud of him. None of us talked much on the drive back to the hotel. I don't remember how much we cried, but the sadness was palpable. We had planned to go to Knott's Berry farm the next day, but the family trip had lost some of its luster. We spent the whole day there riding rides and eating junk food, but nothing felt the same. When you are as close a family as we are, it feels like a part of your body is missing. It hurts beyond

2014/2015

belief. As much as I was hurting and the girls, my husband looked even worse. That was his only son after all.

We made the long drive back home and arrived around 5:00 a.m. We had decided to drive through the night instead of getting a hotel. We even stopped off in Portland Oregon around 2:00 a.m. at a wickedly bizarre donut shop called "Voodoo Donuts." I still can't say if the donuts were worth it because I don't remember, but it was in a horrible neighborhood and was seemingly as unsafe a place as you could get. It was such a dangerous-looking area that my husband sat in the car outside so that we could jump in as fast as possible once we came out of the donut shop. Anyone else would have changed their minds, but that's our family. We get an idea in our heads, and we have to go for it.

When we arrived home, we quickly unpacked our belongings. My husband went upstairs to do something and walked into Justin's room. When he came down the stairs, he had the most painful look on his face I had ever seen. His eyes welled up with tears, and he mumbled he had just walked in Justin's room. I think we all started to cry at that point. When the moment passed we all headed to bed, and about two hours after we had fallen asleep, Tom was awakened by a phone call from his work. The company he worked for had been sold to another business, and he was going to be under new leadership. He was supposed to be off of work still for vacation but ended up having to go to a mandatory meeting to find out what was going to happen with his job. It made for a very special end to a very sad, and painful, goodbye to our son.

The rest of 2015 was adjusting to the emptiness we all felt without having Justin around. I guess in a sense the job change was a lucky distraction for my husband. Since everything was

CHAPTER TWENTY-ONE

new, new insurance, new management structure, and eventually new offices, it kept Tom on his toes. I really wanted to go and see my son in a few months, but we couldn't afford for both my husband and I to go, so I arranged for him to make the first trip out there in January. He went on the trip with Faye. In December, a few weeks before they went out to visit him, we got an opportunity to talk to Justin on the phone. He had been given his habit (a relgious garment worn by monks) and religious name and was enjoying Christmas break. I was devastated when I found out all of the other seminarians in his class had received care packages from their families. Nobody had ever told me we could send them care packages, so I didn't send him anything for Christmas. I was so upset I called his Superior and complained about not being informed. I said I thought they were supposed to be separating from everything they knew, and he said we leave it up to the families to determine how much they want to be involved. A heads up on that sure would have been nice. My son, away from home for the first time, receives no food, gifts, or care packages from his mom or family. How do you think that made me feel?

CHAPTER TWENTY-TWO

2016/2017

So January rolled around, and my husband and daughter flew out to California to see Justin. I sent them out there with gifts for him to make up for the lack of gifts at Christmas. They got a hotel close to the monastery and were able to go and visit him three days in a row. They didn't get a lot of time with him, as that's how visits go, but at least they got to see him, hug him, and just be with him. By this point in time things were going pretty well for him, and he seemed genuinely happy. I think that made things much better for my husband.

Faye and Tom returned home and resumed their activities. At this point in time we were in full-swing with the kids' sports and music. Justin, before he left for the Monastery, had been playing drums for a couple of years, was naturally good at it, and really seemed to enjoy it. He tried his hand at multiple sports, but competed in baseball and golf when he was in high-school. Faye, Agnes, and Alexis had taken some singing and recorder lessons in the past, but their focus was now on their sports. Faye was 100 percent into swimming. As a mom involved in her kids' lives, I volunteered to help with the swimming, diving, and

CHAPTER TWENTY-TWO

dance. While none of these sports always guaranteed the nicest parents, swimming I would have to say was the best environment. Dance was just like they show it in the movies. The dance moms were very crazy, and very mean.

I had the hardest time volunteering at Agnes's dance studio because the moms seemed to like to make it impossible for anyone to fit in. During the shows, I used to work back in the dressing rooms, helping kids get into their costumes, their hair done, and lined up when they needed to be. None of the moms would even carry on a conversation with me. I would try talking to them, and they would just dismiss me. It was always a painfully long volunteer session, but I did it for my daughter. The girls in her dance class were equally bratty and especially cruel to her. I always wondered why she didn't quit. She would just tell me she needed to push through because she loved to dance, and she wasn't going to let these bratty girls take that away from her—she didn't call them bratty, I did. Clearly she was more mature than me.

Around this time we also started hearing some strange rumors that our friend Brother J had left the monastery. We didn't know the details and had been told this through various sources, so we weren't sure what to make of it. The problem, however, was everyone knew our son was in the same monastery and that we were close to this individual, so naturally they assumed we'd know. Not only did we not know, we were afraid to ask. There seemed to be a lot of gossip going around, and we didn't want to spread more of that, so we kept our mouths shut and went directly to the source to ask. Of course the source wasn't answering either. He was out of contact with everyone, from what we understood.

His brother told us there had been some problems at the monastery regarding his schooling and priestly preparation. You can imagine how unsettling this would be as we had just helped move our son there five months prior. I wanted to know what was going on, and I wanted to know from him directly, not his brother. Unfortunately Jacob became the spokesperson because the parents weren't talking nor was Brother J. It was a nightmare for us and it caused us many sleepless nights. We didn't know what to think.

This went on for about six months and eventually I started to realize that this was a struggle specific to Brother J and not to the community of men living at the monastery, or his formation there either. He was a very good man but was in a lot of emotional turmoil and didn't ask for help when he was in the deepest struggles. We found out through his family that he, in a sense, suffered a nervous breakdown and had to leave the monastery. This news never came directly from him,; although prior to that he was texting and calling us fairly frequently. I guess you could say he fell off the cliff and ceased to contact anyone anymore. I wish he had reached out to his superiors before it became critical because I think they would have helped him a great deal.

In the fall of 2016, we made a trip out to California to see Justin. We had talked to him on the phone every month, but I had not seen him in one solid year. We were pretty broke, and I could not justify going into a little bit of debt just to travel out there to see him. If I had been smarter, I would have realized I shouldn't worry about the money, as spending time with my child was more important, but I always struggled financially, and monetary struggles sometimes consumed me. I wish someone had told me to spend the money and go visit Justin. Needless to say, when I saw him for the first time, I thought I was going to cry. I had missed him so much it actually hurt, and I think he missed us also.

CHAPTER TWENTY-TWO

We had a short meeting with the priest in charge of his schooling before we spent time with Justin as a family. That's when we got into the discussion about what had happened with Brother J. As the priest started explaining the situation, he was able to enlighten us on what they had experienced with Brother J abruptly leaving the monastery. As it turned out, the community of priests had actually reached out to him, given him some money and a vehicle to use, and had just asked him not to make any rash decisions but to instead take some time away from the monastery to relax and pray. They tried the best they could to support him, but in the end he chose to leave. This definitely rocked our world, and for a number of months, it moderately disrupted Justin's life as well.

Our visit with Justin was wonderful, and it was so exciting to hear about his life and what had been going on. We were able to take him out to eat, go to the beach, and just in general visit with each other. We also got a couple of opportunities to meet some of his confreres, which we could clearly see was just a bunch of regular dudes coming together to offer themselves over to God and his church. They were a fun bunch of guys, and we really connected and bonded with them all. It started to feel like a real family there, and continues to be that way even to this day.

Things were going well back at home, and our daughters were really improving in their swimming and dance. Faye had been training very hard with her swimming and competed both on a competitive sports team as well as the local high school swim team. She had finally regained all of her strength and race speed, after having broken her arm two times, and her future was looking very promising for college if she should choose to attend. Alexis was also on the high school swim and dive team and was actively working at her diving—she really enjoyed this activity. She swam some with the high school team as well, but her real interest was of course diving. It was a way to use some of her gymnastics skills, and she liked the challenge. She had one small issue that would unfortunately plague her the rest of her diving career; she could not do a reverse dive off the board. It was an extreme mental block for her and very frustrating for all of us to watch. Her coaches knew she had the talent and the ability to succeed at this sport, but they were hard pressed to find a way to get her over this hurdle. As for Agnes, she was our prima ballerina. Just like her other two sisters, she worked and trained very hard to be the best she could be at dance. All three of them set lofty goals for themselves and worked hard to attain those goals.

When Justin had been living at home, he and all three of the girls attended community college in a nearby town. They were able to attend this college for free during their junior and senior years of high school. This was a no-brainer for all of us as it paid for two years of schooling and gave them not only experience in a school setting but the ability to enter a four-year institution if they should choose. In addition, a lot of the four-year institutions accepted the credits from this community college, which would mean they would only have to attend two more years to get their bachelor's degree. To be honest, however, as nice as all of that was, the part Tom and I liked the best was the free part.

As Faye continued her senior year in swimming, she was definitely at the top of her game and one of the top swimmers in her field. She and four other teammates made for some very competitive relays as well. They knew they had a good chance of going to state in a few of these relays, and Faye and another swimmer on the team were always competing neck and neck, which kept them both actively improving their times. It was

CHAPTER TWENTY-TWO

nice to have Faye and Alexis on the swim team together, and I won't lie to you, it was very nice having two of my kids in the same sport. However, these swim meets were not for the faint of heart, and Tom and I put in a lot of hours transporting the girls to and from their meets and volunteering at many of the home events as well. My favorite volunteer position was working as an announcer. I loved an opportunity to get so involved in the swimming, and I really liked getting the crowd involved when possible.

As we were nearing the finish line for Faye's district and state meets, our anxiety was pretty high. Faye had a couple of individual events she could most likely place in districts and state, but in the end, she chose two individual events and two relays. When her district meet was finished, she walked out of there with four gold medals around her neck. Since she was the only one to receive four gold medals, one would think she had won the district swim meet, but that was not the case. Due to some irregular mathematical calculations—created by a highly irregular dude—they gave the title to another swimmer. Mind you, that swimmer did not place first in all of her events. Both she and Faye were confused by the whole thing as well. Nonetheless, we celebrated and prepared for the next and final stage—the state meet. The competition was much more intense at this level, but even with that, Faye medaled once again in all four of her events. It was amazing to see her up on the podium receiving all those awards. We had so much fun reveling in the glory. When she got home, I had her put all of the medals on at once and took pictures. It is a moment frozen in time I remember vividly—my skinny little girl wearing eight medals that probably weighed more than she did. It was a great wrap up to what ended up being her final swim season in school.

2016/2017

As for Agnes, she continued to work very hard at her art, which was dance—specifically ballet. As mentioned before, some of these dancers, and a good majority of their mothers, were the most difficult people to be around. The moms taught their daughters they would not have to work hard if they wanted to achieve their goals because their parents would step in if needed. It was an exhausting and annoying experience for my daughter and I, year after year. Luckily, however, along the way, she ended up with a very solid male dance instructor, and he saw her hard work and talent and took a liking to her. He was only at the facility for a year and a half, but that was just the boost she needed.

Since Agnes did not grow up in that town, or the nearby area, she was not a known entity. This meant some of the instructors took a liking to the other students whom they were more familiar with. This also impacted the types of roles she got in the shows, until Mr. Winn came to the studio. Agnes ended up in some very exciting roles and was lined up to dance in Flowers and Snow for one of the *Nutcracker* performances, thanks to his involvement in the development and choreography of the show.

Through no fault of her own, Agnes ended up getting sick with chickenpox. It was spreading through the family at this point, and we knew that once she got it, it would take two weeks before she could return to the studio. That would give her just enough approved absences to still be in the show. We talked to Mr. Winn and the other instructors to let them know how long she would be gone. She was fitted for her costumes, and everyone that needed to know was made aware of her status. We all agreed that if she recovered in time, she could still perform.

Like clockwork, the two weeks passed and she was starting to feel better. She was still extraordinarily weak, however, from

CHAPTER TWENTY-TWO

being sick. As a side note, this lovely gift of chickenpox was brought to our family channel by none other than me. It was a little gift I received during the emotional crisis that happened when Tina went into the suicide facility. I ended up getting shingles from all of the stress, and with that passed on chickenpox to the kids. Which leads us to the *Nutcracker* show. The first night of dress rehearsal, Agnes and I showed up only to be met with some of the meanest and most unhappy dance moms one could imagine. Some of the girls were equally cruel to Agnes as they had started preparing to take over her role in Flowers. They stood like ravenous wolves over a dead carcass.

One of the moms approached me and said, "The moms and I don't appreciate Agnes coming in at the last minute and taking the roles away from our daughters."

I turned to her and said these roles were not given to their daughters but that they were merely understudies for Agnes. In addition, I asked her if she was actually telling me she preferred my daughter to be sick so her kid could get the part. She stammered at this point, and then I walloped her with a good comment. I said, "I thought you told me that you were a Christian—what true Christian wishes harm or illness on another." She knew I was right, and she knew she was caught in a hard spot. So she just responded by saying that Agnes had missed too many practices and that she shouldn't be allowed to dance. I then told her she had missed only the allotted number she was allowed, and Mr. Winn approved it, so if she would like, we could both go talk to him. She just got up and left at that point—the coward that she was.

I assume Mr. Winn knew what was happening with the other moms because he came to me and told me not to worry about anything and that he would take care of Agnes. I thanked him emphatically, but then I said I was actually more concerned with whether or not Agnes had the strength to do the dances. Both Flowers and Snow are extremely long dances, and neither he, nor I, were sure she could handle it. He just simply said, "We'll do a run through and see how she's doing. If she thinks she can handle it, I will let her, but if she's too tired, then we'll give it to the understudy." She was more than agreeable to this. It was at this point that Agnes told me how horribly the other girls have been treating her, and I said "Yep I'm getting the same." I said, "We'll talk about it later, but for now let's see what you can get done."

After the run through at dress rehearsal, it became pretty obvious to Agnes, Mr. Winn, and I that she wouldn't be able to do both dances. She of course was emotional about this because she had worked so hard to earn those roles, but it was just too much for her poor little body. So he and I talked to her and asked her what she wanted to do. She said she thought she could do Snow but did not think she'd be able to do Flowers. Mr. Winn agreed that this was probably a good choice, and he asked if Agnes wanted to let the understudy know. She said she would.

Now as it turned out, by God's good blessings, the understudy for the role of Flowers was none other than the daughter of the mom that had been talking to me an hour earlier. The blessing part of it was her daughter had been very sweet to Agnes when the rest of the girls were being bullies. She had told Agnes she was glad she was feeling better and was actually very glad she was going to be able to perform in the *Nutcracker*. So Agnes and I were very happy she would be the one to take her role. I love how God always works things out. It was a beautiful show, and Agnes put on a beautiful performance, but when all was said

CHAPTER TWENTY-TWO

and done, we were ready to go home and collapse for a while. My guardian angel probably had something to do with arranging this situation as well so that this girl's mom would not have a comment left to make.

In the meantime, Alexis was going through a mess of stuff herself. She was busy trying to get that last difficult dive under her belt, and we were trying to help her get that done whatever way we could. We went to the gymnastics facility, where Alexis used to train, to try to work the skill out using the equipment there. Unfortunately, when we returned to the pool, it didn't work. At this point, I was so desperate to help her I even drove her all the way up to Vancouver, Canada for diving lessons once a week. There was a large aquatic facility and some amazing dive coaches working up there, so we were trying to take advantage of that. It was a lot of time and effort put into accomplishing this feat, but as it was always the case for me and my husband, we would do whatever we could to help our kids accomplish their goals. The unfortunate news, however, was that during the time we spent there in Vancouver (roughly four months) we were unable to secure the dive. We just couldn't get her over the mental hurdle she was experiencing.

When she returned to the swim and dive team the next year, things had changed significantly. Unbeknownst to us, they had let go of the diving coach Alexis had from the previous season and who she had really grown to trust. The new coach was a young girl, fresh from the dive team in college, and she was put at the helm. She had good intentions, but her lack of knowledge and expertise was not going to get Alexis to the goal she needed. She really wanted to make it to state in diving, and unfortunately she didn't achieve that goal. Like the rest of my kids, however, I could not have been more proud of her. She worked as hard as the rest of her siblings and poured herself into the training. It is this work ethic that has stayed with her into her adult life and career, as is the case with all of my kids. I just wish the poor kid could have had some fun while she was still in school and accomplished her goal at the same time.

Our family was the most important thing to Tom and me, and we gave all we had to their upbringing, formation, schooling, and physical training. We celebrated their many victories along the way, and the defeats that riddled their path as well. There was not a more important job I have ever done or will do in my life. I am so proud to call myself a mom, and I'm proud to call myself their mom.

Once Faye finished college, she found herself itching to get out of the house. I blame myself for this as I had always told the children when you turn eighteen, you can live at home if you're going to college, or you need to move out and learn how to live on your own. This was what was told to my husband and me when we were teenagers, and I guess we kept the same thought process. We must have said this a lot during their early years because that's what they remember most. The unfortunate part was I kind of changed my position on that as time went on, but by then it was too ingrained in their thinking process. Faye always had a desire to prove things to herself and to the world, and I think that moving out early was part of that mission.

Faye was always a sweet and somewhat naive young lady. She wanted to do well by her family and friends and had a soft spot for those struggling around her. In a lot of ways, she was very much like me. The negative part of that mentality is you tend to be drawn toward the wounded individual in an effort to

CHAPTER TWENTY-TWO

help "save them." Naturally you don't know this as it's happening. In a sense, it's like part of your DNA. What I'm trying to say is that she didn't surround herself with the best of friends or influences, and that had caused her some problems along the way and into the future.

Since Faye was determined to move out, we thought it would be best for her to move into a more supportive situation. We didn't want to keep her from taking this next step in her life, but we weren't exactly sure she was ready to be on her own. So a situation presented itself. A young lady who Faye and I had gotten to know had a room available in her house to rent, and they weren't charging much. This was an ideal situation as we knew the parents very well, and both Faye and I had babysat for them on a number of occasions.

We made the arrangements and started moving her in. She got situated fairly quickly, and we came there to see her, and she came to see us quite often. Our two houses were only about ten minutes apart. I was really quite happy and content with this arrangement. She lived there for a while until they took in another roommate. There were some difficulties with the next roommate, so Faye set her sights on moving into her own apartment. It took a little bit of time, but eventually she connected with another one of the lifeguards at the swimming pool, and they decided to move out.

I had to co-sign on the lease for both of them as neither one of them had any rental history. The only thing I asked of her friend was that she made sure to never miss rent, or if she thought she was going to miss a payment, to let us know ahead of time so we could help her and not have it show up on our credit report. They seemed like good roommates, so I was optimistic that it would work well. It did work well for a bit of time, but then something happened between the two of them, and it went downhill from there. To this day, we still are uncertain what happened exactly, but the roommate was very angry with Faye, and it eventually came to a head.

CHAPTER TWENTY-THREE

2018/2019

Before, during, and after these living situations with Faye, she was going through a lot in her personal life, and it heavily impacted our family. She was struggling with the relationship with her cousin Tina and had been for quite a while. Naturally when a person suffers from the level of depression and anxiety that Tina did, it's going to have an effect on her behavior, and in turn impact the people around her—especially those closest to her. Faye was on the receiving end of some of that depression and stress, and it clouded her judgment and self-image. I did not realize to what extent her self-image was harmed until the following year when she opened up about conversations she and her cousin had. I think she saw Faye as too sheltered and wanted to educate her on the "real world." That education, however, was her version of the "real world," which was tainted by her own internal suffering and despair.

Some of the background regarding Faye's experiences and behavior during this time were as follows: lots of boyfriends, numerous car accidents, a wide variety of non-Christian friends with not-great backgrounds—and a huge desire to fit in and party (like I mentioned, a lot like her mom). The car accidents are still very puzzling to my husband and me. To the best of my ability the only thing I can figure out is she had very poor eyesight, and I think it impacted her ability to read the traffic situations and be able to respond. That, I think, combined with the youthful desire to drive fast and ride up on cars, made for a bad combination. She rear-ended a car on her way home from school, which caused the hood of her car not to latch correctly. She had to stop suddenly on another highway because traffic had come to a complete stop from 60 mph, causing her to rear-end an elderly man. She then pulled out in front of a vehicle on a busy road, which caused another accident and cost her a lot of money in fines. She ended up with tickets for all but one of these accidents. All in all she totaled three cars. Weird thing is if you knew this kid of mine, you would find this to be very shocking because she's not an irresponsible person.

After each one of these accidents she became even more financially broke and a little more unsure of herself—one might say even insecure. For a reason known only to her, she seemed to be what you might call "boy crazy"—a trait that definitely did not come from her mother. One of the things she told me later was her cousin had mentioned to her on occasion that she was too skinny and not very curvy and that boys don't like girls that look like that. This is a very cruel thing to say to a teenage girl. So I think she got it in her head she wanted to be as attractive to boys as she could, possibly to prove her cousin was wrong. Either way with her general sweetness and desire to please, she became an easy target for most guys—especially those without a sense of Christian morality.

Agnes and Alexis were also going through their own internal struggles. I mean, honestly, who of us didn't struggle as a

CHAPTER TWENTY-THREE

teenager coming into adulthood? Alexis, for instance, was definitely missing her gymnastics, and without another sport to participate in, she was left with a lot of time on her hands. She had tried over the years to make friends, as did her sisters, but most of the girls they came in contact with were pretty spoiled. In addition, I have found living on the west coast comes with some strange behavior. A lot of the people we met out there had a very secular and paganistic attitude. There was a lot of anti-God sentiment and a strong desire for wealth and status. There's not a lot of kindness that comes out of that mentality.

A good example of this came a couple of years prior, when both of my daughters were on the swim and dive team together and one of the girls from the team had died. The saddest thing of all was she had taken her life. Now both of my daughters knew her, although not closely, and had just been at a swim meet with her the night it happened. As you can imagine, this devastated everyone, and my daughters were no exception. This is when it became very clear Alexis was not part of the inner circle. All of the swim team kids were spending time together inside and outside of school, but they didn't include her.

There was an occasion, one night in particular, that was exceptionally cruel. Some of the kids from the team decided to go to a pumpkin patch together before Halloween. Alexis was invited along, and when they got back to the pool, they decided they would all meet at a friend's house, carve pumpkins, and then go trick or treating. She came home so excited and told me she would have to leave in an hour or two. I think she ate dinner and waited for her friends to text her. When she didn't hear anything, she reached out a couple of times, and they kept changing the plans. They said they had changed their mind about carving pumpkins, and they may not even go out trick or treating. Alexis just said,

"That's okay. I can come and hang out with you guys anyway. That'll be just as good." The next excuse was they were tired, and they were just going to go to bed. It became very apparent they did not want her there.

So here I am looking at my daughter, whose friend had just died, and the rest of her friends can't even include her in a simple Halloween activity. She was so upset, and all I could do was hug her. It got even worse, if you can believe it. A social media app had just come out called "Snapchat," and most of the girls were using it. So the next thing you know, Alexis sees some photos on her friend's Snapchat page showing them trick-or-treating together without Alexis. The meanest thing about this is everyone who follows those girls on that app can see her story, which made it public to the people in our town. This behavior is basically a public way of humiliating people. God used this opportunity to make Alexis strong, confident, and independent. She no longer looked to friends for her value system; she turned toward God. Her faith grew through the process. Truth be told, however, it broke her mama's heart to observe the whole thing unfold.

Agnes had no shortage of those same kinds of behaviors with some of the girls in dance, as mentioned previously. She had actually formed a friendship with one of the dance girls though, and oddly enough, she seemed to be reliable. If they made plans to go to her house or come to ours or go out somewhere, she usually showed up. If she wasn't going to make it, then she would call ahead and let her know. The people on the coast don't even follow these most simple matters of decorum. They might tell you they're going to come to your party or event, but if something better comes along, they'll just blow you off. My mom would have whipped my butt if I had ever done that to someone.

Agnes was coming into her senior year, and she was waiting

CHAPTER TWENTY-THREE

to see what part she might get in the *Nutcracker*. The dance studio, and more importantly its members, had somehow shifted though, and the parents and students alike were a much nicer breed. In other words, it changed for the better except for a few bad seeds left behind. Much to our surprise, and of course her talent and hard work, she got the role of Sugar Plum Fairy. This was the most desired role in the *Nutcracker*. We were so excited and just couldn't believe it had finally happened. She had a lot of work ahead of her, but she showed up to every practice and worked her tush off.

When Agnes got the role, some of the claws came out. The young lady, who had the role as understudy for the Sugar Plum Fairy, got very upset with Agnes. Apparently she thought she could do it better than my daughter, and she could not hold back her anger.

"This sucks!" she started yelling at Agnes, and said Agnes wasn't taking the role seriously, and therefore didn't deserve it. The teacher immediately removed her from the area and had a private talk with her. She also called her mom, and me as well, and explained what had happened. Up until this moment, the young lady had been one of the more neutral dancers at the studio and had never really treated Agnes poorly. That's what made this kind of a shock. When all was said and done, she apologized to Agnes, her mom and I left things alone and chose not to interfere, and we all moved forward.

The show came and it went beautifully. For the last two years, I had taken over the role of working backstage, which came with two benefits: 1) it got me out of the dressing room with the mean mommas, and 2) I had some authority, so they couldn't push me around. It was great because I got to see my daughter from the wings. The new set of moms in the dance studio, however, were nice and very helpful, and it appeared they were all creating a new and positive environment. It was a great finish to a stressful few years. My daughter danced beautifully in the role of Sugar Plum Fairy, and I could not have been more proud.

During this time, Agnes and Alexis started having trouble with Faye. Faye had told us multiple times how much she missed her brother and how lonely she felt without him there; Justin and Faye were always very close growing up, and his absence seemed to have a profound impact on her. She had started to pull away from the family and was spending a lot of time with her roommate and some other friends. I think Agnes and Alexis wanted some support from their big sister during these difficult times, but it was a combination of issues that led to some distance being formed between the two younger girls and their older sister. For one thing, they were really frustrated with her because of all the car accidents she was having, and for another, they didn't necessarily approve of her choice of friends.

Something was clearly going on with my oldest daughter, and she wasn't really forthcoming. We had done a lot to help Faye along the way, but she was not pulling herself together, and we needed to change tactics. It was time for some tough love since she didn't seem to show much regard for how frustrated we were. We were trying to help her get a better direction in life, but she just kept falling into the same traps. The worst part is she thought she knew what to do, she was trying to do it her own way, and she didn't want to take any advice. Does that sound like any teenager you know?

Faye was also being very secretive. It seemed as if she was living a very worldly life and not much concerned with doing the right thing by us, or more importantly God. She was absolutely broke and at the end of that year was working in a fish packing

CHAPTER TWENTY-THREE

plant. It was a miserable environment to work in as it was freezing cold, and she was in that facility for eight hours a day. She always looked cold, sad, and miserable when we saw her. She had also lost a lot of weight, and her clothes were falling off of her. She had always been a very skinny girl, but this was a whole new level of skinny. This was very disturbing, to say the least. However, until she was ready to face us about what was going on, we couldn't do anything except stand by and watch. Faye was a lot like me and preferred to do things on her own, so she wouldn't accept any money from us. It was heart-wrenching.

As the story of my health continued to decline, I had another hurdle to overcome. I had always experienced very difficult menstrual cycles. They were painful, debilitating, and long. I was in my fifties and not showing any signs of menopause. I was still having a cycle every month, which meant I was in pain for five days out of every month. Not to mention that I also experienced some ruptured cysts along the way, which was excruciatingly painful. Even my naturopath seemed confused as to why I hadn't started showing signs of menopause. After a couple of years of trying to heal myself naturally, it became clear I would probably have to have surgery. Toward the end of 2017 and into 2018. I met with a surgeon and scheduled a hysterectomy.

The original date was at the end of 2017 after Christmas. I had a lot of problems taking medicine and was definitely afraid to go under anesthesia again. So what ended up happening, you might ask? I ended up getting sick, very sick, two days before the surgery. I had a fever and sore throat, and I knew they wouldn't take me into surgery in that condition. I wasn't going to lie about it because I knew the back end and healing was already going to be hard enough, but it might be even worse if I did it with a compromised immune system. So I had to reschedule the surgery, which they couldn't do for six weeks. I was so scared of having surgery, and to have to put it off for another six weeks was like torture for me. I was convinced I wouldn't make it out alive and was so scared I actually wrote "goodbye letters" to my whole family. What a way to spend six weeks.

The day finally came, and I talked to the anesthesiologist before the surgery. My sister came out to be with me for the surgery, and she and my husband sat with me and the anesthesiologist to go over all the details before the surgery. It was so good to have them both there and have the support around me. The anesthesiologist did a perfect job, and I made it out of the surgery without getting sick and without feeling panicked. I was so overjoyed things had gone so well, but not too surprised to find out she had to remove almost everything because there was so much scarring and endometriosis. Needless to say, I was in a great state of mind and health for the first couple weeks after surgery, and then everything went to the proverbial hell in a hand basket.

I was very low on estrogen because I no longer had any ovaries, and my current naturopath just kept increasing the dose on the cream I was using. It eventually became clear that was not working. I slipped into a very severe depression and felt incredibly alone and confused about what was going on with me. My husband and my kids treated me very strangely, and I couldn't understand why. We were fighting all the time, and I felt anger, fear, and panic. I started looking on forums for support. The problem with that is there were a lot of very scary outcomes for some of these women, and reading that when you're already scared and paranoid is not comforting. There were nights I would lay in bed and pray to my Guardian Angel, and God to please keep me alive because I was afraid I was going to try and kill myself.

CHAPTER TWENTY-THREE

I was afraid some dark force inside of me would take the choice out of my hands.

As it turned out, my husband and kids had noticed the change in me and were very scared. The problem was Tom never approached me to tell me he thought I was going through some hormonal changes. Because of the difficulty I had with postpartum depression I was afraid I might have similar responses after the surgery. Before I went into surgery, I begged my husband to please let me know when and if he thought something was changing in me. Of course when push came to shove, and my extreme anger came into play, he basically chickened out. He was afraid to make me upset and never confronted it.

One day I came to him and said things had gotten so bad two nights before, and that I almost didn't make it. He looked at me confused, and that's when I told him I was very close to taking my own life. He told me the kids and he had been talking, and they were afraid I was going through hormonal changes, and Agnes even told him he should talk to me about it. She said, "Mom told us to tell her if she starts acting strangely." I was so angry and felt so betrayed because he promised me he would tell me if he thought anything was changing in me. I said he almost missed a chance to ever talk to me again.

Shortly after this conversation with my husband, I reached out to my younger sister who had been through the same surgery a few years prior and told her I wasn't doing well. She immediately got on the phone with my surgeon's office and explained to them I needed a different type of hormone product. She explained she was only able to use the patches to metabolize the estrogen. So they quickly filled the prescription for me, I started using the patch, and I slowly started crawling out of the very deep hole I had landed in.

2018/2019

About six weeks after my surgery, which was about the time this had all started happening, I went in for my six-week follow-up. While I was in the doctor's office, waiting for her to come in and see me, my daughter Faye walked through the door. I looked at her surprised and asked why she was there. She got very serious, looked very scared, and said she had something very important to tell me but wanted to wait until we were out of the doctor's office. So as soon as we left the office, she and I went out to my car to sit and talk.

By this point I was seriously concerned, and I asked her to tell me what was going on. She immediately started crying and slowly started to explain to me what had happened. She wasn't forthcoming with all the details, mind you—those were going to come later—but she explained to me the most important aspect of it. As it turned out, she had been "catfished" by an individual posing as a cancer victim. This was done via social media of course, and he kept telling her lies about how soon he was going to die if he didn't get some cancer treatments. He asked her to wire money to him via Western Union to pay for the treatments. This went on for months, and she had depleted what little money she had left and was borrowing money from everyone she knew. She was afraid to stop giving him money because he had threatened her. This was why she was being so secretive and had lost so much weight. Finally, one night, someone intervened at the Western Union office, got on the phone with the guy doing this, and then told him she was going to call the police. Luckily, that woman did just what she said she would and called the police. Faye was a wreck at this point in time because I think she was slowly realizing he had used her. This wonderful woman was like a "Guardian Angel" to her and put a stop to all of it. The police showed up, and Faye filled out a report.

CHAPTER TWENTY-THREE

To say I was in a state of shock is an understatement. I immediately asked for his information and name. I called Tom at work, and he looked the guy up and within five minutes had his real name and location in Texas. Everything that happened after that feels much like a blur. We met with the police officer the next night and got a few more pieces to the puzzle, and that night the whole family met for dinner, and Faye revealed to her sisters what had happened. They couldn't believe it and were very angry at Faye for letting this guy do this to her. It was very hard for them to understand she was a victim. They didn't understand how this guy was able to manipulate her and convince her to send him money. It just made them mad because she had refused to listen to any of us for months on end, and she could have saved herself the pain and suffering. It takes a while for kids to understand those kinds of things.

My husband was probably the angriest because, from the time they were little, he always warned them not to put any personal information on the internet and especially not on social media. He warned all of them it was the quickest way for a person to find everything out about an individual and use that against them. He had been in this line of work for twenty-plus years, and he couldn't believe one of his own kids would fall for this scam. The girls, on the other hand, were angry because she had kept this from them, and they felt betrayed. I knew Faye was very wounded and had truly been victimized, which broke my heart, but I also understood where the others were coming from. In other words, I was stuck right in the middle.

The next steps we had to take were to get Faye to completely cut off contact with this individual. We suggested she change her number, but for the meantime, we told her to not respond to any of his phone calls, text messages, or emails. This is when things

2018/2019

really began to unravel, and we started to see how twisted and psychopathic he was. He bombarded her with phone calls and text messages and wrote ridiculously long and hateful emails to her as well. As if she wasn't broken enough, he just kept trying to knock her down. Finally, when she wouldn't respond anymore, he took it up a notch—he contacted my husband's work.

When he got ahold of my husband's contact information, he started doing the same thing at his job that he was doing to my daughter—bombarding them with calls. After the first one or two calls, my husband let the helpdesk people know he was not to be transferred back to Tom. He didn't stop, however, and my husband called me, and we decided it was time to go to the police in our town. We showed up at the police station and briefly explained to the lady at the front desk what was going on. She quickly walked us back to meet with one of the sergeants. We couldn't have asked for a better person to handle this situation because he jumped on it without hesitation once we told him what he had done to our daughter and to us. My husband told him the criminal background on this guy, so the Sergeant asked if we had his telephone number, so we gave it to him, and he proceeded to tear into this guy. The guy was on probation no less and had been in jail as a sex offender, so he had a lot to lose. He wouldn't keep his mouth shut and started trying to fight with the officer. It didn't end well for him though because the sergeant told him if he hassled us or our daughter again, he would contact his parole officer and put him back in jail.

That ended the conversation, and in the long run ended the multiple phone calls. He finally stopped calling and texting Faye, but by then she had already changed phone numbers entirely, so there was no way for him to contact her. I asked her if she wanted to file charges against him and put him back in jail, but she did

CHAPTER TWENTY-THREE

not want to do that. It wasn't that she didn't think he deserved it, but she was so emotionally devastated she didn't have the capacity to do anything more. To this day I wish we would have nailed him for this crime so that he could have gone back to jail. In the end, however, it wasn't my choice to make.

There was so much fallout from this, and I was not in a healthy state of mind to deal with it all. Even as I write this, I can remember how physically horrible I felt, as well as incredibly sad, scared, and confused. Remember that I was still recovering from surgery and all of the depression and suicidal thoughts. Now I had this disaster to deal with. We found out shortly after that Faye had actually betrayed the girls in other ways as well. I know it was in desperation to keep her secret from being revealed, but she had lied to them, and they caught her in the lie, and they were very angry about it. They came to their dad and me to let us know what happened, and I thought my husband was absolutely going to lose it. It was at this point in time the three of them decided they didn't want any contact with Faye. While I knew they had every right to be as angry as they were, I was also concerned we could lose our daughter if we didn't keep in contact with her. I was certain she would go deeper into the black hole, and I did not want that.

So the net result of this dilemma was Faye retreated and kept some distance from us. When she did go places with us, for instance down to church, it would always end up in a huge fight. Tom, Agnes, and Alexis said I was always taking her side and didn't support them, even though they were the ones who had been used and mistreated by Faye. I tried as hard as I could to make them understand how compassionate I was for what they'd been through, but that I was very nervous we might lose Faye altogether if I didn't keep connected to her. As if I hadn't felt alone enough, now my family was pulling away from me too. I was stuck in the middle, reaching with one hand to hold on to Faye and the other to hold on to Tom and the kids. It was brutal, but all I did was pray, constantly ask for direction from God, and follow what he told me to do. I feel most surely he wanted me to stay close to Faye, and that is what I did.

The months and years that rolled out following this event were very difficult. It almost tore us in two and destroyed the close relationships we had all developed. We needed to reach out to Justin as well to inform him of what was happening, but it was difficult to give him any kind of real details until we could meet with him in person on our next trip to California. When we finally made it to California to see him, Tom, Agnes, Alexis, and I tried to explain at length what had happened with Faye. In part he was completely baffled and utterly confused, so there wasn't much input he could give us. Besides he had his own stuff to process as he was trying to determine whether or not he was supposed to be a priest.

It was going to take a number of years for us as a family to work everything out, but we got ourselves to a more functional place, and we started moving forward. Sadly enough, a month or so later, Agnes's dog Sadie started to go downhill. It got to the point where she couldn't walk outside to go to the bathroom anymore—I would have to carry her out there—and she wasn't eating. About a month prior to that, Sadie had actually had a seizure when Tom and I were upstairs in the kitchen. That was a very scary situation for us, and we knew it probably wouldn't be much longer before she passed. I did everything I could to care: giving her baths, blow drying her fur because she couldn't shake off anymore, and hand feeding her when she needed it. The day before Agnes's birthday, we knew she was nearing the end. We

CHAPTER TWENTY-THREE

decided we would take her to the vet the day after our Agnes's birthday—and unfortunately Sadie was her dog, which made it even harder for her.

The day came, and we loaded her up in the car. It was Agnes, Alexis, and I that went to the vet. We stopped by my husband's work to see if he was going to come as well. He said he couldn't handle putting down another dog after seeing Mattie die so we left him at work and headed over to the veterinary office. The girls and I sat in a room with Sadie, loving all over her and saying our goodbyes. When we decided it was time, the girls headed out into the waiting area—neither one of them wanted to be in the room when it happened. So I sat there holding Sadie on my lap, and they gave her the injection. In just a minute or so it was over. It was an incredibly difficult thing to witness. As I sat in the room with our sweet dog Sadie, having just died, I felt an overwhelming sense of loneliness once again. I think that is just one of those things I will probably struggle with for the rest of my life—the feeling of loneliness. There have always been so many moments of loneliness in my life. I just have to remember it's God that always fills that void and nobody else.

Shortly before Sadie got so sick we decided it was time to get Tom the Corgi he had wanted. After a lot of searching, we found a litter of half Corgi/half mini Aussie puppies and drove over to pick one out. When we brought this puppy home the two dogs snubbed him (secretly Sadie probably knew he was her replacement). We named him Joe schmoe and he has been about the craziest dog we've ever owned. He weighs 25 lbs and has eaten more chocolate than any dog I know, loves to bark and whine and talk, and can jump higher and is more athletic than probably any dog in the universe. Quite frankly, he's a pain in the rump, but he's our pain in the rump and we love him.

2018/2019

Luckily, after all that had happened with Faye, she ended up getting a job at Starbucks—and getting out of the fish-packing plant, which was a move in the right direction. She was finally working in a better atmosphere and making more money, so we were very glad for that. She really enjoyed her coworkers and enjoyed the job. She was desperate to make back money as quickly as possible because of the damage this event had done to her bank account and finances. So she was working two and three jobs at a time to do just that. However, once the month of July rolled around, she found herself in a predicament. Faye got very sick and came to me and Tom for help.

I could tell she was not just sick with your run-of-the-mill cold or flu; this was something more serious. I had my suspicions, but we needed to go to the doctor to confirm it. At this point in time, she was working at a Starbucks closer to her apartment as well as working some hours at the coffee shop in our town—because she knew the owner personally. She worked an early shift on the Fourth of July when I came over to see her. She was very bad off. The following day she went to the clinic up by her house to see if they could run some tests. Once again I was suspicious she had mononucleosis just like my son a few years before. She asked the doctor if she could test for it, and she said to my daughter she didn't fit the symptoms. So Faye just looked at her and said, "Listen, my mom is convinced that I have mononucleosis, and she is usually right; either way can you just check?" The doctor thought that was a reasonable request, so she went ahead and ran the test. And lo and behold the kid had mono.

I told her to pack up some things from her house and come and stay with us so I could take care of her. When she got there, I set up an appointment with our doctor to run some more labs. Her liver count was very high, which explained her severe

CHAPTER TWENTY-THREE

abdominal pain, and it was clear she was very sick. The doctor wrote her a note that she couldn't work for two weeks, and then we loaded her up and brought her home. My husband actually had to call her boss at Starbucks because they weren't going to let her have time off. Once he talked to the boss, however, they quickly agreed and let her stay home. I took care of her for the next few days.

She slowly started to get her strength back, and in the meantime, she had been getting to know a young man by the name of Andre. I had asked her if she was dating anyone a few weeks prior, and she fessed up. As it turned out, he was in the military and just happened to be a friend of this couple she knew and was close to. They started to see each other more frequently, and one of the times the girls went up to see a movie with Faye, he joined them. Agnes and Alexis both liked him and thought he seemed like a pretty decent guy. My husband and I also eventually met him and thought he was very nice. We were all very guarded, however, and it took a long time for us to work through our emotional baggage from her past. In other words, we were kind of hard on the guy because she didn't have the best track record for choosing friends/boyfriends. It appeared, however, this guy was going to stick around for a while.

CHAPTER TWENTY-FOUR

2020/2021

I can't believe I actually wrote down the year 2020 and didn't go into cardiac arrest. I don't think there's anyone on the planet that doesn't know what 2020 was. I can't say I want to relive any of it, as I'm sure no one else wants to either, but I think there are some nuggets of information I have to present to complete my story and help you understand the impact it has had on me and my family. So let's start at the beginning of the year.

The very first crisis that landed on my lap had to do with my younger sister Lisa. She was out on a mountain biking trip with her husband and dogs down in southern Colorado. I did not know they were out there, but it wasn't uncommon for them to take little mountain biking trips. I had called my sister because we hadn't talked in a while, and I think I owed her a phone call. I wasn't able to reach her, so I left a message. The following day she called me on the phone sounding exhausted but not giving anything away.

I jabbered away for a little bit, and then I finally asked her how she was doing. Her response was very intense, and her tone was serious. She said she was in the hospital and had been

CHAPTER TWENTY-FOUR

throwing up all night long. She was very sick and definitely very scared. I asked her what had happened, and her response was she had taken an oral live typhoid vaccine, and within a couple hours started having gastric distress. She said Brent—her husband—raced her to the hospital. When they arrived, the doctor that saw them in the ER did a quick assessment on her. He was of the belief she had an intestinal blockage, and in the long run, they would most likely have to do abdominal surgery to open up the blockage. He was at the end of his one-week shift and would not be returning again until the following week. I was so freaked out and scared for her and asked her what I could do to help her. She told me to pray for her and to please not tell anyone what was going on. Can you believe she did that to me?

Normally I try to respect people's wishes—okay, when I think they make sense, I try to respect them—but this was not going to be one of those situations. My sister Anne was out of town on a vacation, and Lisa did not want to disturb her. Nonetheless I called her because I knew she would be very upset if we didn't let her know, and I didn't want to share this burden alone. I told her that she didn't need to head home early, but that I would keep her posted on what was going on. We agreed that, once she got back in town, she would head over to the hospital. In the meantime, I called our cousin and a couple of other people to keep them informed.

The next call I got from Lisa sounded like she was really struggling, and it was clear her condition was worsening. As she was talking to me, she said, "I'm going to be sick," and she jumped off the phone. She was my only point of contact at this time, so I had to sit and wait for updates, which was more than nerve-racking. I can't remember exactly what the order of events was in regards to her worsening condition, but over the course of the next couple days, it became clear things were critical, so my husband and I started making plans for me to fly out there and be with her.

I was continuing to keep everybody in the loop and had notified them I was going to be coming out there to be with her in the hospital. While I made the plans and arrangements I got another phone call from Lisa, and this is when I knew things were dire. She was in tears and told me they were going to have to do surgery because they thought she had a bowel obstruction. As she was crying, she asked me if she could talk to Justin, because she wanted to do some form of Confession (a process in the Catholic church of confessing one's sins to a priest and asking for forgiveness). As I had mentioned before, he was in a monastery preparing to become a priest, I told her I wasn't so sure I could get ahold of him, but I would do my best because I could tell she was very scared and didn't think she would make it.

I jumped through hoops and was able to contact my son. Once I got him on the phone, I quickly explained to him what was happening and then proceeded to conference call my sister in. She was so excited to talk to him and asked him if he could hear her confession. He told Lisa he wasn't a priest yet, so he couldn't hear her confession, but not for her to worry because it's actually Jesus doing the confession, not the priest. So he asked Lisa if we could get a priest to her, and she agreed. I got off the phone with Justin and proceeded to call my brother and sister-in-law, who scrambled like crazy for two hours to find a priest and get him down there.

I headed out the next morning to go to Colorado and be there with my sister after her surgery. At this point in time, she had been in the hospital for four days, and they had not handled the situation very well. They put a tube down her nose and into

CHAPTER TWENTY-FOUR

her stomach multiple times, which should have only been done once, twice at the most. The hospitalist and the surgeon kept disagreeing on the best option moving forward. This apparently went on for a couple of days. I wish I had been there because I would have been ready to battle. It just doesn't make sense to have a person in that much pain and that sick and just sit by and let them struggle knowing they're not going to get better.

I was in contact with my family, some of whom were down at the hospital with her at this point. I knew I couldn't make it there in time for her surgery, but she would have a long recovery, so I could be there to help in the early stages of that. My brother picked me up from the airport, and we drove down to the hospital, and I was able to go into her room upon arrival and visit with her as soon as I got there. She was exhausted and weak but very glad to be done with the surgery. I visited with some of my family and my cousin until it was time to leave. We stayed at a hotel that night. We woke up early the next day and went to the hospital, which is where I stayed the rest of the time.

I stayed by Lisa's bedside virtually every moment, other than to take little breaks to go for a walk or make a phone call to my family back home. As a side note, I remember a very strange exchange I had with one of the nurses assigned to my sister. She started talking about some coronavirus in China and said we all needed to watch out because it could spread and could be very lethal. I didn't think much of it because it always seemed to me there was some kind of virus or bacteria health authorities were warning against. So I just mentally dismissed it. A few days later, they decided it was time to release Lisa so she could go back home and start the recovery process. We got her loaded up in the car and sent them on their way, and I went to my brother's house to stay till my flight home. Sadly within about twelve hours of her being released from the hospital she was taken by ambulance to another hospital in Denver where she stayed for a few more days until they could get her stabilized. My poor sister spent the next year and a half in and out of the hospital and suffered from various intestinal episodes. She eventually turned a corner, but it was a very long haul, and I think it kind of mentally and emotionally changed her.

When I got home from Colorado, Agnes told me about a litter of golden retriever puppies she had found online. She was very excited to get a new companion dog after having lost Sadie the year before. She asked me if I wanted to drive with her to the breeder and go choose one of the puppies. My response; "You mean you want to know if I want to go and look at a litter of eight Golden retriever puppies?"

"Of course I do—as if you even had to ask." So we did just that, and found this chubby, clumsy, adorable little puppy, and Agnes put down a deposit. A few weeks later, when the puppy was old enough, we drove back over to pick him up and brought home sweet little Murphy. It was the first time we had a male dog, and it became quite an adventure. Murphy is the sweetest and snuggliest dog you could ask for. In addition, he's a good protector and very strong should anyone try to hurt Agnes or Alexis.

After I got back home and got settled in, my husband and I planned for our anniversary trip. We had decided to do our anniversary a couple of months early—since our anniversary always bumps into other events in June—so we decided to go to Monterey, California. We had a wonderful trip, went to the aquarium, drove along Big Sur, went down to Carmel, and nerded out at a Catholic Traditional Latin Mass Convention. The convention was the real reason we were down there, and we loved and enjoyed it immensely. We visited with some of the priests and

CHAPTER TWENTY-FOUR

some of the religious sisters and of course the guests. We were really growing in our faith, and I can honestly say I was in love with Catholicism.

On our flight back home, we started noticing some strange stuff going on in the airport. We noticed people were walking around in masks, and we were pretty confused. In addition, the young woman sitting next to me on the plane had her cell phone in a plastic bag and was typing on it through the bag. She said there was a threat of some kind of virus, and she wasn't going to take any chances. It was like being in a sci-fi movie, and my husband and I just looked at each other and kind of shook our heads.

A month or so after we arrived back home is when things started to get crazy. By then this virus was on the news and being talked about everywhere. People were starting to be pretty panicked because it had made its way to the United States via an individual/s that had been in China and had returned home, or so we were told. The first known cases at that time actually started in a nursing facility in Seattle. A number of the residents had died. They were not letting people go in or out of the facility after they determined it was probably coronavirus. This was the saddest thing to watch because these poor people were separated from their families and were watching friends of theirs be wheeled out of their rooms on gurneys.

By then everything started to explode. They started talking about shutting down businesses, limiting flights, and shutting people in their houses. There were plastic tents being put up outside of hospitals across the country to test the people coming in. On top of all of that they chose a particular type of test to be used to determine if someone had "Covid" (the new name they have given Coronavirus) but said they didn't have enough tests to go around, so they sent a lot of people home that were

2020/2021

demonstrating symptoms of the disease. This was puzzling to me because everyone knows the best time to treat something is early on, but apparently for this "deadly disease" they determined it would be better to go home and get sicker.

I remember the last trip we took down to Seattle before everything got shut down. We, as a family, all had tickets to go see a concert, and the drive down was amazing. There was no traffic on the road, no congestion, it was just easy. As soon as we got near the concert venue, we easily found parking and set about the task of getting to the venue. My husband, kids, and I all laughed that if Covid made it this easy to get into Seattle, maybe it should stay around a while. When we made it to the concert, there were quite a few people wearing masks, but the band we were seeing seemed utterly baffled. They made some comment about our toilet paper shortage, and we all started to laugh. You see, we made news as the first state with a Covid patient, and secondly as the first state to seemingly run out of toilet paper. Now don't ask me why anyone would think the toilet paper was the most important thing to stock up on if we were going to run out of supplies, but somebody started it, and the rest followed.

About a week after this I ended up getting super sick, and the following day we got the news that all of the businesses were going to shut down, and they sure did. It was the strangest thing to see all of the businesses and stores in our town not operating and so few people out on the roads. It didn't help I was not feeling well either as that just played into the worry. There was a twenty-four-hour, seven-day-a-week news cycle of absolute panic and fear. If someone had not lived through it, they would never be able to understand what this felt like. I even started to get nervous and wondered if I had this mysterious illness. Luckily, I have a husband with a very rational brain, and he gave

CHAPTER TWENTY-FOUR

me articles and fed me information so that I could get a handle on things. Once I started reading and learning more about the illness, it calmed me down.

The good thing about Covid was that it finally allowed my husband to work from home, which was something he'd been wanting to do for years. After about eight weeks—which started in the middle of March—businesses were slowly allowed to open again. The joy of that would not last long, however, because starting around June, in Washington state, they issued a mandatory mask requirement everywhere in public. People in other states were doing it too, and the intensity of this varied from one place to another. Let's just say the West Coast took it to a whole new level of crazy. For me, personally, I was verbally attacked, bordering on physical attacks in stores, other businesses, and even outside on hiking trails. A sort of group psychosis started to happen, and anyone who didn't buy into the idea of masking was public enemy number one. At least I was number one at something.

There were all kinds of division going on by this point because some people were buying into the whole fear and panic of Covid, and others were more suspicious there was something more sinister than just the "virus" going on behind the scenes. Not surprisingly, being individuals that never just blindly trust authority figures, my husband and I did not trust the decisions and proclamations brought down by those in authority. In other words, we thought they were full of doodoo, and that there was more to the story and much better ways to handle the situation. In addition, those authority figures themselves couldn't remain consistent and kept changing their minds and the rules.

These differences of opinion, however, ended up making their way right into the middle of family relationships, and mine

2020/2021

was no exception. I talked to Lisa on the phone during this process, and she was definitely of a different mindset than me. She thought the closing down of businesses and the request for masking was the right thing to do. I realized that with her having just had abdominal surgery a few months before, and her healing struggles afterward, she was probably very scared, but I was trying to assure her it wasn't as bad as what was previously thought and that there were treatments. I don't think my words conveyed that, as she was very hyped up, as was I, and not wanting to hear my opinion. So sadly we ended up in a fight, and we didn't talk a whole lot for the rest of that year.

As if there wasn't enough going on in our lives and in the world, we got a call from our son. This was the fifth year of his formation in the monastery, and he was getting ready to take his next set of vows (a promise to remain in the monastery for a period of time), which would keep him there for another year. He had been struggling a lot for the five years he was there and was not experiencing much joy. The priests working with him couldn't make the decision for him, but they had told him that if things didn't improve by the end of that fifth year, he should probably consider leaving. He was torn on what to do but decided it was time to leave. So we planned for him to come home in May. That's right; straight out of a quiet, peaceful monastery and into a dystopian movie "Covid and The World of Tomorrow."

I think in some ways this was probably the hardest on him because Justin didn't even have a chance to get used to the "real world" again because there was no "real world" left. We were living in a kind of sci-fi alter universe where everything we knew from before was gone and was now replaced with health authorities (a.k.a., dictators), hospital regulators, and a random bunch of men and women from government agencies (some of which we

CHAPTER TWENTY-FOUR

had never heard of) telling us what to do with our own bodies and even our own businesses and livelihoods. To make matters worse, Tom and I were dug in with our position and were ready to go to battle to defend it. The whole experience was surreal.

I have a lot of compassion for Justin during this time and all the years preceding. Five years prior he walked away from his family entirely and was only allowed to see us every 4 months, as mentioned earlier. He did not see 3 of us for the first year he was in the Monastery. He was only 19 when he entered and it must have been a hard blow for him. He was always the family's confidant and counselor before he left and we realized how much he had done for us over those 19 years. What a blessing he has been to us and unfortunately, we couldn't help him adjust to being on the outside. Interestingly enough, the men that he had been in the Monastery with (his brothers and his new family) were the ones that helped him on this journey to the outside world. We love that community in California and always will.

The kids, after a couple of months of listening to Tom and I rant and rave, just didn't want to hear it anymore. They believed the way we did, but they kept explaining to us they didn't have the capacity to stay angry and in the fight as long as we had. Basically, what they were saying is we're young and we still want to enjoy our life, which means not talking about Covid, business shutdowns, or masking every minute of every day. I honestly tried my best to balance things, but I'm sure I didn't do a very good job. It's hard not to be angry when one feels an injustice is being done, but every now and then I need to be humbled and the kids were kind enough to do it.

One of the wonderful things we did as a family during Covid, however, was to build a deck in our front yard. We decided on the plans and headed to the hardware store to get supplies. Yes,

2020/2021

apparently when other stores were locked down, large corporate businesses were allowed to stay open. I think Covid must have known not to enter those places. Anyway, we picked up the needed materials, headed home, and started the process. It didn't take us long to build this beautiful deck. We had fun as a family doing the project together, and once the deck was built, it became a meeting place for us and anyone in the neighborhood that wanted to stop by. I officially deemed it Covid deck, but I'm sure I could come up with a better name than that.

While all of this was happening, we were also in the process of planning a wedding. Back to the story of Faye and the military gentleman she had met. Well as it turned out he had decided to stay around. He asked Tom for her hand in marriage, received his blessing, and four months later asked Faye to marry him. Not only that, he had been going to Mass with us on a regular basis for about a year and decided he wanted to become Catholic. He started taking classes with the priest from our church, and in December of 2019, he became a Baptized and Confirmed Catholic and received his First Holy Communion.

Fast forward to June of 2020, and we were in the process of trying to make wedding plans. If any of you got married during 2020, my apologies go out to you. This was the hardest thing to arrange. At first we could have 150 guests, then it was down to forty guests, then it was back up to fifty. We were hoping to have it at our parish, but even that became a problem. The invite list changed, the location of the reception changed, and even the food changed—multiple times. We were at about the end of our wits when we finally decided we would do the ceremony "Nuptial Mass" down in Seattle at our parish and the reception back at our house. We only had two weeks' notice to do it at our house, so we scrambled like crazy cleaning the house, windows, mowing and

CHAPTER TWENTY-FOUR

trimming the lawn, and decorating. When it was all finished, it looked beautiful.

For a good deal of time we had been talking as a family about moving out of state once the kids had all finished school. We weren't sure exactly where we wanted to live, but because of the cost of living being so high in Washington and us not particularly liking the people there, we decided we needed to move. Because of Covid, we could see which states were the most conservative and that helped us narrow down where we wanted to go. We went on a multi-city trip—Tom, Justin, Alexis, and I—to flush out where we should live. In the end, we decided on Oklahoma City. The area surprised us and looked like a very clean and nice place to live. Add to that the kindness of the people, and it was an easy decision to make. Once we all decided as a family, we determined we would leave after the wedding was finished, so October 1st—to give us time to pack.

The wedding was planned for September 5th, and since we couldn't have very many guests, we just had immediate family: both sets of his parents and my sister since my dad couldn't travel. To make matters worse, the restaurants, if opened, were limiting guests, so our company didn't have anywhere they could eat. I had to plan multiple meals to feed all the family members for all four of the days they were with us. Although everything turned out fine, I would not recommend this for anyone. It was a nightmare trying to figure out how many people to feed at any given time for any given meal.

Everything about Faye's wedding was perfect minus two issues; her leg waxing and my injured toe. When Faye got her legs waxed it caused welts all over and she was hurting for a few days afterwards. I ended up injuring my toe, was not able to walk on it or put pressure on it, and was in massive pain for four days.

2020/2021

The rest of it, however, went as smoothly as one could expect. The Mass was beautiful, the music was wonderful, the bride and groom were gorgeous, and the reception turned out to be amazing, as did the catered food. One of the highlights to this beautiful event was the stretch limo I rented. The limousine driver showed up in a stretch Hummer, which had extra seats, and all of the young kids got to ride in it. To this day they still talk about what a great time they had in that limo.

After we managed to get our beautiful daughter all married up, we helped her start packing her stuff up as well. You see, she had decided to move out to California where her now husband was stationed. He was in the Navy and getting ready to deploy on a ship for eight months, so they decided to take advantage of the two weeks they had beforehand. When she was ready and all packed up, we said our goodbyes to her, and she headed out. Almost immediately we raced back to the house and started packing our belongings knowing we would be leaving in about three weeks.

Once we got everything staged and ready to load into the truck, the day came for the actual move. My two daughters ended up getting sick, which is not too surprising, but they worked hard anyway. We loaded everything up in the truck and the three cars. Our friends came to help us clean the house. So while they were loading up the vehicles, my girlfriend and I started cleaning all of the rooms one last time. It was a very emotional day for us as we had been living in that town for twelve years and had gotten to know their family very well. I still remember all of us crying and saying goodbye as if it was yesterday.

The drive out to Oklahoma was a long one for sure and took three days. My husband's vehicle broke down twice on the way, and we blew out a tire on the trailer. All in all, however, it didn't

CHAPTER TWENTY-FOUR

delay us, and we arrived on time. We stayed in a hotel the first night we got into town and the next morning went and signed the lease for our apartments. Justin, Agnes, and Alexis all decided to rent an apartment together, and Tom and I got our own place. Right off the bat, I loved the new apartment and the location. We were just across the courtyard from our kids' apartment, so it was easy to get to. We had a workout room on the premises, which was super convenient. During the summertime, we also had a pool, which my daughter and I used quite frequently.

Our kids got jobs very quickly and started making money almost immediately. It was impressive to see how fast they were able to purchase dishes, furniture, and housewares. They did a great job of making a home for themselves. I was so glad to be out of Washington that the peace and calm was almost palpable. Even though some of the people in Oklahoma were still wearing masks, nobody treated me the way I had been treated in Washington. There were just a couple places that wouldn't let me come in if I wasn't wearing a mask.

It was so easy to talk to people when we got here and so easy to connect and make friends. It took the kids a little while to get to know young men and women their own age, but after about a year, it finally started to click. Prior to that they had actually met a couple of people in Tulsa, and that was who they did their social activities with. These young ladies and their families have been so gracious to us. I am very grateful for their friendship.

A couple of Agnes and Alexis's friends came out to visit them in December. In addition, Faye also came out to spend time with us. That was a nice, helpful transition for them having only been in Oklahoma for two months at that point. It just so happened we ended up with some snowy weather while they were here, and we were snowed in for a few days. That all worked out fine, however, because we got to play outside in the snow and visit, eat food, and laugh with one another the rest of the time. We took the girls to go see Christmas lights—which in this area are extremely abundant. We also went ice skating, and a few other Christmas activities, like baking cookies, etc. . . . It was a great trip, and we were glad to have them here.

In January of 2021, I headed out to California to visit Faye for her birthday so she wasn't alone. Her husband had already headed out to sea, and although she had made quite a few friends out there, she still felt very alone at times. Luckily before he left he bought her a puppy, a cute golden retriever puppy they named Samantha. This way she had a companion to go places with all of the time. We had a great trip and a great time together, but sadly I had to go home. I didn't want to leave her, but I also was missing my husband.

When I got to the airport, I received a phone call from my dad. As it turned out, he ended up in the hospital again with breathing issues. I was very grateful that on our trip in June we had stopped in Denver on our way back home to go to visit my dad. He was in an assisted living facility at this point, which only happened because he had flooded some of the rooms in his house and had to move out. We weren't allowed to go into the assisted living facility to see my dad, so I had an idea. The plan was to go and meet him outside of his window and get on our cell phones and talk to each other. He was on the first floor after all, and there would be glass between us, so it shouldn't be a problem. We visited with my dad for only a few minutes when one of the workers came out and saw us there. She went to get a manager, and she quickly chased us away. I was just happy, and so was my dad, that we all got to see each other.

Months later, when my dad got sick during my return flight

CHAPTER TWENTY-FOUR

home from visiting my daughter in San Diego, I found out they had taken him to the hospital. For whatever reason they had transported him over to a different hospital than he usually went to. My dad and mom had been going to the same hospital for about fifty years, so I have no idea why they took him to another hospital. He was not treated well at this facility, and I'm not even sure they actually treated him for what he came in for. As it turned out, he had bacterial pneumonia, but during Covid, hospital systems were getting paid extra money to treat Covid patients. If someone didn't have Covid, and just had a myriad of normal ailments, they didn't get any extra money. So what this created in hospitals across the country was an elevated desire to make every diagnosis seem like Covid. So that's what they tried to do with my dad, and within the first twenty-four hours of his time in the hospital they tested him four times for Covid, and all tests came back negative.

There were all kinds of scary things that happened while dad was in the hospital and some funny ones as well. At one point in time, we were told my dad was actually about to die, so we all got on a Zoom call to say goodbye to him. The weird thing was he seemed rather normal, and not particularly sick other than the BiPAP machine he had to wear for breathing purposes. He was interacting with us, writing notes, and seemingly happy to have us there. After we all got off the call and my siblings there with him in the room asked him how he was feeling, he said fine. The doctor took my family out in the hallway and asked what they wanted to do. They were confused and said, "He's completely coherent; why don't you go ask him what he wants?"

So as it turned out, they were about ready to take him off the BiPAP machine. The funniest part of it came when I called my dad the next day. I asked him what the heck had happened because they thought he was dying. He said, "I don't know. All I told them was that I don't want to do this anymore." I proceeded to ask him what it was he didn't want to do anymore, and he said the stupid BiPAP mask was annoying him, and he didn't want to wear the damn thing anymore.

I started laughing so hard and said, "Oh, they thought you had given up on living, and you were telling them you were ready to die."

He said, "Oh my gosh, I think you're right," and the two of us laughed.

Eventually he made it out of the hospital despite their seeming efforts to help him die. At the hospital they had asked my dad how he was feeling and if he thought he could recover and get back to where he was before. He told them he thought he could and his goal at that time was to make it to the age of Ninety, which was only a couple of months away. When he started to feel better, he was released into a rehab facility. We all wanted to help our dad make it to ninety, so we were willing to do whatever it took. Sadly things started to take a turn for the worse.

In February my sister Mary had been notified by the doctor my dad was getting worse, and he didn't think he would make it twenty-four hours. So the doctor suggested my sister call everyone from out of town to let us know. She asked the doctor if she could come and see our dad, and he said not until he is "actively dying" because of the Covid restrictions. She called my brother and me in case we wanted to travel out, but as it turns out, that very night he died. The worst part of the whole thing is they never called my sister or brothers to let them know he was dying. When my sister asked why they hadn't called her to let her know, the nurses said, "The doctor told them that nobody was going to be coming." My dad died without any of us around, and my

CHAPTER TWENTY-FOUR

sister was only ten minutes from the facility, and nobody bothered to call.

We had a funeral for my dad a week later. Faye drove up from California to come to the funeral and was going to spend some time with us afterward. The funeral was beautiful, and it was so great that everyone showed up. A couple of our relatives had died during 2020 and those poor families were never able to have a funeral and a proper burial for their loved ones, so I find it quite a blessing we were able to do that for my dad. It was very sad but a great opportunity to see everyone and get together again because everyone had been apart for so long. The smell of Covid was still in the air, so there was a mixture of masked and unmasked people at the funeral. Either way I was just grateful we were able to have a funeral Mass and bury my dad.

The rest of 2021 was largely devoted to the implementation and mandating of the Covid-19 vaccine, or, as I like to call it, the "jab." From the moment it was announced they were going to try and fast-track a vaccine, never before created, using a brand-new technology, I dove into the research. I read anything I could on the jab, what was in it, how it was made, and what the side effects might be. I was naturally leery of this option because of my health problems and because of my friends who had suffered vaccine injuries themselves, and now they were going to bypass any of the safety testing and try to bring to market an untested and unknown vaccine technology.

Even if I hadn't been concerned with the health risks involved, I had moral problems with using it. We now entered into the worst part of the whole pandemic in my opinion—the mandatory vaccine requirements. Suddenly all of these institutions i.e., . . . the military, schools, hospitals etc. . . . started mandating everyone get the Covid-19 vaccine or lose their job.

2020/2021

It was unbelievable to me to watch our whole country, better yet the whole world, willingly line up, stick their arms out, and let some random person inject them with a substance they didn't even know. Worse yet is these same people thought the rest of us should do it as well. They thought we should not have a choice in whether we wanted to inject ourselves with potentially toxic chemicals.

Some of the people I knew personally, who were real health fanatics, had no problem shooting this stuff into their veins. Some of these health fanatics wouldn't even consider eating fast food, but a nice little chemical cocktail was fine. This was the definition of insanity to me. In addition, they didn't even allow exemptions for health problems. My son-in-law refused the vaccine for multiple reasons: health as well as moral, and they discharged him. Recently, the Navy contacted him, admitting they made a mistake, and begged him to come. These soldiers were the target of threats and harassment by so many members of the military, and now they just want these men and women to jump back onboard? I think Covid must have messed with their brain cells as well.

During all of the drama going on, my sweet daughter Alexis decided she was ready to have a dog for herself. After all they were living in an apartment that allowed dogs, and since her sister had Murphy, they might as well have a mate for him. We all started shopping online again for different breeds of dogs and available litters. Alexis finally landed herself on a litter of mini-Aussie puppies, and she fell in love. The litter was about two hours away from where we lived, so she sent them a down payment, and when the time was right to go pick up her dog, Agnes and I drove down with her. It was so amazing to see where these puppies grew up. They were in an area called Texoma and

CHAPTER TWENTY-FOUR

grew up on a horse farm and ranch. All of the little puppies were running around next to the big dogs and horses off in the pasture. It looked like a Hallmark card, and secretly we were a little sad to take this poor puppy away from her paradise. Alexis picked out the one she wanted, and we scooped her pretty little tushy up and took her home with us. She is about the prettiest dog I've ever seen and as cute, funny, and sweet as could be. Between three homes, we had six dogs by this point in time. I guess you could say we like dogs.

CHAPTER TWENTY-FIVE

2022/2023

At the end of 2021 my husband and I decided we should start looking for a house to buy. The market was still pretty crazy as demand for houses was high and inventory low, which created a bit of a battlefield. Homes were selling for sometimes $20,000 and $30,000 more than their asking price, and we were in the middle of that. I, in my stubbornness, did not want to be in the middle of it, so I found a way around it. After putting offers on two different homes and ultimately getting outbid, I decided to look elsewhere. Then one day, as if by magic, I found this beautiful subdivision with some pretty houses on ¾-acre lots.

I was so excited I couldn't get my husband out of the apartment fast enough. He was kind of dragging his feet, but eventually I got him out to the houses. When we got there, there were quite a few houses in the process of being finished and were open. So I took it upon myself to go tour them. We both actually really liked the design of the houses, floor plans, and layouts. So we picked the style we liked best and grabbed a pricing sheet. The next day we contacted our realtor and asked if we could do an official showing. Of course the realtors representing the builder

CHAPTER TWENTY-FIVE

didn't bother to come and meet us, so once again we walked through the open houses on our own.

Our realtor was surprised by the area as well because he had not even heard of this particular subdivision. We put an offer on the house, and it got accepted. Then began the process of the paperwork. It really did not take long at all. It took a month to six weeks for us to turn in all the paperwork and be processed. Lo and behold we were about to buy ourselves a new house, brand new for that matter, which we hadn't had in fifteen years. We did the walk-through toward the end of January and moved in a week later. Our late Christmas present to ourselves was a new house in January of 2022.

We started working on the house and the yard immediately, and there was no shortage of work to be done. The yard, as mentioned, was very huge, and there were a lot of branches, leaves, and debris that needed to be cleaned up. Upon living here for a short while, we witnessed all the drainage issues. After a few good rain storms, we could see all of our soil washed down across our driveway and into the neighbor's yard. The strange thing was the builder did not sod the entire front yard. We contacted the landscape person, and he ordered some more sod for us, and we got it in the ground. In addition, we decided to have him put in a sprinkler system.

I decided I wanted to start gardening, so I got myself a planter box and some large pots and started my garden. The following year my sweet husband made another planter box for me so I could expand my garden. I think I am missing some gardening skills because while my plants are very green and luscious, they don't seem to be producing much fruit. I think it will take a while for me to get really good at this, but I'm willing to do the work.

2022/2023

The kids lived in the apartments for quite a while after we moved out. Things had been so good there during the time my husband and I were living there, but it ended up taking a turn for the worse. One of the days my daughters were home, they saw multiple police cars outside of their apartment and a suspect who was handcuffed and placed in the back of the patrol car. We found out later he had actually been in a nearby apartment complex and had pulled a gun on one of the men there and shot him.

Another night someone had actually gotten into the apartment complex and broken into some cars, and stole various things. My poor daughter walked out to her Jeep and saw somebody had taken a knife to the soft top and cut through it, had broken the middle console, and ultimately stolen her catalytic converter. This took us about six months to get everything fixed and the Jeep to get somewhat back to normal. This Jeep was a very precious gift given to Agnes by her great-grandfather. She insisted he sell it to her, so in all technicality it wasn't just a gift, but he didn't charge her very much. This beautiful Jeep belonged to Tom's Uncle Steve, and it's one of the few things we have left to remind us of him.

As it became more and more apparent this so-called secured and gated community was no longer so secure, they decided it was time to move out. It was actually fairly easy for them to break the lease because the apartment complex had not managed to keep the gates closed and were responsible for having let some of these criminals into the apartment complex. So the manager told them to let her know when their move-out date would be, and she would approve the breaking of the lease with no penalty.

In the meantime, Justin had started working as a school teacher and a youth minister down south. This job was a very good fit for him because he's so good with kids and knows how

CHAPTER TWENTY-FIVE

to relate to them. As mentioned before he has the gift of counsel and uses it well. When I go to the school the kids always tell me he's their favorite teacher. Needless to say, his work was down in Norman, and he was driving about forty minutes every day, in a lot of traffic, so he decided it would be better to move down there. As luck would have it, one of the students' parents had a house for rent and were hoping to get him in it. Tom and I went down and looked at it with him and couldn't believe how nice the house was. They had just renovated it, and it was very well done, and the rent was very cheap. So he signed his lease as well, and we set up a moving date and a moving truck to be shared between the three kids. We decided to move them all the same day, which was quite entertaining because they were moving in opposite directions.

Agnes and Alexis had been looking for a house to rent as well, and managed to find themselves a beautiful home. It was really quite cute and had a big backyard with lots of space for the dogs. They decorated it so cute with all of their belongings. They moved out with a friend of Agnes from work. She was just getting to know this young lady when they moved out together and unfortunately didn't have enough information on her. It would later become quite a difficult roommate situation. To be honest, I think things got kind of squirrely right from the beginning with her.

At this point in time, Agnes had gotten herself a really good job at a restaurant and the tips were very high. She and Alexis both worked at a medical clinic together, which they also very much enjoyed. They did a lot of things together at that medical facility, and even though they don't work together anymore, they still do social activities even to this day. Alexis was working at the clinic and working at a restaurant to make enough money to pay her bills. The interesting thing is, when Alexis started at

2022/2023

the clinic, within a couple of months they had her working as a medical assistant. They lost the medical assistant they had, and Alexis was such a quick learner that they just shifted her into the position.

When everyone finally moved into their new houses, we came back home and collapsed. We had been doing a lot of moving in the last few years, and my husband and I were starting to feel the wear and tear on our bodies. It definitely isn't as easy as it used to be. We kept saying that we wouldn't move again, and yet we ended up ALWAYS moving again. Now that we've purchased a house, I'm feeling a little more certain we are going to stay put for a while. After all, I really love my house and love the big backyard. I also don't mind living where we live, since it's out of the city and in a more rural area, but I sure hate how much driving I have to do. The girls live about twenty-five minutes away from us by highway, and our son lives an hour away. It's a lot of driving around to see everyone, which makes me wish I could get my guardian angel to fly me there instead

In October of 2022 we got word from Faye and Andre that he was getting discharged from the military, and they would be moving to Oklahoma. So when the release date got close my husband rented a truck from here to drive out to California—truck rentals in California were three times the price—and loaded all of their belongings and brought them home. Faye had been working like crazy to get everything packed and situated for the move and was exhausted by the time they arrived. All of them were.

In the year 2021, Faye had been having some struggles getting pregnant, so she went to a doctor recommended by some of her friends. After multiple tests the doctor determined she had a condition called PCOS (polycystic ovarian syndrome) and that it would make it harder for her to get pregnant. Luckily this doctor

CHAPTER TWENTY-FIVE

had worked with a lot of women and was able to restore fertility for quite a few of them. Not to mention the fact he had an open mind and was familiar with a lot of holistic treatments and had no problems with Faye using all the resources available to her. They even collected blood samples over an entire month to see what her endocrine system was doing. Sadly this is just another way she's like her mommy.

After getting all of the lab work done, working with a Naturopath and nurse on her fertility cycles, and working with the OBGYN who had her taking progesterone, she finally got pregnant. The funny thing is she didn't know it until she moved out here. They arrived shortly before Thanksgiving, so they basically arrived here, unloaded all their belongings, and about two days later went on a four-day trip with us to a cabin in the woods for Thanksgiving. Apparently she was suspicious she might be pregnant even on that trip and decided to wait till she got home to do a pregnancy test she made the announcement a week or two after Thanksgiving. She of course was very nervous that she might not make it full term, so she decided not to tell a lot of people until later. In July 2023 my sweet grandbaby Isabel decided it was time to be born. Since we never can do things simply, I knew we would have to have some complication with this too. As it turned out, my husband, two daughters, and I had been planning a trip to Norway and Portugal. The trip had been planned for quite a while before we knew Faye was pregnant. I tried to convince them to push it out a year, or to just do it at a different time, but they were not having it. They did not want to change the trip, so I was not able to go. I am so glad I wasn't in Norway when my sweet daughter went into labor. I needed to be here, my girls knew I needed to be here, and God must have surely known I needed to be here.

2022/2023

The labor was insanely long, and to this day we still don't really even know why. She labored for fifty hours before that midget decided to come out and visit us. I don't think I've ever seen anything quite like it and was so amazed at how strong my daughter was through the whole thing. Unbeknownst to us, the baby had turned sideways in the birth canal, so when she came out, her head was pretty morphed. I kind of laughed, because that's what I do, but unfortunately her daddy was worried something was wrong with their head. The doctor said it would go down in twenty-four to forty-eight hours, and he was definitely right. Sad thing is I didn't get a picture of it while it was morphed. When Isabel finally came out, she actually started nursing fairly quickly. I couldn't believe she actually latched down as easily as she did, but what can I say, my granddaughter's a genius.

Tom had done a lot of research before they headed out to Norway so he could track down the family farm and hopefully the gravesites. He did a good job with the research as they were able to find the tombstones of his family members and they were pretty sure they located the family farm. Alexis planned the whole trip from Oklahoma to Norway, around Norway, from Norway to Portugal, and Portugal to home. This was no small feat and she did a great job. They also walked a 65-mile pilgrimage across the countryside in Norway which ended with a Mass at the Cathedral and dinner with the local bishop and the local parishioners. It was good thing they walked the pilgrimage as Faye went into labor right as they were starting their walk and they were able to offer a lot of prayers for her wellbeing and for a safe delivery. They have very fond memories of Norway and I think they plan to return there someday in the future—this time they better take us. Faye and Andre took to parenting very easily. They've both

CHAPTER TWENTY-FIVE

done a great job with this beautiful daughter of theirs, and I'm very proud of them. It's always amazing to see new parents and how much love they have for their sweet little child when they're born. They lived with us for a couple more months after Isabel was born, and then Andre decided it was time to get a house of their own. They shopped around for a few months trying to find a place, and then by magic they finally found a house, were able to make an offer on it, and bought it quite quickly. And yes, once again, Tom and I helped move. You think we would clue in at some point. We want to make sure our kids are well situated and have a good launching-off point to be able to handle the obstacles life will throw in their way. They are doing just that, and God provides them obstacles for lots and lots of practice.

As for Justin, it took a while for him to feel settled in and comfortable in his new job. The journey after he left the monastery was a very long and difficult one. He ended up getting a job in a fish-packing plant (like his sister) when we were still in Washington, and it was a miserable job, but that seemed to be the only one he could get at the time. When it was getting closer toward time to move to Oklahoma, we sat down to talk to him about it. You see, he did not want to make the move initially and wanted to stay in Washington. We talked about it, but there seemed to be no good options. He couldn't afford to live on his own with the job he had, and there wasn't anybody he could share an apartment with or rent a room from. He hadn't had time to establish himself.

Justin's struggle was that he had been moving around so much, and Oklahoma was another move. When he was in the monastery living out in California, he ended up having to move to Toronto, Canada for some of his classes in 2019. He lived out there for four months and then came back to the monastery in

2022/2023

California at Christmas time for a short break. After the break was over, he headed back to Toronto to continue his school work, but when Covid happened and Canada decided to do a complete lockdown, they sent all non-Canadians back home. So Justin ended up back at the monastery two months later, was there for two months, and then discerned out and came back to Washington. He had only been back in Washington for about four months, and then we were getting ready to move. You could see how that would be an exhausting process for someone.

When he got here to Oklahoma, he was in a very sad state. He was definitely angry at me, and I think his dad, and was very depressed. It didn't help that his sisters were also feeling the same way when they first moved out here. I think for a little while the three of them kind of fed off each other in a negative sense. Anyway, I didn't know what to do for him, and no matter how much I tried to talk to him or help him, he just always seemed angry at me. I just felt like I couldn't do anything right by him. He blamed me for forcing him to come to Oklahoma. I told him he didn't have to come with us, as he was a grown adult, but that he didn't have any money and didn't really have any options for remaining out in Washington. I don't think any of that mattered because I think he just wanted to be sad and angry for a while, and after everything he'd been through, he had every right.

Once he got his new job teaching at the middle school, however, things seemed to start turning around. He started to seem less depressed, and he started to be more confident again. Even though teaching is very hard, it gives him a sense of purpose, and he knows he's doing God's work. It is really a special gift when we get to see him at school with the students because they love and respect him so much. He is well suited to the task, but I'm

CHAPTER TWENTY-FIVE

sure he doesn't know how long he'll last with teaching. The kids and parents never want him to leave.

While everybody is well situated now, and things have been going really well for all of us, there were some sad things that have happened at the end of 2023. My sister-in-law's mom got very sick in August, and she ended up dying. She was a very wonderful woman, was always very kind to me and my family, and she will be greatly missed. Shortly after she had died, Tom's mother died unexpectedly. She was having some bleeding issues, oxygen problems, and overall weakness. She had been in and out of the hospital a couple times, and one week before she died, we had the opportunity to be there with her and her siblings, as well as Tom's dad and brother. It was a great visit with her, but I could tell even then that she wasn't doing well, and I was not so sure she was going to make it.

We went out to the funeral in Colorado Springs, and both of my sisters and sister-in-law came to the funeral. They all knew Sue pretty well from our time together over the years, but overall it was just nice having my family there. We spent an extra day there with Tom's dad after the funeral, and I'm so glad we got to do that. I think he really needed his two sons by his side. He was and is utterly heartbroken.

The day after I got home from Colorado, I received a very serious phone call from my sister Lisa. She informed me she had been diagnosed with breast cancer and was going to need a lot of blood work done and a lot of appointments to decide what steps to take moving forward. After all that she had been through with her surgery in 2020 and the struggles with her health over those following years, I couldn't believe she was dealing with this now too. She kept me informed and let me know the date of the surgery. I stayed in close contact with my older sister Anne, who was

2022/2023

there in the hospital with her, to find out how everything turned out. She actually made it through the surgery fairly easily and returned home in short order.

I traveled out to Colorado once again to go be with my sister for a few days during her recovery. I could not believe how well she was doing considering the major surgery she had, but she just looked really good. I was able to take her down to her appointment to get her drains pulled out, and I was so glad to be there for that. I got to hold her hand and comfort her in probably the worst time of her life. While we haven't been that close in the last four years there's something about serious health struggles and tragedy that bring human beings together; it makes us forget all the opposing viewpoints and focus on what really matters—people. God working in all of us is what makes that true love come out.

As I painstakingly wrote down the events of my life, it led me to a deep study of the subject matter I was writing—me. The subject of me has been the one subject I have avoided throughout my life. I avoided it because I thought I was undesirable, unwanted, and most of all unlovable. I had no problem showing love and forgiveness to so many people and could never do that for myself. I thought the truth of who I was would be detestable to the one entity that mattered most to me—God. That however, was not the case, and the one who helped me understand this was my guardian angel. He was always doing what he could to protect me, redirect me, and sometimes save me from my self. He did this quietly and silently every single day of my life, as your guardian angel is doing with you right now. He's there in all of the big moments, and most importantly a million small moments that you don't always take notice of. He's holding your hand when you're crying, hugging you when you need it the most,

CHAPTER TWENTY-FIVE

and always trying to reconnect us with God, because he knows how much better our lives will be if we just let him in. The truth of the matter is, however, that he is the ONLY one that has the capacity to love us at our very worst, so how would he not love us at our best? It's okay that I don't do things like I think they should be done, or that I am stubborn, hardheaded, and even that I sin, because I'm human just like everyone else. We all do things we shouldn't—and as long as we say the "I'm sorry" part to our loved ones and to God every day and make amends for the things we do wrong, we are going to be okay. The most important thing I've learned through this process is really quite simple—God is my friend—always has been my friend - and always will be my friend. He is everyone's friend, and what he desires most is for us to let him in and let him show us what he has to give. I promise you won't be disappointed.

Thank you, God, for giving me these opportunities and helping me grow in my faith. Thank you as well to my wonderful husband and kids for being my greatest achievement. My life has been filled with adversity, love, tragedy, chaos, and beauty. I am completely and utterly blessed to know God, Jesus Christ, the Holy Spirit, and last and not least my beautiful family—immediate and extended—and my friends. In addition, thank you to my best friend, soldier, companion, and comforter, my Guardian Angel who has never left my side for even one moment this whole time.

ACKNOWLEDGEMENTS

To my wonderful, supportive, comedic, somewhat cranky, sarcastic, and onery husband I thank you for just about everything. You have endured so much with all my mental and physical health struggles and have always kept showing up day after day to do the tough stuff. You were sweet to me when I was my most vulnerable and broken, as well as being my fiercest defender. As I peeled back the layers of my self-created shell you have never pulled away from my stories no matter how awful or gruesome. You are the smartest, and most stubborn creature I have ever known, and you use all those skills to lead me, and the children, towards a greater life and future for ourselves, mentally and most importantly spiritually. Most of all you are my moon, and my stars, and my sunshine, and I will always love you.

To my one and oldest son I have thanked God for you from the moment he placed you in my womb and every day since. You are the heart of this family with your compassion and gift of counsel, and we tend to lean on those talents of yours quite heavily. From the minute you were born you had that spark in your eye, and I knew you were going to set the world on fire—little did I know it might be literally as well as figuratively. You were so fun

ACKNOWLEDGEMENTS

to raise, so incredibly intelligent, and a beautiful and Godly man. Dear son of mine, you have always been a loyal, and trustworthy human being, which is why you have so many close friends and continue to collect them every day and everyone loves you. You will do even more amazing things in your future, but your greatest achievement will be the gift of your fatherhood either with your own kids, or even with those you teach.

To my oldest, and one of my favorite daughters. What an inspiration you have been to me, and the rest of the family. With all the hardships you've endured it has never stopped you. You just keep moving forward. You are a talented artist, a gifted athlete, and a fierce competitor. Even as a little kid you had such an infectious personality, a deep desire to learn and try new things, and most of all a desire to meet new people. You have been my source of support while writing this book and refused to let me give up. When I was ready to throw the whole thing in the trash you stopped me and told me what I needed to hear "Mom you will finish this book and I will help you do it." In that moment you found the path forward for me. You are a beautiful human being, smart, kind, as well as a great mother, and wonderful wife.

To my son-in-law I want to thank you for your massive contribution to my book as well as the creation of our beautiful granddaughter. You sacrificed time with your wife so she could help me write my book. You are such a good, kind, humble, and loving person, and genuinely make the world a better place. When you came into our crazy family we were not on our best behavior, and probably made your life painful, but you never gave up. I have watched you take on some long painful deployments in the military, as well as monotonous civilian jobs, without

ACKNOWLEDGEMENTS

giving up, and you did this all for the sake of the family. You are far smarter than you think, handsome, creative, and talented. You are a blessing to this family, and I don't want you to ever forget that.

To my second oldest, and one of my favorite, daughters. As I sit here writing about you, I have a big smile on my face. From the moment you came into this world you made your presence known in a big and beautiful way. You were beautiful, smart as a whip, clever, sassy, quippy, and overall, a force to be reckoned with. Even when life got tough for you it never controlled you. You have this perfect balance of empathy and logic, and can quickly assess any situation and make the right decision. You are the life of the party, and instantly know how to end the sadness, and bring in the fun. This is a much-needed gift, and you have it in large quantity. I have enjoyed watching you over these last 24 years and want to thank you for your love, the gift of your music and singing, and the depth of your heart.

To my youngest, and one of my favorite, daughters. You are an amazing child, talented, extremely witty, funny, and have an infectious smile. When you were very young, and eager to start doing school with your siblings, I wasn't quite sure you were ready. Well, it didn't take me long to realize that you were incredibly smart (talented in so many ways) and there wasn't anything you couldn't learn. Just like your dad you have a gifted intellect as well as a talent for using your hands to build things. As you've gotten older, I see how incredibly compassionate, charitable, and loving a human being you are to everyone around you. You show me that kindness when I need it the most, and you show that kindness and love to everyone around you. I know you will make

ACKNOWLEDGEMENTS

an amazing mother, because you are so good with that sweet niece of yours and are such a natural when it comes to taking care of young children. You are beautiful, smart, strong and faithful and you make this world a better place just by your presence.

Special thanks to Joseph Salomon for this inspiration!

www.ingramcontent.com/pod-product-compliance
Lightning Source LLC
Chambersburg PA
CBHW010429190426
43201CB00047BA/2333